Fife

Genesis of the Kingdom

Fife

Genesis of the Kingdom

Adrian C. Grant

Troubador Publishing Ltd
Unit E2 Airfield Business Park
Harrison Road, Market Harborough
Leicestershire LE16 7UL
Tel: 0116 279 2299
Email: books@troubador.co.uk
Web: www.troubador.co.uk

ISBN 978-1-80514-384-0

British Library Cataloguing in Publication Data.
A catalogue record for this book is available from the British Library.

Printed and bound in Great Britain by 4edge Limited
Typeset in 11pt Minion Pro by Troubador Publishing Ltd, Leicester, UK

Dedicated to my former students at Viewforth High School,
Kirkcaldy and their parents, especially those with whom
I was delighted to work in the successful campaign
to upgrade from Junior High to full High School status.

Contents

Appendices

List of Illustrations

Colour Plates

Glossary

T&M:	Simon Taylor and Gilbert Márkus, the authors of the enormous (5 volume) "Place Names of Fife"
PNF:	"Place Names of Fife": the number which follows is the item number in the online database version of T&M's work
SCLLE:	My own "Scottish Clans: Legend Logic & Evidence" (2012)
ALLE:	My own "Arthur: Legend Logic & Evidence" (2017)
YGM:	Y Geriadur Mawr (leading English/Welsh dictionary)
GSP:	Geriadur Priysgol Cymru (online English/Welsh dictionary)
ASC:	Anglo-Saxon Chronicle
Dwelly:	Illustrated Gaelic-English Dictionary by Edward Dwelly.

I also use shorthand to refer to many of my own papers. See the Bibliography for the full names.

Introduction

All Fifers should know about their home patch, but we don't. Until the publication of this book no-one alive today or for several hundreds of years has known what "Fife" means or where the name came from. There are far too many people who think St Serf was a Culdee! And then there is Macduff – a character invented in the 1200s, but too few people know that. And why is it "The kingdom" of Fife anyway? In this book all these things and more are answered and explained in a detail never before available.

It all started because a few years ago I watched a BBC "Reporting Scotland" outside broadcast from Kirkcaldy railway station. I was not happy with "Cair Chaladain" – the *faux* Gaelic version of the place name on the signposts – so I decided to investigate the origins of Kirkcaldy. Soon I discovered that Kirkcaldy's name had indeed been written down during the time when Gaelic as a language was at its peak – and it was nothing like Cair Chaladain! I expected that this could lead to a short booklet which I could publish in conjunction with the Kirkcaldy Civic Society.

As my researches progressed I came to realise that I could not fulfil my intentions without addressing the origins of Fife as a whole. In turn the origins of Fife could not be understood without understanding the origins of Scotland – and the true story turns out to be very different indeed from that which which has been a "well known fact" for far too long.

To publish here all that I discovered in the course of this research would have imbalanced the book. So I have written up the many of the conclusions I have come to about Scottish history but which have relatively little bearing on Fife as such and put them into the public domain in my collection of papers at

www.academia.edu.

Very often these papers went through more than one version because they benefitted from discussions with other interested members on the site – so several of my initial ideas needed substantial modification in the light of the expertise they were so good as to share. These papers are referred to liberally throughout this work and are accessible freely to the reader.

I had no idea where the research would take me and I have been very surprised – shocked in some cases – by the conclusions I have had to come to.

In most academic books the author normally never uses the word "I"; such books are written on the assumption that so definitive is the work that there can be no argument, no alternative. In this work the reader may note that "I" is used a lot. This is not a matter of egocentrism: on the contrary it is rather to emphasise that this work is essentially speculative. Although I have dis-covered many items – facts – entirely unexamined and unaccounted for by academics at any time, there can be no definitive proof of the narrative into which I have woven them and I may well have made mistakes of detail. This work is not "ex cathedra"! What I am offering here is my opinion about the best way that such facts as there are can be formed into a coherent narrative. Of course I will defend it all robustly but one should always expect the unexpected.

I hope that you, the reader, will enjoy the book. In places I do expect you to be surprised – at least the first time you read it!

Notes on the Front Cover Illustration: The Caledonian Warrior

The front cover depicts a Caledonian Warrior dating to around 200AD. The image is based on two descriptions written by contemporary Roman writers and the image they made of themselves which they displayed on Pictish standing stones, four of which remain to the present day, one in Fife.

1. Roman Author 1 – Herodian

Herodian lived through the times of the Severan campaign. A brief overview of his life can be found at https://en.wikipedia.org/wiki/Herodian. Here are the key sentences regarding Caledonian warriors:

> *6. Most of the regions of Britain are marshy, since they are flooded continually by the tides of the ocean; the barbarians are accustomed to swimming or wading through these waist-deep marsh pools; since they go about naked, they are unconcerned about muddying their bodies.*

> *7. Strangers to clothing, the Britons wear ornaments of iron at their waists and throats; considering iron a symbol of wealth, they value this metal as other barbarians value gold. They tattoo their bodies with coloured designs and drawings of all kinds of animals; for this reason they do*

not wear clothes, which would conceal the decorations on their bodies.

8. Extremely savage and warlike, they are armed only with a spear and a narrow shield, plus a sword that hangs suspended by a belt from their otherwise naked bodies. They do not use breastplates or helmets, considering them encumbrances in crossing the marshes..
source: http://www.tertullian.org/fathers/herodian_03_book3.htm

2. Roman Author 2: Cassius Dio

Cassius Dio, (for whose life see https://en.wikipedia.org/wiki/Cassius_Dio), another contemporary, adds this:

3 They go into battle in chariots, and have small, swift horses; there are also foot-soldiers, very swift in running and very firm in standing their ground. For arms they have a shield and a short spear, with a bronze apple attached to the end of the spear-shaft, so that when it is shaken it may clash and terrify the enemy; and they also have daggers.
source: http://penelope.uchicago.edu/Thayer/E/Roman/Texts/Cassius_Dio/77*.html

3. Image on Pictish Standing Stones:

For a picture of the Collessie Standing Stone see photograph in the Colour Plate section.
I have used computer software to draw over the image which is otherwise hard to discern. In the relevant text I explain why this is specifically a Caledonian Warrior.

The image has been drawn by and remains the copyright of Craigrothie artist Kirsty Whiten (www.kirstywhiten.com) based on the data above and discussion of the brief with the author.

Time Line

Time Frame	**Event**
BCE	
c6 300	Final retreat of ice-cap from Fife: people can move back in! Arrival of Mesolithic peoples
c4 000	Arrival of Neolithic peoples: Balfarg Henge built thereafter
c2 500	Arrival of Beaker people
c1 000 x 650	Arrival of Cymru
c600 x 350	Arrival of Caledonians in northern Fife (inc Kinross) and Maeatae in southern Fife
c200	Arrival of Falcon Tribe which displaces Caledonians in north Fife and Kinross
c100	Arrival of Menapians who briefly rule the lands of the Maeatae

CE	
78 x 82	Roman invasion of Scotland I under Agricola – Fife not involved
200 x 204	Roman invasion of Scotland II under Severus: Carpow a major base
205 x 220	Caledonians re-conquer north Fife Abernethy becomes administrative HQ
c225x30	Foundation of Caer y Caledy: Kirkcaldy
c300	Fife incorporated into the new federal Kingdom of the Picts
302 x 304	Roman invasion of Scotland III under Emperor Constantius - No details available

c507	Battle of the City of the Legion: 'king' Arthur defeats Picts at Abernethy
580 x 600	St Raguel ("St Rule") establishes a church at St Andrews and a Culdee hermitage at Dysart
c600	King Nechtan establishes nunnery at Abernethy
640	King Oswy of Northumbria brings Fife &c. under his rule
685	Picts drive Northumbrians south of the Forth, Fife expanded to include Dunfermline area. Administrative centre moved to Cupar, Kennoway and Dunfermline
695	Arrival of St Serf: Catholicism spreads through Fife
717	Columban clergy expelled from Pictland
732	St Acca brings the bones of St Andrew to St Andrews
850	Kenneth Mac Alpine conquers Pictland, kills all the nobles in Fife. Member of the Cenel Angus imposed as Mormaer of Fife Columban Christianity reintroduced Fothriff, including Culross, re-allocated to the Culdees People have to learn Gaelic and largely forget Pictish
850x65	Foundation of Old Kirk in Kirkcaldy dedicated to St Patrick
900	Catholic clergy largely expelled from Pictland including Fife
c1025	Mormaer of Fife seeks Canute's protection from King Malcolm II
c1029	Battle of Falkland Muir – Mormaer of Fife and others killed
1030	Siward, brother-in-law of King Duncan I, appointed Thane of Fife

1045	Macbeth's men kill Siward's family at Kennoway but he escapes
1054	Thane Siward killed in battle helping Malcolm III to reconquer SE Scotland Osulf mac Siward appointed Thane
1068	King Malcolm III and Margaret Atheling married at Dunfermline
1072	Norman King William I meets King Malcolm III at Abernethy, forcing Malcolm to become his vassal.
1075	Foundation of All Saints (Catholic) church in Dunfermline to replace St Patrick's (Columban) church
c1076	Aethelred son of Malcolm III appointed Mormaer of Fife aged about 5.
1085	Aethelred leaves Fife to become Mormaer of Moray. Members of the family of the Mormaer of Angus fill in as locum mormaers
1124	All Saints church, Dunfermline, becomes an Abbey
1130	End of the Moray Risings: Duncan I appointed first Earl of Fife FIFE BECOMES A 'KINGDOM'
1270	Prince Alexander (son of Alexander III) appointed Earl of Fife until Earl Duncan III comes of age: Fife as a "kingdom" exposed as a myth.
1286	King Alexander III dies at Pettycur by falling off his horse Earl Duncan III appointed a Guardian of Scotland MACDUFF MYTH CREATED by Earl Duncan III and his uncle Macduff.
1288	Earl Duncan III murdered by Sir William de Abernethy
1298	Macduff killed at the Battle of Falkirk (fighting on the Scots' side)

1306	Edward I burns Dunfermline Abbey – foundation charter destroyed New 'Foundation Charter' faked.
1315	Earl Duncan IV resigns his earldom to King Robert Bruce for a regrant END OF THE KINGDOM OF FIFE
1371	Countess Isabella resigns earldom. Earldom reassigned to Duke of Albany.
1389	Death of the Countess Isabella of Fife – end of the main line of the Earls. Wemyss family now the senior line of the family.
1425	Murdoch Albany forfeits his lands END OF THE EARLDOM OF FIFE
1426	Establishment of Kinrossshire as a separate entity.

LOOKING FORWARD

2030 Like any cathedral, for example, the building of the fort at Kirkcaldy will have taken some time. Given that the Caledonians only settled on Kirkcaldy after they had given up on Dunfermline, We may usefully use the date 230 as the approximate date of its completion, making 2030 the 1800th anniversary.

2030 In 1030 Siward was appointed Thane – the king's representative in the then Mormaerdom of Fife. 2030 thus represents the 1000th anniversary.

It is remarkable that it is a direct descendant of his, Robert W Balfour, who serves currently as Lord Lieutenant of Fife: the king's representative.

2030 In 1130 Duncan, the grandson of Aethelred, was appointed as first Earl of Fife. 2030 thus represents the 900th anniversary.

His direct line descendant, Michael Wemyss remains a key figure in the County and resident at Wemyss Castle, despite the attentions of King Edward I.

1. In the Beginning

1. The Ice Age and Mesolithic (Middle Stone) Age

There is a meaningful and quite recent beginning to the story of Fife, because 20,000 years ago it did not exist! Of course the land was here and people had been here, but at that time the land lay under ice a mile thick. The ice did not melt in one go. In Fife it melted – sometimes altogether, sometimes partially – and then refroze and expanded again several times. We know that people ventured in during at least one of the 'retreat' periods – but because the re-expanding ice forced them away again, they had no impact on what happened later.

Fife has been inhabited continuously only after about 6,300 BCE during the Mesolithic Period (Middle Stone Age) the last time the ice retreated from our land.

2. The Neolithic (New Stone) and Bronze Ages

In very general terms the Neolithic period started about 4,000 BCE. The earliest sign we have of what we could call political or social organisation in Fife belongs to this period: the Balfarg Henge complex in Glenrothes (Canmore site 29990). This site was developed by the Neolithic people, but based around an even older existing Mesolithic site.

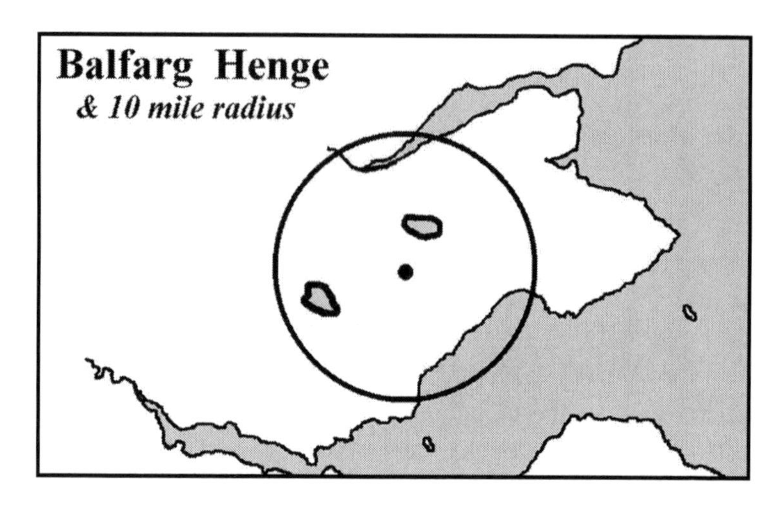

Apart from the henge itself, travellers on the A92 road can see a set of wooden poles in the ground (Canmore site 29959). These are actually a replica – the original site lying a few yards away now under the dual carriageway (see photograph in the Colour Plates section).

The most widely held theory is that this was an excarnation site – where dead bodies were laid out to be scavenged by birds – a practice similar to the Sky Burials which were commonplace in the Himalaya in general and Tibet in particular until quite recent times.

It was during this Neolithic period that Stonehenge was built and with recent research suggesting a connection between Stonehenge and Orkney – with Orkney being the older site – we may reasonably guess that some of the people who used the Balfarg site may have travelled, whether to Stonehenge or to the Ring of Brodgar. These proto-Fifers were part of a wider culture and we do not have any reason to suppose that they were entirely isolated.

Even if the original wooden poles would have been easy to erect, the stone circle was a mammoth effort requiring a lot of people working together to create it. Within a ten mile radius are Kinghorn in the south, the Tay coast in the north, Kinross to the west and Lundin Links to the east; twenty miles takes you to Tentsmuir, Culross and the Ochil Hills – so it seems likely that the Balfarg complex served all of Fife (and Kinross) north of Kinghorn and Loch Leven.

The Beaker People arrived some time after 2,500 BCE, bringing the Bronze age with them. These new people very largely replaced the stone-agers. This is well summed up at https://www.nhm.ac.uk/discover/news/2018/february/the-beaker-people-a-new-population-for-ancient-britain.html

The Balfarg site continued in use for religious purposes after the arrival of the Beaker People (although not necessarily used in the same way for all that time) – so it is interesting to note that this religious function persisted there for considerably longer than there has been Christianity in Fife.

The idea that Balfarg Henge served people living in the Kirkcaldy harbour area is reinforced by the fact that one can still trace a road running directly between them. Not the current A92 nor even the old main road running through Thornton and Woodside, but rather this old road can be seen now starting where Randolf Road crosses the railway line. From there the road runs parallel to the railway line keeping straight on to Thornton Farm where the Railway bears east. From there the route of the road follows farm tracks and field boundaries and then along the Tyke's burn behind Bankhead Industrial Estate. From the western boundary of Coaltown of Balgonie the line is rather lost in fields (but much can still be seen on old maps) before crossing the River Leven between the West and Middle Mills whence on to Sweet Bank on the Markinch road. Of course the Balbirnie Estate has been very seriously landscaped in the intervening period and in recent years a whole chunk of the northern part has been built over. But on old maps the road from Balbirnie Mains to the North Lodge exactly aligns with Sweet Bank. So too routes directly to the henge complex from Kennoway, from Leslie and from the North can be discerned.

Note on the Rossie Loch

The reader may have been bemused by the body of water shown on the map north of the Henge. This was the Rossie Loch. It no longer exists because it was drained finally in 1806 after an attempt a few years earlier had not prevented considerable re-flooding every winter. So it was a major feature in the Howe of

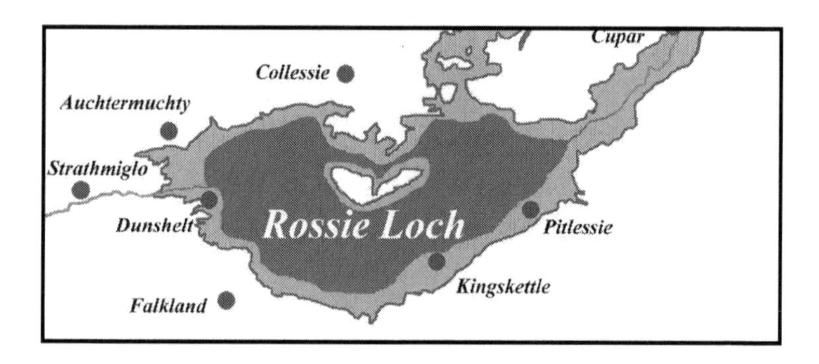

Fife or the whole of the time period covered in this book.

The edge of the loch as shown is indicative rather than precise. The outline here is the 150ft contour line. Britain was resurveyed so that contour lines could be shown on maps in metres; from this it would appear that people were confident in building on most land above 40m (131 feet). On the one hand "Shorehead" in Kingskettle is a clear indicator that the loch came quite close to the settlement and "The Harbour" at Dunshelt (at the bridge over the River Eden) may not be as fanciful as it might at first appear (see also below, Chapter 13). On the other hand there were clearly many more islands in this loch than I have shown and in many places it is likely to have been shallow enough to wade through. As this loch will not be familiar to any reader, it will normally only be included on maps here where it is directly relevant.

The surface level will have varied somewhat depending on the season, rainfall etc. Surrounding the loch was an area of marshy wetland (generally indicated on the map); 200 years of farming since 1805 will also have altered the land surface considerably from how it was back then.

Balfarg Henge and Falkland Hill

Balfarg Henge sits at the foot of Falkland Hill (aka East Lomond) – and we shall see the key strategic function which the Lomond Hills held in later chapters. The view from the summit commands the whole area within the circle illustrated and far beyond. But it is pleasing to note that archaeological investigations currently under way (July 2023) demonstrate how people continued to use them as an important defensive location – and a place to live – at least until the end of Chapter 9!

3. The Iron Age

3A The Cymry

There was a major influx of Celtic tribes into Britain. Although these tribes had many separate names, some of which have come down to us, they also had a collective identity – they called themselves the Cymry.

Their name: For a long time this name has been supposed to be from a hypothesised Brythonic compound word "Kombrogi", meaning "fellow countrymen". While I can see how this idea has been arrived at, I prefer "branches off the same stem" – which is not dissimilar. Either explanation suggests that they knew they were disparate but wanted to assert a shared identity.

Date of their arrival: It is normally suggested they came some time in the period 1000 and 850 BCE. We should be cautious about this proposed dating. The assumption is that these people spoke P Celtic, but this really did not develop before about 700BC – so either the influx of Cymry was later than is normally suggested (so perhaps 600 BCE) or they were so comprehensively overwhelmed by later arrivals that their own language disappeared all over Britain.

Their spread: It is clear that there were substantial numbers of them in much of England and Wales. Despite the 'normal' interpretation I think that even the name of the River Humber is related. In Scotland their name seems mostly left on the boundaries of lands later settled by others. Thus names like Cumbrae, Cumberhead and Cumnock make clear their continuing presence in greater Ayrshire. In Roman times Ayrshire was the home of a tribe called the Damnonii – but I think that these were mainly a ruling class who had imposed themselves on the locals. Even centuries later this area was known to be "Welsh" and it was difficult to distinguish it from "Cumberland".

Other echoes in Scotland will be discussed below in relation to the arrival of the Agathyrsoi and Cruithin, their names defining the limit of how far they got. This includes a residual enclave of Cymry who retained their identity in the South of Fife see "**The Cymry and Fife**" below. However it is difficult to see what legacy, if any, they left here in Fife – or indeed anywhere in northern Scotland generally.

3B The Coming of the Picts part one – Eastern Scotland

"The Chronicle of the Picts and Scots" (ed. WF Skene 1867) ends with this statement:

> "... this is the sum of years of all the kings of the Picts and Scots, one thousand nine hundred and seventy-seven years and nine months and eight days to the coronation of Johan de Bailliolf."

John Balliol was crowned on St Andrew's Day: November 30th 1292. Take off nine months and eight days and we have February 22nd. 1977 years less the 1292 at the coronation takes us to 685 BCE.

So there we have it. According to the Chronicle, the Picts first landed in Scotland on February 22nd 685 BCE (686 BCE if, like Scotland in the time of John Balliol, the new year only started in late March). Sadly this is not as straightforward as it appears. There are many errors in the Chronicle and many other claims which need deep and detailed interpretation to wrest any truth from them.

As I have discovered and set out in various papers, there was no people called the "Picts" until around 300 CE (we shall come to this later). They were an amalgam of several distinct groups.

The Agathyrsoi and the Maeatae

As I write this part, the city of Mariupol lies in smouldering ruins. Sadly this is not the first time this area has been devastated by invaders. The area between Crimea and the estuary of the River Don was known to the ancient Greeks as the Maeotian Marshes. Their neighbours inland have come down to us as the Akatziri. There was a third group: the Geloni. These people were of Greek origin, but had created a settlement on the north shore of the Black Sea – probably between the mouth of the river Dniepr and Crimea. It was due to them that a mythological link was forged in which it was claimed that both the Geloni and the Agathyrsoi descended from Hercules.

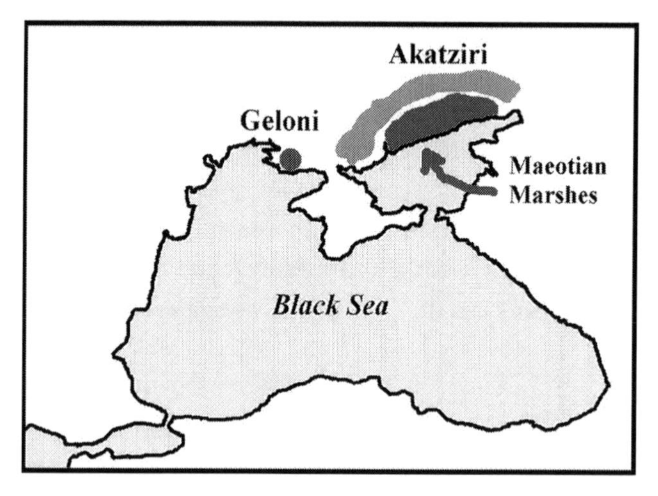

In the 700s BC a tribe called the Scythians swept in from the Steppes of Asia, leaving the bulk of the members of these tribes with no option but to flee. Not all fled in the same direction, but our interest is in those of them who ended up walking rather more than 500 miles to reach Transylvania where they were able to re-settle. Herodotus knew of and recorded the Akatziri as the Agathyrsoi. The names on the map below will prove significant.

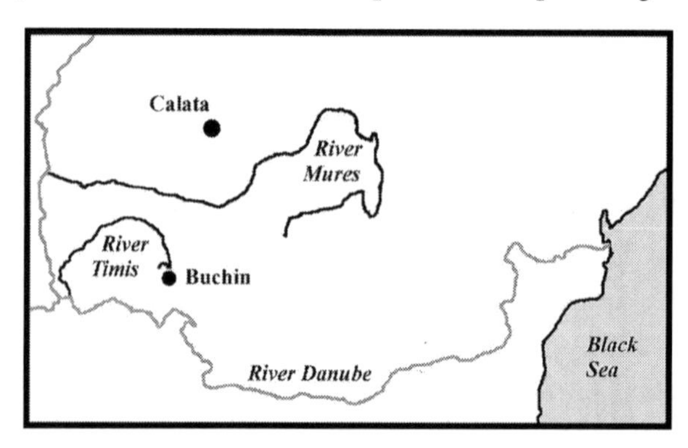

[By the time of King Darius' expedition against the Scythians (c513 BCE) such Maeotians who had stayed behind had moved 'out of the way' to the southern shores of the Sea of Azov. The Akatziri/Agathyrsoi had been forced west – closer to the Moldovan border around Novi Bun and the Geloni had relocated, founding a new city ("Gelonus") near Bilsk, some 50km north of Poltava on the Vorskia tributary of the Dniepr, nearly 200 miles east of Kyiv.]

Unfortunately for these tribal groups who had resettled in Transylvania, the Scythians continued their advance. And so it was that a significant part of these peoples felt the need to move on again – many of them ending up in Eastern Scotland. [For a full discussion of the whole migration see my papers OPS, PS1, PS2]

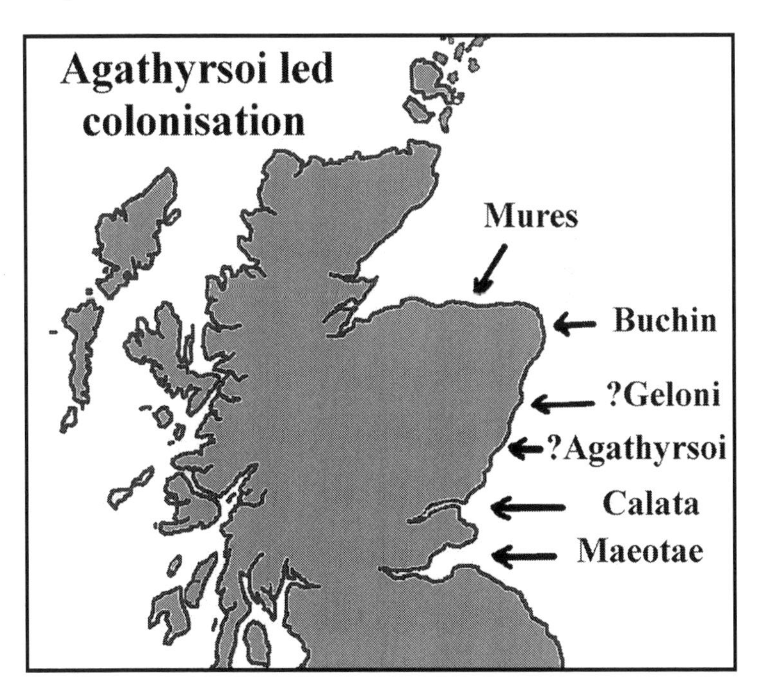

When the invaders reached Scotland they appear to have established several separate beachheads. Two are of interest to us:

1. The Maeotians (known to history as the Maeatae) settled in the Forth Valley, occupying both shores including the Dunfermline area of Fife, probably as far north as Kinghorn. Note that there is no meaningful difference between the "a" and the "o" – on the one hand they gave their name to the hillfort Dumyat and on the other hand to Myot hill. [No-one knows what the name means, but I suspect that it is cognate with Proto-Indo-European "Mia" meaning "to smudge, dirty". The nearest Greek words mean "bloodstained" or "polluted", "bloody" and "murderous"!]

2. The Caledonians (the name means "the hard men") were of the stock of the ancient Calata people of the hills above the valley of the Mureş in Transylvania who gave their name to the Călata river there. They settled in the Tay Valley, and, like the Maeatae, there is no good reason to suppose that they did not settle both banks. So it is reasonable to suppose that the Caledonians settled Kinross and Fife north of Kirkcaldy and Loch Leven. It should be noted that Gibbon ("Decline and Fall of the Roman Empire") tells us that in some stretches the River Tibisis was known as the Teyis – so this may be the basis of the name of the River Tay.

It could be argued that the chronicler scribes were familiar with Herodotus and other writers and so just made their tales up. They could have connected the Agathyrsoi to the Caledonians on the basis (i) that both practiced tattooing, (ii) both boasted that they did not farm and (iii) they did not believe in marriage. But:

- they did not mention the Maeatae (who were only incorporated into Pictland in the late 600s CE – see below Chapter 8)
- they took no account of the placenames we have noted
- they were unaware of the god Amadokos which the Caledonians brought with them and who was still being invoked in the 200s CE (see discussion of Lossio Veda's plaque below and in Chapters 2 and 3).

[Just as with the exodus from The Sea of Azov, so too not all those who left Transylvania made it to Scotland. Some of the Calata people stayed on on the North Sea coast (perhaps giving their name to the River Scheldt) until they were forced to move on, finally settling in the Pays de Caux where they came to Julius Caesar's attention in the Gallic Wars: he called them the Caletes. So too another group, possibly of Agathyrsoi, made it all the way to the Poitou area of Western France – The Romans called these people the "Picti".]

Western limits on their range

On the map above I have not indicated how far inland these Agathyrsoi/Maeatae penetrated.

- In Strathearn we may note the name "Comrie". This is normally explained via the concept "coming together" and indeed it is a place where various tributary rivers join what is now called the Earn. A Keltie Burn joins what is now the Shaggie Burn to join the River Earn at Crieff. This suggests that this may have been the border between the Caledonians and the Cymry north of the Earn. River names have changed a great deal over the years – and often the name which applied originally to one stretch only is now applied to the whole river. So one possibility is that "Comrie" really refers to the River Earn above Comrie, perhaps even above

Crieff and roughly here was their border. Thus the fort site at Dundearn may have been in use a very long time ago!

- Over the hills south of Loch Earn and very near Callander is the "Keltie Water". This should be parsed "Kelt-ie" where "-ie" means "burn". Place name people cannot make up their minds what to make of this: they suggest (a) that it derives from "caled" meaning "hard" (which gives rise to several rivers called "Calder") or (b) that it derives from "Coill" meaning "wood" (originally hazel wood). I am sceptical about both of these and bizarrely the same (a) argument is used as an explanation for the name Callendar! I prefer the idea that the Keltie Water juxtaposition implies that the Maeatae stopped their advance where the Keltie enters the Teith, leaving the high land to the Cymry and then later, when the Caledonians annexed Menteith (see below) they established a forward base at Callander.
- The same thing occurs in Strathtay near Kenmore where there is the "Keltney Burn", just below the mouth of which is Comrie Castle suggesting that the Caledonians halted their initial advances at Dull.
- Just across the Spey about 7 miles upstream from Aberlour is Knockando. The burn which enters the Spey here is now called the Knockando Burn, but 400 years ago it was called the Cumbrey. Again I think that a very long time ago the glen in which this burn sits was occupied by an enclave of Cymry.
- Yet another Kelty Water is a tributary of the Forth west of Buchlyvie. Because its course is East/west not only may more of the Forth have had this name in years gone by, but it makes it difficult to interpret. Nevertheless its mouth does continue the same general line. Further east along the Forth lies Gargunnock whose name may date from as late as 1296 (see "Scottish Clans…" Vol 2 p 244/5). Further to the east the Forth comes very close to the higher land of the Touch

Hills at Craigniven. So it may be that, at least in the first instance, the Maeatae halted their expansion at eg what is now the Baston Burn or the Gargunnock Burn. However it is clear that the Maeatae (who were experts at living in marshy land) did indeed expand westward – and the mouth of the existing Kelty Water may represent the limit of that further expansion as they drove the Cymry westward.

- **The Cymry and Fife:** There is of course another Comrie – in Fife [PNF 313]. This too is traditionally explained as another confluence of streams. The problem with this explanation is that there are many confluences of this size in this area, so why is this one special in any way? I cannot think of one reason. On the other hand if one wanted to make the argument for a group of surviving Cymry in the area, it would really have to be up in the Cleish Hills at the head of what is now the Blair Burn and the Cowstrand Burn – ie between Saline Hill and Craigluscar Hill. And flowing out of the Cleish Hills to the east is… the Kelty Burn [PNF 209]. Is it possible that, at least in their early times, the Maeatae left a population of Cymry alone in the Cleish Hills? Surely we cannot rule it out, but rather more "evidence" is required before we can be properly confident.

Note on the timeframe

As we have seen, the legend tells us that the arrival of these groups under the umbrella of the Agathyrsoi was in 685 BCE. This would be very tight. Some time before 700 BCE, the Scythians started spreading into eastern Europe from the Asian steppes. It is only around this time that the language now generally called "P-Celtic" which became the basis of Pictish and, indeed, modern Welsh was developing. The other problem is that there is no supporting evidence for any date from 700 BCE to about 200 BCE. So I think that it is more likely that this date may represent the occasion when the tribes decided to move from Transylvania – and frankly we have no idea how long it would have taken them to migrate to the coast or indeed how long they may have tarried there before moving on. To this we can add the problem that, as we saw above, the Cymry had arrived before them and there must have been enough time for them to settle and establish themselves before the Agathyrsoi arrived. So we can say that something important happened around 685 BCE and that the Agathyrsoi and their fellow travellers arrived in Scotland some time after that – perhaps as late as, say, 400 BCE.

Lossio Veda's Plaque (Part I)

In compiling the chapters in this book, I have tried my best to follow the time sequence, but already I have had to depart from this. A plaque was found in Colchester which is extremely helpful to our understanding:

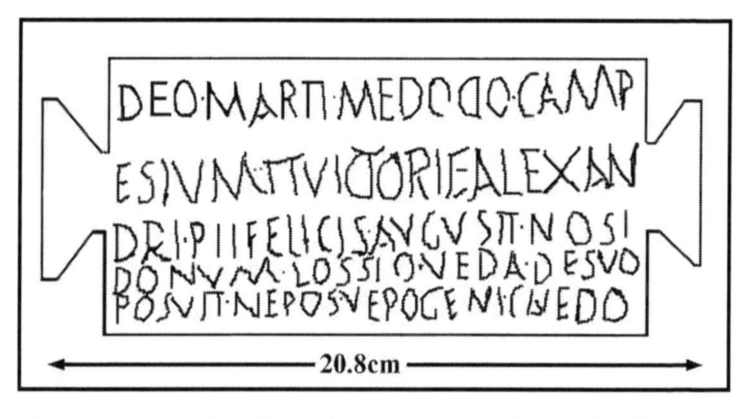

[For an image see http://www.britishmuseum.org/research/collection_online/collection_object_details.aspx?objectId=1363164&partId=1]

The plaque says:

> Deo Marti Medocio Campesium et Victorie Alexandri Pii Felicis Augusti nos(tr)i donum Lossio Veda de suo posuit nepos Vepogeni Caledo

This has been translated as:

> To the god Mars Medocius of the Campeses and to the Victory of our Emperor Alexander Pius Felix, Lossio Veda, grandson of Vepogenus, a Caledonian, set up this gift from his own resources.

Perhaps we should start with the name itself. Lossio Veda probably means "magnificent spear". [Compare modern Welsh "Llost" = spear (amongst other meanings) and "(G)wedd-" = comely (in general terms – the initial "g" was only added to many words in the 500s CE). [Compare this to St Kessog whose name really means "Little Spear" (in Gaelic).] Next we may pin down the date. It is the mention of Alexander Pius which specifies the date of the time window for the creation of this plaque to 222-235 CE. We will return to this later.

Mars Medocius proves the Transylvanian origin

Before getting to our main subject it is well to consider the God "Mars Medocius". First we should remember that the Roman practice to recognise local gods as personifications of their own – thus elsewhere in Britain we have Mars = Camulos and Minerva = Sulis. So who was "Medocius"? He is otherwise unknown in Britain, but there were two Thracian Kings of the Odrysae (ie covering most of Bulgaria and some surroundings) called Amadokos (the name Latinised as Medocus) who lived around 400 BCE. So where did their name come from? At a battle in 279BC this is told of the Hyperboreans (see https://www.theoi.com/Phylos/Hyperborea.html):

> "When the forces engaged, not only were thunderbolts and rocks broken off from Parnassos hurled against the Gauls, but terrible shapes as armed warriors haunted the foreigners. They say that two of them, Hyperokhos

> (Hyperochus) and Amadokos (Amadocus), came from the Hyperboreans, and that the third was Pyrrhos son of Akhilleus (Achilles)."

From this we can see that "Medocius" / Amadokos was a god and understood to be a Hyperborean. Anyone consulting the internet will find a wide variety of places sited as the home of the Hyperboreans. The increasing range of opinions reflected the way that explorers expanded the Greeks' understanding of the world. But the earliest reference is made by Homer. He located Boreas in Thrace (roughly modern day Bulgaria) and hence the Hyperboreans were immediately beyond there – ie in Transylvania... the area where the Caledonians came from!

It is worth pausing here to note just how remarkable this dedication was. The plaque was found in Colchester – which in Roman times was known as Camulodunum because "the" British god of war was Camulos. Camulos was known and recognised as far north as Falkirk – the village now incorporated into the town is still known as Camelon. There were several Roman forts erected here at different times and dedicated to this god. So the normal equivalence was Mars-Camulos, yet here was Lossio Veda at the heart of Mars-Camulos territory dedicating his plaque to Mars-Medocius! That is some commitment. It is truly impressive that this god should have remained in Caledonian culture so long after their leaving Transylvania!

LOSSIO VEDA WAS A CALEDONIAN

Lossio Veda identifies himself as a Caledonian ("Caledo"). The Picts spoke a version of Brythonic/Old Welsh; the modern Welsh word for a Welshman is "Cymro" (say "Come-roe"). So we may be confident about "Caledo". [We may go on to presume other parallels with Welsh – so that the Caledonian word for the land they occupied would be Caledu and the plural for Caledo would be Caledy (there is no difference in the pronunciation of these two words say "Caled-i").] Again we will return to this later. "Vepogeni" will be discussed below.

3C The Coming of the Picts part two – The Animal Tribes in Eastern Scotland

Fife's name takes root

According to my calculations (see my paper LKP), sometime around 200 BCE north east Scotland experienced a new wave of immigration; it was almost certainly from the Low Countries and the immediate cause may have been a major flooding event caused as a prequel to a more general climate change which took hold around the year 150 BCE. However these tribes were probably in any case under pressure from other tribes (like the proto-Saxons and the Goths, for example) pushing westward. These tribes identified with totemic animals and they had a drastic effect on the Caledonians and the others north of the Maeatae. Their leaders bore the title "Brude" which we should understand as meaning "priest/king". [Compare this with modern Welsh ""Brudiwr" (the "-wr" meaning "man") meaning "Soothsayer"/"Magician" etc. Even Scots Gaelic has "Bruadarach" (again "-ach" means "man who") meaning "Visionary".] Their settlement took this form:

- The **Hound** tribe settled Buchan (Welsh "Ci" means hound)
- The **Badger** tribe settled Strathdee and Strathdon (Ptolemy's "Taexali" are mirrored by the island of Texel in the Netherlands, the Germanic tribe the Texandri, the American badger being called a Taxel (taxidea taxus) and the German word for a badger being "dachs"). Thanks to

Nigel Lindsay for bringing the island to my attention and to Dr Martin Counihan for making the connection to the Gaulish language.

- The **Wildcat** tribe settled Angus and the Mearns (Welsh "cwyrcyn" means tom cat)
- The **Stag** tribe settled Strathearn (Welsh "Hydd" became Gaelic "Fidach")
- The **Falcon** tribe (see below) settled that part of Fife and Kinross previously under Caledonian control.

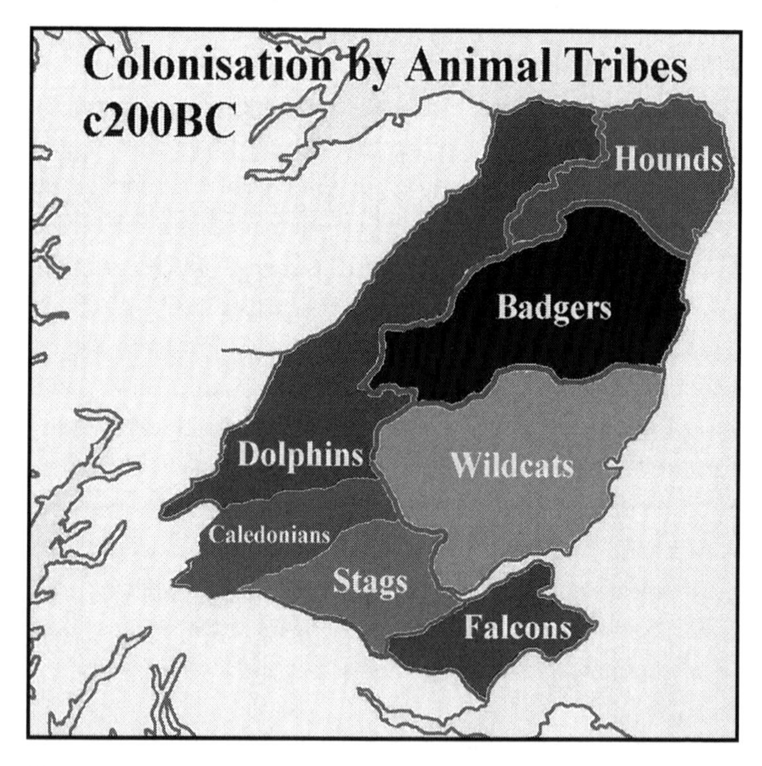

The effect on Fife

Key idea: The P-Celtic word "Uip" means falcon. In modern Welsh "Gwipia" means sparrow-hawk; cognate forms include the English words "quip" and "whip" – so the underlying concept is speed. The bird we now call the Peregrine Falcon is the fastest bird – the fastest animal – in the world, reaching over 200mph in its hunting "stoop". No wonder a tribe would take such an animal as its emblem. This word was used as a personal name and as an element in other personal names in the historical record and many people today have names which are not too dissimilar. So the establishment in around 200 BCE of this kingdom with this name within a confederation of kingdoms represents the beginning of the story of Fife as a name. How "Uip" became "Fife" will become clear later.

Where the Falcons came from: We cannot answer this for sure, but we do have a hint – remembering that the Calata people spread in several directions.

The Romans did recognise a tribe called the Uberi (Pliny calls them Viberi) who occupied the Valais region – the upper valley of the River Rhône centred on the town of Sierre and the ski resort Crans Montana. Clearly the Falcons did not come to Fife from Switzerland, but in the valley, just below Crans Montana is a village called Lens. There is a larger town of Lens in the Pas de Calais department of France and it is by no means clear what this name means – so there is a good chance that it is very old. So it looks to me as if, when the Falcons were forced to leave their 'home' in the Pas de Calais, some came north with the other animal tribes while others went south – and as they travelled they were not welcomed so they were pushed on and on until they found themselves in the high Alps where few people in their right mind would choose as a home at that time.

Lossio Veda Part II

As we saw on the plaque above, Lossio Veda also identified himself as "nepos Vepogeni".

"Nepos" is a difficult word to understand. Normally it means "nephew", but it can mean "grandson" (as the translator has supposed here) or, rather more loosely as "younger male relative of…". And so to

"Vepogeni". The assumption has been that this is simply a personal name. As we noted above, this might be possible. Other personal names with a "uip" element include a "Brude" called Uip, a king of the Picts called Vipoig and Gwipno, a member of Strathclyde Royal Family. So too there are several names from that era with the ending "-genos" (eg Artogenos – "bear born") as well as those which have survived through to modern names such as Eugene/ Euan. So we could understand Vepogeni as the genitive form of the name Vepogenos and translate it as "falconborn" which could be taken to imply "imbued with the spirit of the Falcon" – or of the Falcons as a tribe. We do have the name Macbeth and many Scots are named "Scott". If the Falcon were seen in any way as godlike then we could compare the name to "Luguvallos" (Strength of Lugh) or Thorkettle (vessel of Thor).

On the other hand why would you mention an uncle or grandfather rather than your father? The Welsh dictionary (GPC online) tells us that "Sais Geni" means "An Englishman ['Saxon'] by birth" – from the Welsh verb "Geni" meaning "to be born". So too for "Cymro Geni" it says "born Welshman". Thus we could construe the "Vepogeni" as "Vepo Geni" – ie "Vepo by birth", or "born a Falcon" or even "born in Fife".

In this scenario we can see Vepo having the same form as "Caledo". From this we may suppose that the name of Fife at that time was "Vepu" (which is close to pronounceable as "fifi") – with nepos Vepogeni meaning "a young man of Falcon tribe stock". The fact that he is a Caledo means that by this time the

Caledonian annexation of Fife was complete – or he would still have been fighting against them.

It could just about be argued that when the Falcons took over it was not necessarily the case that all the Caledonians were expelled, so Lossio Veda could have been born in Fife of Caledonian stock. However as this is 400 years after the Falcons took control it is extremely unlikely that his family's religious commitment to Amadokos would have survived so long – so we can rule this out.

I should be clear here that both Dr Alex Woolf of St Andrews University and Professor David Willis of Oxford University – both towering experts in their fields – have no doubt that "Vepogenos" is a personal name and I am most grateful to them for their time and advice. Nevertheless I prefer the alternative explanation. The difference, while interesting, is of little fundamental importance. Given the hostility between the Caledonians and the Falcons it is vanishingly unlikely that a Caledonian would have named his son "Vepogenos" – so in either event we may be confident that Lossio Veda was a Fifer.

Effects and subsequent events on the rest of Eastern Scotland

The result of the invasion by the Animal Tribes was that

(i) the existing tribes north of Stonehaven were squashed against the river Spey, with their eastern border possibly at the Deveron. They seemed to have acquiesced with the new régime and a very small amendment to the name Mures allowed them to become the "Sea Monster" or "Dolphin" tribe. [The Welsh for dolphin is "Morwch", the Gaelic equivalent is "Moruach" and later the Earls of Moray featured mermaids in their coats of arms.]

(ii) the Caledonians as such resisted the take over as best they could, but still had to accept the overlordship of the "Brude" priest kings. They were confined to the Braan and upper Tay basins and pushing out any remaining Cymry made their "capital" at Drummond Hill near Kenmore. Schiehallion was on their northern boundary and their fort Rohallion (now "King's Seat") near Birnam on their Southern boundary (see my paper Schiehallion). The Caledonians were not happy with any of this – and over time they gradually re-took control over the mountains so that by about 50 BCE they were able to declare independence and have their own kings again.

Meanwhile, perhaps at the same time, perhaps even 100 years later

(iii) a contingent of Menapian settlers imposed themselves on the territory of the Maeatae, calling their kingdom Manau and giving their name to places like Clackmannan and Slamannan. So too Dalmeny was originally Dyn Mannan or some such, possibly suggesting that the lower reaches of the River Almond may have served as their eastern border. However I have not found any evidence that the Menapians themselves settled in any of what is now Fife. While the name for the kingdom Manau stuck, the Maeatae regained control – so that they were once again the dominant tribe in that area by the time the Romans arrived.

There is a similar problem in Angus and the Mearns – for

(iv) while the name Cwrcyn (Shakespeare's 'Circinn' in Macbeth) remained, Ptolemy records the name of the tribe living there as the 'Venicones'. I accept the analysis of

> thehistoryfiles.co.uk that these were a group of Veneti who had been attacked and largely expunged from their base in the Vannes area of Brittany in 56 BCE by Julius Caesar's troops. [Another group of them fled to Ireland.] As they were great seafarers it is little surprise that it was they who came to Roman – and hence Ptolemy's – attention in Scotland. How much of the Angus coast they actually occupied is a matter for speculation, but it certainly included Monifieth and their main base was probably at Montrose. It seems that they were able to get on well with their Wildcat hosts, which should not be a surprise as it would bolster their defences against raiding Caledonians.

The Veneti were near neighbours (about 30 miles by sea) of the Picti of Poitou – and it is only too easy to see how this would have led to confusion in the minds of later historians trying to make sense of "The Picts". Indeed it may be the Veneti themselves who embedded the "obvious" connection they observed in the minds of those whom they came to live amongst.

3D The Coming of the Picts part three – The Cruithin in Western Scotland

Irish annalists normally refer to the Picts as "Cruithin". Almost all historians and indeed linguists will tell you that "Cruithin" is a corruption (by Q-Celtic speakers) of the name "Pretani" – essentially meaning "ancient Britons" (remember that in Gaelic "-in" often means the plural of something). This is not true for at least three reasons:

1. First of all there was no concept of "Ancient Briton" at the time in question. There was a collection of tribes – some rubbing shoulders, others contesting with each other for territory. The idea of "Ancient Briton" was only made

possible by the stability provided by 300 years of rule by the Roman Empire. At the time we are talking about Britain was generally known as Albion (usually translated as "white" – supposedly a reference to the White Cliffs of Dover, but I think more likely a reference to Barley which Britain produced in great surplus at the time – and pearl barley is in essence white – I am grateful to Proto-Indo-European language expert Eduard Selleslagh-Suykens for advice in this matter).

2. In the modern Welsh dictionary we can find "crwydr" meaning "wandering" and , "crwydryn" and "crwydrddyn" meaning "wanderer" containing the element "cruith-". When we consider the time lapse and the same corruption between languages which those who argue for "Pretani" rely on (remember it is Irish people who used this term), this is a far closer match. We should bear in mind also that the Irish entirely invented the name "Cruithne" as the personification – supposed name father – of the people. [In Gaelic the suffix "-ne" is an emphatic, so "Cruithne" (Cruith-ne) was not real, but so far as the Irish were concerned he was "The" Cruith! After all if the people are the Cruithin it "stands to reason" that the progenitor (they assumed there was one) was called Cruith!] So it is clear that they invented the name as an archetype.

   Whether the word "Cruithin" as written is a corruption of the modern Welsh (eg Crwy(dr)ddyn) or whether the modern Welsh is an elaboration of an older Brythonic (and we do know of other parallel linguistic developments) we may be confident that there was a P-Celtic word which accounts both for Cruithin and for Crwydr and that Cruithin means "wanderers".

3. The word "Pretani" is plural. We may presume that the singular is "Pretanos"- and here there is an extra syllable – indeed the root name is normally understood as "Pretanike" which has yet another syllable.

The reader is advised to beware books and webpages where a name is preceded by an *asterisk. What this means is that the author has no clue and so is making it up. Etymonline.com (June 2023) says:

> In 4c. B.C.E. Greek they are recorded as Prittanoi, which is said to mean "tattooed people."

"Said to" is a helpful caveat. [Many people have "said" many things – but that does not make what they said true!] As we have seen above, the practice was sufficiently specific to the Caledonians as to have been remarked upon by Roman writers. So this is actually quite unlikely.

Taking a different line altogether bitaboutbritain.com mentions an explanation currently out of fashion which derives 'Britain' from the Phoenician '*baratanic*' *meaning "land of tin"*. I regard this as substantially more likely.

Thus there is no good reason to doubt that, just as the legend says, the Cruithin left Thrace (in the time of King Darius the Great – around 500 BCE) eventually making their way from Spain to Ireland where they landed in the south west (around the Dingle peninsula – A on the map below). So too, just as with the boatloads of migrants crossing to Britain and other European countries in the last several years, the overwhelming majority are young males. So how to found a family? The only source of women would be from the local population. Why would the indigenous Irish not put in the proviso that if they were to allow these people to marry their girls then the *quid pro quo* would be that inheritance should be though these and subsequent generations of females? This would be the basis for the legend behind the matrilineal tradition amongst the Picts.

By some time rather before 300 BCE they had seized the High Kingship of Ireland which they retained for rather over a century. But the Irish did not like it and eventually – around 209 BCE – they rose in revolt successfully.

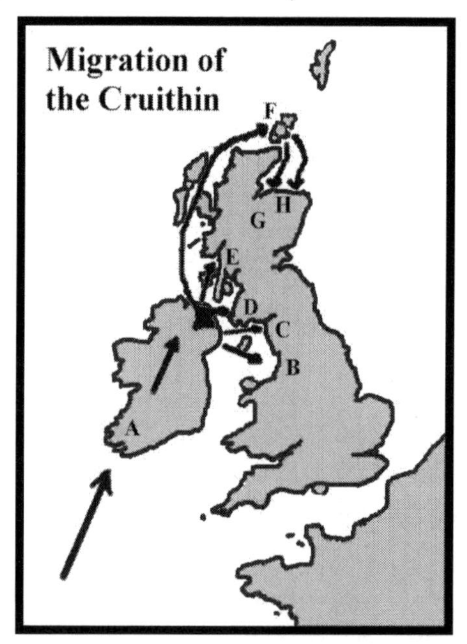

Many Cruithin were expelled and they went in several directions: some to the coast of Lancashire (B: the Setantii), some to Galloway (D: the Novantae) and some to Kintyre (E: the Epidii). [The Senchus Fer n'Alban refers to a king "Eochaid Muinremor" and if he was the leader of this group he may be the 'name father' of the Epidii – for "Eochaid" (say "Jocky") means 'horse rider' – and this is the real reason why so many

Scotsmen are called "Jock".] Another group of these exiles may have been D: the Carvetii of the Solway Firth with their base at Carlisle.

However the most important group went to Orkney. Clearly this was a place fraught with danger of attack – they reacted to this by building the brochs in which they were relatively safe (in this regard they may have copied or developed a practice which was already starting). From Orkney they spread onto mainland Scotland where they faced fierce opposition from the tribe there which they called the Smaertae (recorded by Ptolemy). They reinforced their occupation by building more Brochs, spreading onto mainland Scotland, especially down the coast of the Moray Firth. [My view is that the real name of the Smaertae gave us the name "Cataibh" (from which Caithness) and that this name meant "The Warriors" – see my paper Brochs.]

By the time the Romans came, the Cruithin had taken overall control of the lowlands along the shores of the Pentland Firth and the western shores of the Moray Firth and all the lands east of the Great Glen and west of the River Spey (G: The Vacomagi – which means "the Cattlemen"). [H refers to the Verturiones, the Ploughmen, who were invited in much later to help the Moraymen.]

[Meanwhile a considerable number of Cruithin remained in Ireland. The reinstalled High King of Ireland took hostages from these people confining most of them in two contiguous areas:

- One was the area round the Glens of Antrim extending from Garron Point in the South to Kinbane Headland beyond Ballycastle in the north. They may also have held Rathlin Island. They were known to the Irish as the "Robogdii" (a

Latinised version) meaning "the Broken Men"/"Outlaws". The land was known as "Dalriata" meaning "the plains of the Foreigners".

- The other was the area now focussed on Oriel County (the Irish name Airgialla or Oirghialla means "the land from which hostages are taken"). Today this is mainly the main part of County Tyrone.

These two groups shared a border with each other, making Airgialla a buffer between the Dal Riata and the rest of Ireland. Both of these groups are directly relevant to Fife and will feature in later chapters below.]

Footnote on Islands in the Firth of Forth

It has been quite widely suggested that the Isle of May might have been a (royal?) burial ground for the Maeatae. The basis of this is that there are many old burials on the island and that "May" includes a bit of "Maeatae". A facilitating idea has been the assumption that the Maeatae controlled the whole of Fife. As we have seen and will see further this was definitely not the case – so much so that the proposition is left with no foundation.

There are weaknesses also in the supposed place name equivalence:

(i) In the cases of Myot Hill and Dumyat the "t" has remained in place even to this day.

(ii) It is hard to justify the vowel shift from "Myot" ("Eye" and "-ot" as in got) and "Dumyat" ("Eye" and "-ut" as in gut) to "May" (as in say).

However the general idea of burying people on islands is deeply embedded.

- In the case of Iona it is true that many bodies had to be taken a very long way, but (i) there were very special (Christian) religious implications and (ii) the final journey across the water was only a mile or so.
- In the case of 'king' Arthur, The Isle of Avalon, in Loch Lomond (probably Inchtavannach), is again only a mile or so from Luss and even closer to other convenient points on the shore.

The islands in the Firth of Forth all have had strong religious connections in Christian times and the archaeology on May does imply that this represents a resonance from older times. However if the Maeatae were inclined to Island burials then Inchcolm presents an ideal location, failing which Inchkeith (2.5 miles from Maeatan shores) is very convenient. [Relevant archaeology may well be hidden under more recent archaeology etc.] Conversely the Isle of May, 25 miles even from Kinghorn is an unnecessary distance to travel; on the other hand at just 5 miles from Anstruther or Crail it would have been reasonably convenient for the Falcons.

The idea of the Caledonians using it before the arrival of the Falcons cannot be ruled out, but it would have been very inconvenient to any Caledonian "central place" or "capital" so it is quite unlikely. The best that could be supposed is that it may have been used by those of them living in Fife.

All in all we may be confident that the name "May" does not imply a connection to the Maeatae.

Summary

1. After the ice had finally retreated (about 6,300 BCE) Fife was occupied by Mesolithic people, to be replaced after 2,300 years by people of a Neolithic culture. After another 1,500 years the Beaker people arrived and spread out quite widely.

2. Sometime after 685 BCE there was a major influx of people from Transylvania. The Maeatae took control of Fife south of Kinghorn and Loch Leven while to the north the invading settlers were the Caledonians.

3. Sometime around 200 BCE there was another influx from the Low Countries. The Caledonians lost control of their part of Fife to the Falcon tribe. In the south the Maeatae seem to have held on to their part of Fife, even if they were temporarily eclipsed in their heartlands by the Menapians whose name lingers on in Clackmannan.

Further consideration of the Timeframe

We noted above that the legend of the Agathyrsoi was that they arrived in 685 BCE, but that this was tight. The key problem is the development of P-Celtic. However because both the Cruithin and the Animal Tribes arrived around 200 BCE and both spoke P-Celtic, it is not actually necessary to assume that the Agathyrsoi did so when they arrived. We have noted the huge cultural gulf whereby Camulos was the god of war in much of Britain while Lossio Veda gave thanks to Amadokos – and the same applies to other cultural habits like their attitude to marriage. So it is feasible to suppose that when the Agathyrsoi arrived they did NOT speak P-Celtic, but came to do so under the influence of the Brudes – and this in turn makes the 685 date a good deal more possible.

2. Along came the Romans

As we saw in the last chapter, the Caledonians seized back their independence from the régime of the "Brudes" somewhere around 50 BCE; thereafter they gradually expanded their control over the highland area of the Grampians. They established hill forts at the mouth of the glens from where they could mount predatory raids on the lowlanders, taking away booty, especially agricultural produce – because, famously, they did not do any farming themselves. So there was no love lost between the Caledonians on the one hand and the animal tribes on the other hand.

The Falcons in Fife were largely unaffected by all this because we did not have a common border with the Caledonians: from their nearest fort at Rohallion they would have had to fight their way though 20 miles of Wildcat and Stag territory before reaching us.

1. Agricola's Expedition

In 78 CE the Roman general Agricola was sent to conquer Scotland. There was a brief skirmish with the Damnonii of Strathclyde, but they quickly came onside as "fœderati". Understanding the local politics, Agricola hoped to do the same with the east coast tribes and initially they welcomed him. As he went north he set up forts at the mouths of the glens opposite the Caledonians' own forts (sometimes there were only a few hundred metres between the opposing forts) and the Venicones of Cwrcyn allowed him to set up a supply base supported by the navy ("Orrea Classis") at Monifeith. For a full discussion of the Geography of Scotland at this time and Agicola's campaign see my book ALLE.

Agricola was very successful. He defeated the Caledonians in a pitched battle at Mons Graupius (near Bennachie); the army reached the river Spey. Expeditionary units may have been sent beyond that, perhaps as far as Inverness and he sent the navy on expedition to prove that Britain was an island (which they did). But this very success proved Agricola's – and the Romans' – undoing. Back at Rome jealousy arose along with worry that Agricola might try to seize control as Emperor – so he was recalled and the Roman army melted away from Scotland.

The Immediate Aftermath

The Caledonians were furious with the tribes who had helped the Romans and as quickly as they could they attacked and defeated the Cwrcyn/Venicones and the Taexali – the Wildcats and the Badgers – in particular, annexing their territory. It seems that this was probably achieved in stages rather than all at once.

The first evidence of this is the village Kirkton of Kingoldrum 3 miles west of Kirriemuir. The old spelling was Kincaldrum – which is clearly kin-cald-drum: the headland of the Caledonians' ridge and on the northern end of this ridge is Castle Hill on which there is a "prehistoric" fort. This is well in front of the mouths of the glens (of the South Esk and Provan) and the Roman Fort at Inverquarity. But it is only a small Caledonian advance. So it looks as if this represents one stage illustrating that the Caledonians had to fight their way to the coast in stages.

A further stage is illustrated by Kinpurney Hill on the Sidlaws 7 miles NW of Dundee – the clue being that the entrance is on the west side. There is also another Kincaldrum Hill by Hayston Hill some 5 miles SW of Forfar (but this hill may take its name from the nearby Kincaldrum house (now in ruins) so one cannot rule out this being a transferred name). However it is broadly in line with Kinpurney Hill and Turin Hill. I.5 miles SE of the Fort on Turin Hill is a standing stone featuring the "Caledonian Spearman" (we will return to this in the next chapter) saying to the locals "Thus far and no farther". But this was still only half way to the coast, so it looks as if the Caledonians paused once they had stormed this second line, regrouped and took their time to gather their strength for the next push forward.

We do not know how long this process took – surely more than 10 years, so perhaps 20 or even 30.

The same applies to the lands directly to south of the Caledonians. Here the Romans had been free to occupy the Gask Ridge and put forward operating bases at the mouths of the glens.

Phase one: At this stage the Caledonians hoped that the valley of Almond would 'do'. A Caledonian Spearman standing stone was found near the fort Bertha at the mouth of the Almond suggesting a phase one of the attack taking them to a line not too far away from the A85.

Phase two: But a second wave is suggested to occupy the Gask Ridge (above and to the North of the Earn, for at the eastern end of this ridge Coldwells Wood and Callarfountain (Mailer Hill – where there is a standing stone) suggest the name of the Caledonians – this line culminating in the formidable Moncrieff Hill.

Phase three: The third phase would have seen the establishment of the forward positions at Kay Craig, Dunning and Forgandenny to be discussed in the next chapter.

Again Fife was not involved in this, but appreciating this background is highly advantageous for understanding what happened next.

2. And then

The Caledonians and the Maeatae continued to mount predatory raids into Roman Britannia. The Romans' first reaction was to build Hadrian's Wall (c120 CE) but, this proving unsatisfactory, they pushed back north, establishing the Antonine Wall (c140 CE) hoping that their friends the Damnonii in Ayrshire and the Gododdin (whom they had brought north from Northumberland into the Lothians) would be able to hold the line. But they proved to be unequal to the task. In particular a major raid was undertaken in 180 CE when a legion was destroyed. [This is the likely occasion for the creation of the 'erratic' Pictish Symbol stone at Trusty's Hill in Dumfriesshire.]
The Caledonians and their fellow "Agathyrsoi" confederates the Maeatae were thorns in the flesh of the Roman Empire and "something had to be done".

3. Severus' Expedition

In the late 190s CE the Roman emperor Severus was feeling the need for a "Triumph" – a military victory which would gain official recognition and associated celebration at Rome. He concluded that annexing Scotland would be a suitable project which would give him his triumph while solving the all-too-real problem we have noted above.

The main Roman supply base for this expedition was at South Shields on the River Tyne (in Roman times this port was called Arbeia). Severus determined on opening two fronts – one to attack the Maeatae, the other to attack the Caledonians. [The Severan campaign did have a third front – for the Roman fleet sailed all the way round Scotland, even reaching Shetland, no doubt landing and pillaging at will as they went.]

3A The campaign against the Maeatae

A forward supply base was established at Cramond – as close as they could get to Manau while still being based in friendly, Gododdin-controlled, territory.

Against the Maeatae Caracalla carried out a deliberate campaign of genocide on Severus' explicit orders. Cassuis Dio [77, 15] reports that Severus gave orders to his soldiers in these words (Bill Thayer's translation):

> *Let no one escape sheer destruction*
> *[Let]no-one [escape] our hands, not even the babe in the womb of the mother,*
> *If it be male; let it nevertheless not escape sheer destruction.*

The name Dunipace (Dyn-y-bas) actually means "fort of death" – it was the base for Caracalla's sadism of the sort later to be seen in the sons of Ragnar Lodbrok in England in the later 800s and in the sons of Saddam Hussein in Iraq at the turn of this millennium.

3b The campaign against the Caledonians

For the northern campaign Monifieth was no longer available to the Romans as a logistics depot, and Cramond was too far away. This is where Fife enters the story for the first time, for the site chosen was Carpow by Abernethy.

The Roman army marched their way up through Strathallan and along the Gask ridge from which Severus took Agricola's line – up Strathmore, and nearly reaching Stonehaven. The tactics of the Caledonians was the inverse of 'scorched earth'. They melted away into the glens, refusing a head-on confrontation and they left animals in their wake deliberately – to lure the Romans further and further in, stretching their lines of supply and reinforcement which made them open to opportunistic attack.

Huge numbers of Romans were killed in this way – many by the Caledonians but also many by their own side – Romans who had been injured but not killed by the enemy then killed by their comrades to prevent their falling into enemy hands. Casualties were high on both sides.

3c Analysis

However much Severus may have wanted to complete the conquest of Great Britain, his efforts turned out to be more a punitive expedition than a meaningful attempt at annexation. In-fighting between Severus and his sons and Severus' own ill-health may have played a part – but there is no need for us to concern ourselves with the details here.

Severus died at York in 211. Caracalla returned to Rome and the Caledonians and Maeatae were left to lick their wounds and pick up the pieces.

3D Fife's involvement

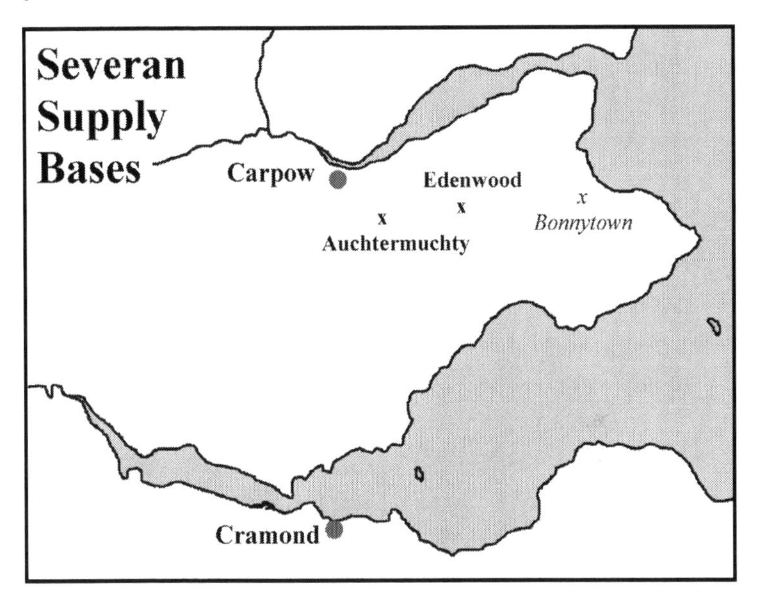

As shown on the map, apart from Carpow itself, there are two Roman camps in Fife – at Auchtermuchty and at Edenwood near Cupar – which are understood to date from this time. We may be confident that the locals were delighted to be bolstered by the Roman presence, indeed they may have hoped that a Roman victory would have seen off permanently the threat to them posed by the Caledonians. On the other hand the Romans were grateful for the opportunity to base themselves at Carpow and we may see Roman artefacts including coins which originate from this time as a measure of the largesse associated with this gratitude. So there is no need to suppose the camps in Fife to be part of the Roman punitive expedition. A show of force to inspect the area round Carpow in detail and to warn off any dissidence, yes; perhaps a tour to instil confidence.

Consideration has being given to possible third and fourth camps:

(i) at Bonnytown, some 3 miles south east of St Andrews; at 11.4 miles from Edenwood (as the crow flies, so considerably longer on the ground) it is an over-stretch from the normal 10 mile distance Romans marched between camps and the archaeological evidence on the ground is equivocal enough for the balance of opinion to be that there was no camp there.

(ii) at Collessie – according to CANMORE [ID 268730] – in the field immediately to the north of Newton Farm Steadings. There is nothing to be seen on the ground and in 2003 the view was that there had been an enclosure but it was unlikely to be Roman. As Auchtermuchty and Edenwood are within a day's march of each other, even if the Collessie site were Roman it is unlikely to be contemporaneous, but there is nothing to have stopped a Roman contingent from Carpow marching out and pitching camp at Collessie to 'show face'.

4. Postscript: Fake History

1. There were no pontoon crossings of the Forth or the Tay
2. There was no Roman Camp at Auchterderran
3. There was no Roman Camp at Carberry Farm
4. General remarks

The Severan campaign in Scotland is very poorly understood – and this has not been helped by too many recent authors not being able to draw maps – which has led to errors of understanding which in turn has made it all too easy to come to the wrong conclusions.

4.1 The Pontoons

Writing in the 1970s, Nicholas Reed got very excited about the illustrations on a coin or two showing the Romans crossing a river on a bridge of boats. The Romans did indeed do this on occasion – on the continent. He went on to suppose that this applied in Scotland and that the Romans marched across the Forth at Queensferry marching on to Auchtermuchty via Auchterderran! He went on to claim that the Romans used the same resource-intensive solution to cross the Tay at Carpow.

(a) The Forth: Just imagine how many boats you would need to "waste" making a pontoon bridge across the Forth! The Romans would have been mad to build and maintain bridges of this sort when far easier and cheaper logistic solutions were readily available.

To this we may add that:

(i) we know that the army went up through Dunipace, Stirling, Auchterarder and then along the Gask Ridge. They could ford the Forth and the Teith without specific difficulty just as Agricola had done a century or so earlier.. and

(ii) Carpow was supplied by the navy – that was the whole point of it!

(b) The Tay: This is a slightly different matter – but the army was far better served by marching on land from Carpow to the fort at Bertha (now on the northern edges of Perth and importantly on the west bank of the Tay) where they could ford the Tay to reach the fort at Grassy Walls (in the grounds of Scone Palace). This march was no farther, was a much easier prospect and it means the Romans could use their boats for their originally intended purpose!

4.2 Auchterderran

Particularly because there was no pontoon across the Forth, there is no logic to any supposed camp at Auchterderran – and there is no evidence for any such camp. [It should be noted that the argument used to be that Carpow would be reached via Auchterderran. Beyond the sea-based access to Carpow, this in itself would have been a logistic nightmare as the Romans would have had to cross Falkland Hill in the process – imagine tramping up there in full armour! – not to mention the extensive marshland east of Loch Leven at the time.]

4.3 Carberry

This is a good point to dispose also of the idea given an airing in the New Statistical Account and rehearsed uncritically by Torrie and Coleman ("Historic Kirkcaldy" 1995) that there was a Roman station at Carberry Farm (now by Mitchelson Industrial Estate, Kirkcaldy). It is thoroughly illogical.

- As Rebecca Jones ("Roman Camps in Scotland" 2011) has made clear there is no evidence of this.
- Like Bonnytown it is about 11.3 miles from the Edenwood camp as the crow flies – but this translates to about 15 miles on the ground – so a (non-existent) intermediate camp would have been required.
- The basis of the claim is the naive parsing of Carberry as Caer + Berry. However not only is there no evidence of a "caer" (a stone built fort) but
  - the oldest spelling we have for Carberry is "Crefbarrin" [PNF771]. This should probably be taken as Welsh "cref"= "strong" and "barru" = "to bar/close securely" – thus a guard post or even a toll gate, which may well fit. [Another potential interpretation might have been that "Cref" was a corruption of "Tref" = house, but then why would the T revert to C? Moreover there is no comparator, so I think not.]
  - elsewhere Carberry is actually an Anglicisation of the Gaelic personal name and/or title "Cairbre" (the

name means "charioteer" (compare this with the British title "knight")

So we may be sure that Carberry was NOT a Roman fort; it was probably a local guard post.

4.4 GENERAL REMARKS

There has been too much talk about proto-Pictland coalescing into two groups: the Caledonians and the Maeatae. This has arisen from a lazy and unquestioning acceptance of the cursory remarks of Cassius Dio (who lived c155-235 CE and, as we have seen, wrote about Severus' campaign in Scotland). While it is widely recognised (and recorded) (i) that the Maeatae and the Caledonians were the "main players" as far as the Romans were concerned and (ii) that they often teamed up with each other – particularly when it came to raiding in the south – the danger lies in over-generalisation. To prove this point we need look no further than the Epidii who would become the Scots. They were not absorbed by either of those mentioned by Cassius Dio, yet they were well north of the Antonine Wall.

The un-thought-through and too frequently supposed extension of this lazy thinking is that Fife was an integral part of realm of the Maeatae. This also is not true – as the previous chapter set out. Not only that but the clear line of hillforts (see next chapter) shows that the northern boundary of the tribe occupying what would become "Fife" regarded their neighbours to the north as at least potentially hostile. The intensity of these defences alone makes clear that this is not the interface of two groups (the Caledonians and the Maeatae) who were often friends and allies.

Given that the Romans intended the genocide of the Maeatae, it is ludicrous to suppose that the Romans could have sited their main resupply base in the territory of the Maeatae (which would have been the case if the Maeatae had controlled the whole of Fife). If that had been possible there would have been no need for the security of using Cramond which was so far away from the main action. [See also Rebecca H Jones' "Roman Camps in Scotland".]

5. The Aftermath: The Caledonian decision to re-conquer "Fife"

The Caledonians were not about to forgive the Falcons for having welcomed the Romans onto their lands. On the contrary as soon as they had recovered from the drubbing they had been given by the Romans they would exact their revenge and further secure themselves against any future expedition of this sort by annexing the Falcons' territory. In particular this would ensure that Carpow could not be used again by the Classis Britannica – the Roman fleet in Britain.

While Carpow was their key target, the Caledonians were also determined that the Romans would never again exercise control of the Gask Ridge – so the Stags of Strathearn too had to be annexed.

Conclusion

The Caledonians' decision to annexe Fife was founded on:

(i) the desire to punish the residents for their hospitality to the Romans

(ii) he need to add to their security against attack from the South, especially by the Romans,

(iii) to facilitate their own raiding in the South.

The details of how this was done is the subject of the next chapter.

Afterword

The Romans did invade again. The Emperor Constantius I and his son Constantine mounted a punitive expedition into Scotland. The situation is very well summarised by a well referenced paragraph in the Wikipedia page on Constantius:

> In 305, Constantius crossed over into Britain, travelled to the far north of the island and launched a military expedition against the Picts, claiming a victory against them and the title *Britannicus Maximus II* by 7 January 306. After retiring to Eboracum (York) for the winter, Constantius had planned to continue the campaign, but on 25 July 306 he died.

Unfortunately there are no details of this expedition anywhere.

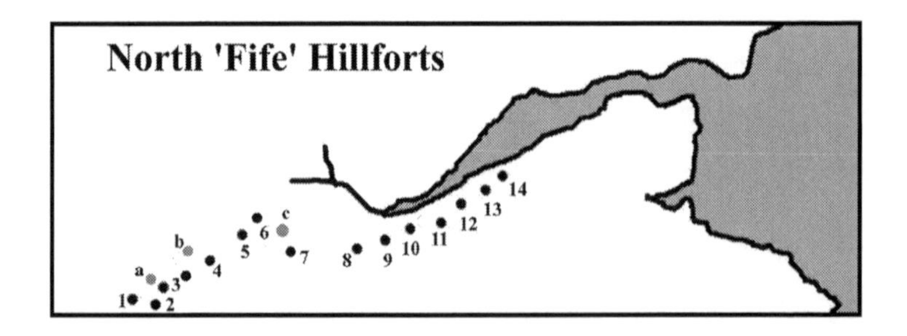
North 'Fife' Hillforts
a
b
c
1
2
3
4
5
6
7
8
9
10
11
12
13
14

3. The Caledonians re-conquer 'Fife'

As we saw in the last chapter, as soon as Severus had retreated, the Caledonians were determined not only to punish the Falcons for having given aid and succour to the Romans, but also to annex their territory to preclude the possibility of a repeat performance. Their overall plan was to use what was now a tried and tested strategy: They would move forward only so far as resources would allow taking over the territory one tranche at a time.

1. The Campaign

Just how much the Falcons feared attack from their Caledonian neighbours can be seen from the density of the hill forts facing this enemy:

The 'Falcons" hillforts identified on this map *left* (in black) are listed below:

1 Ogle Hill	2 Ben Effrey
3 Castle Craig	4 Rossie Law
5 Ha' Tower	6 Jackschairs Wood
7 Castle Law, Forgandenny	8 Castle Law, Abernethy
9 Black Cairn	10 Clatchard Craig
11 Kinnaird Hill	12 Glenduckie Hill
13 Norman's Law	14 Green Craig

Three forts (in grey) I interpret as Caledonian forward positions:

a. Kay Craig b. Dunning c. Forgandenny

This interpretation is based on the lie of the land where the forts are situated and, where available, where the access to the fort is situated.

There is a caveat, however, for there is little specific dating evidence for most of these forts. Nevertheless 14 forts covering 38km (24 miles) is remarkable; so even allowing for the possibility that not all of them may have been occupied simultaneously it is still a very intensive line of defence!

[For as full an appreciation of the distribution of such forts as is available see https://hillforts.arch.ox.ac.uk/. I am particularly grateful to Ms Sophie Nicol of Perth and Kinross Council for her time and expertise discussing these forts and their environment with me and bringing to my attention the helpful and Scotland-specific website www.pastmap.org.uk.]

In the previous chapter we saw that the Caledonians overwhelmed the Wildcats in particular in waves or stages. This strategy having proved successful – and the best way of marshalling their limited resources – they adopted the same strategy in Fife.

Phase 1: Securing Carpow and a surrounding salient

In order to avert a possible renewed assault by the Romans in the short term, the Caledonians' immediate objective was to occupy the area round Carpow. However the evidence on the ground shows what a stiff resistance the Falcons offered.

Their first task was to capture such of the 'Fife' forts from which attacks could be launched on to Carpow – these are shown on the map below:

1. Castle Law, Forgandenny 2. Castle Law, Abernethy
3. Black Cairn Hill 4. Clatchard Craig

The problem with the first two of these forts (from the Caledonians' point of view) is that they do not offer good line of sight to spot an enemy detachment on the warpath from the south until it is nearly too late – and they offer no chance for the Caledonians to impose themselves on the local population from which such a force might be drawn. So a new line of forts would need to be built – but for them to be effective they would need to be far enough below the tops of the hills as to be out of any direct communications. Although the distances are small enough that runners could take a message fairly quickly, signal stations would be an advantage.

New Caledonian defences:

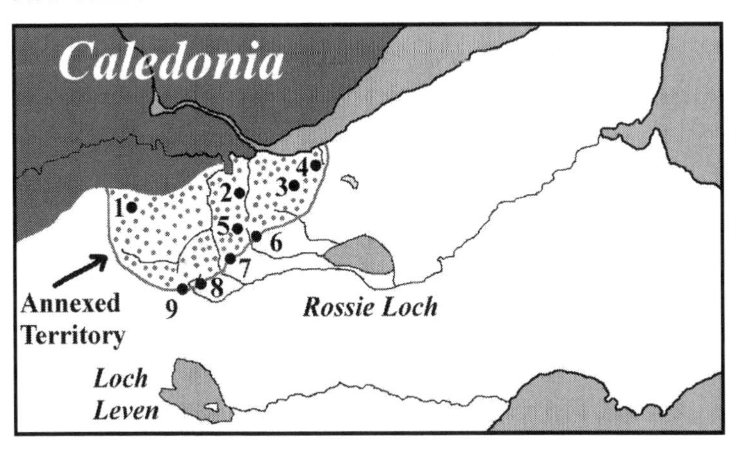

5. Wester Pitlour (6. Beins Law) 7. Corrinzion
8. Carmore 9. Duncrievie

The main route from Abernethy was up the glen of the Nethy and over the hill into Glentarkie. The Caledonians established a fort on either side of Glentarkie – at Wester Pitlour and at Beins Law. While the fort at Wester Pitlour is well identified on the ground and well placed as a base from which to exercise control over the North part of the Howe of Fife, its drawback is that there is no line of sight back to headquarters (eg Castle Law), so the higher site at Bein's Law was also required. For a long time now nothing has been left to see of the fort at Beins Law, but the site is shown as a fort on older OS maps. This is significant, however, because it demonstrates the old adage "absence of evidence is not evidence of absence" in this context.
If attackers were to choose a bit of a flank attack and so to drive through Glenfarg, then the easier of two routes would be from Gateside up the Morton Burn (clearly called the "Lochie" – the Black Burn – in Pictish times) and over to The Bein Inn. To guard this route another fort was set up at Corrinzion.

Again there is the problem of a lack of line of sight back to headquarters, But Bein's Law should have been able to solve this problem as it did for Pitlour. The exact site of the fort at Corrinzion is unknown, but it is likely to have been at Castle Wood – some 400 yards ENE of Corrinzion farm house itself. Here it would also have prevented the 'Fifers' from bypassing the fort at Wester Pitlour.

The earliest spelling we have for this name dates to 1494: "Carrynane" – betraying the "Caer" first element (meaning stone built fort). The rest of the meaning of this name is unclear [PNF 3168]. With any name the first problem is parsing, but in this case the stress today is corrINzion, suggesting that it is NOT a case of Caer – y – something. It would not be appropriate, nor is it necessary to seek a Gaelic explanation here. Possibilities cognate with modern Welsh include "einion" meaning 'anvil' but there are other possibilities: for example 'onnen' (Gaelic 'uinnsean') means "ash tree" – however such has been the intensity of land management that there is no native treescape in the area to help us assess this.

The Collessie Spearman: This new border was further marked by the Standing Stone near Collessie with the carving of a "Spearman" on it. There are a few such stones with identical carvings. From their locations I think it is safe to say that they featured specifically Caledonian warriors. This stone stands on a bluff facing south and says to the Falcons unequivocally "Thus far and no farther!"

For details see the "Notes on the cover illustration" and for the Collessie stone see the Colour insert pages. The image picked out is approximate in some places because it is so heavily covered in lichen. [I am delighted to be advised that at the time of writing Fife Council is in discussion with Historic Environment Scotland with a view both to removing all the lichen and taking a detailed laser scan of the stone and its image before any more deterioration takes place.]

The reader will note that this too was not an innovation. They had placed one of these stones in front of their fort at Turin Hill (in this case they seem to have 'repurposed' an existing stone; whether or not they moved it we cannot say). Two other such stones have been identified. The other two are at (i) Perth (probably, like Turin Hill, part of their expansion after Agricola) and (ii) at Rhynie which is more difficult to date – it could be from before Agricola, or as a stage in their retreat some time later. For a paper on all of them by Helen Mackay see https://www.academia.edu/39103695/

In passing it is worth noting that:

(i) the "-tark-" in Glentarkie does derive from turk/twrch, but this does NOT mean "wild boar" – it refers to domestic male pigs (probably mostly castrated) who were raised in this glen;
(ii) the females ("muc" means "sow") were reared separately in the next glen – the Muchty…
(iii) Meanwhile it seems likely that there were wild boar in the area: this is implied by the farm name Bannaty near the Kinross border (and again misunderstood in PNF). [While Hadrian's Wall was garrisoned, one of the forts was called Banna and its garrison the "Venatores Bannienses" – the boar hunters.]
(iv) There are huge numbers of words for "bog" in Gaelic – some deriving from Pictish. Mostly they each refer to specific types of bog. The element "-mig-" in Strathmiglo is Pictish and can be compared to places like Meggetland on the river Leith in Edinburgh, Migdale just north of the Dornoch Firth and The Maggot Glebe in Inverness. It refers to an area of land beside a river which is boggy because it is likely to be inundated when the river is in spate. "Strathmiglo" makes clear that the River Eden was liable to regular flooding in this area – only modern engineering has allowed eg Bankwell Crescent to exist.

Rather more out of the way was an advance up what are now labelled as the headwaters of the River Eden and on to the so-called Carmore Burn. Carmore is now the name of a farm. The meaning is "obvious" (Caer Mawr – big fort) but there is no evidence remaining on the ground. One good site for the fort would have been around the trig point at Yellow Hill – with the added advantage of a natural defence on the southern side – but actually there is a plateau stretching from near Carmore farm in the west to Balcanquhal very near the Gateside/Bein Inn road on the east, so it may be that the fort occupied a more central position on this plateau which would have enabled the garrison to react more easily to either side. In this regard we should note that the old road came from the smithy at Burnside on the A91 straight up to crest the hill on the edge of the field to the east of Yellow Hill (whence on to Arngask etc.), so the woods one field further east on the escarpment is another potentially inviting site. [Balcanquhal is a much later name dating to the middle ages.]

On the other side of the river lies Duncrievie - the Dun of the "Crieve-ie". This lets us know that the 'proper' name for this tributary of the Eden is the Crievie. Duncrievie is in a relative hollow, so will probably have had to rely on Carmore for signals. [The name Crievie is not immediately apparent, but the Welsh word Criafol refers to the Rowan tree and, as it happens, despite all the human disruption in the area (roads, railways, houses, farming) there are still rowan trees growing wild in the area - so the valley may have been really "Rowan Glen" and the stream the "Rowan burn". Alternatively Welsh crëyr/crehyr means heron - and the earliest spelling for Pittencrieff in Dunfermline is "-creher" so the corruption may be parallel.]

So all in all what we can see is that the Caledonians had their work cut out making any inroads into 'Fife' at all and had to be very muscular even in the defence of their small early gains. The fact that these forces were so evenly matched suggests that the invasion took place before the Caledonians had recovered properly from the ravages of the Severan invasion, so we should estimate a date soon after 210 CE and probably before 215 CE.

Phase 1 result: The first salient had pushed the Falcons south of the upper reaches of the river Eden and the Rossie Loch. It had been successful in securing Carpow against any sneak attack.

Phase 2: Advance to the River Eden

So we may now put ourselves in the position of the Caledonian Field Marshal and ask ourselves how we would tackle the problem. In my view a critical consideration is the avoidance of a counter-attack on the flank – and there was only one potentially exposed flank – the eastern one. This would be particularly so if the Caledonians had tried a frontal assault on Falkland Hill – which would be a mammoth task given the lie of the land. So the next task was to complete the take over of the Tay-facing forts identified on the first map above. Any attempt by the Falcons to reoccupy these would be weakened if the Caledonians occupied Cupar. Securing Cupar would, in effect, cut off the whole Tentsmuir/Leuchars area north of the Eden which could then be mopped up and secured at leisure.

[The earliest reference we have to the Castle Hill site is early mediaeval; the extensive works there at that time would have obliterated any earlier archaeology. But the same considerations which led the Earls of Fife to make this an important site – so important that it remained the County Town into the 20th Century – already applied in the times we are discussing here.]

This would be the time also when the Caledonians would have set up a forward position at the so-called Agabatha Castle (next to the old Trafalgar School house at Collessie) to control access to the Collessie Den.

Phase 2 result: Thus the end of the second stage was the securing of all Fife between the Tay and the Eden.

Phase 3: Annexing the East Neuk

We may now go on to consider the layout of hill forts in the centre of Fife.

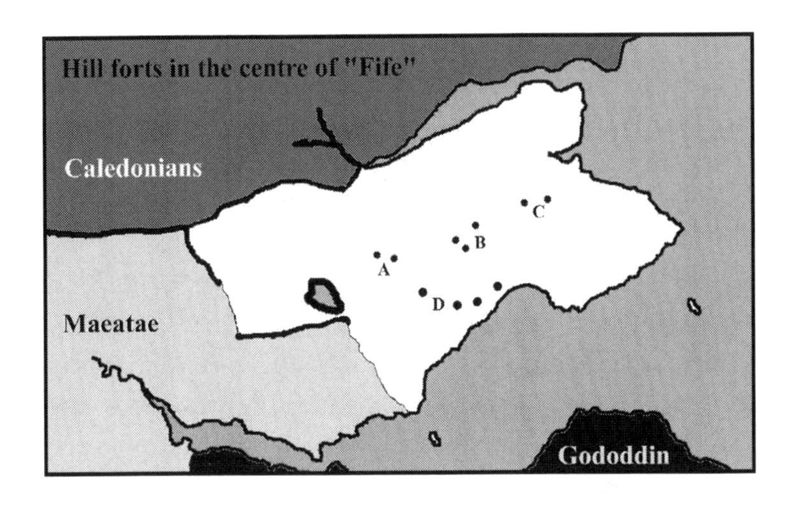

[There is no need for concern about the apparently large distance between Loch Leven and the forts at A, for in between is the massif of the Lomond Hills which descend steeply to the shore of the loch. Not only that but the whole area between the loch (as we know it today) and Auchmuirbridge has only been drained (and the river canalised) in relatively recent times. Thus the Caledonians were faced by a near impenetrable cordon. The place/river name "Leven" [PNF 948] here is one which cannot be explained with certainty. It may refer to

- a significant stretch of the river (around Balgonie) running fast but smoothly (Welsh "llyfn", Gaelic "liobhann"); or
- it may have run though elm trees (Welsh "llwyfen", Gaelic "Leamhan") or
- it could refer to the often flooded land mentioned above (cf Welsh "llif" meaning "flood"]

Group A: Right in front of the Caledonians were the four forts on the Lomond hills: Maiden Castle between East and West Lomond, East Lomond Hill itself and other forts at Purin and Netherdrums farms. For reasons which will be made clear, Maiden Castle will be considered separately below, but this aside and despite the fact that the latter two were comparatively easily attacked, this was a formidable obstacle because of the steep northern face of Falkland Hill – and West Lomond is even steeper. So the Caledonians' plan was surely to leave these alone in the first instance.

Group B: Two more forts to which the Falcons would have retreated – Bowden/Fronthill and Walton Hill (variously Lady Mary's Wood) – face the Howe of Fife. Storming these from the Howe would be difficult (which is why the sites were chosen!) because of the substantial steep slopes below them. Behind them lies Down Hill fort – which may have been part of the previous 'normal' infrastructure but was less suited to a front-line role.

Missing from the map is a location between Group B and Group C which I am sure was also a fort. On the top of Hill of Tarvit (previously Wemyss Hall Hill) is a site labelled "enclosed settlement". Half a mile to the south-east is Scotstarvit Tower; three-quarters of a mile south of the "settlement" is Craigrothie [PNF 981] which T&M agree contains the element "roth" (fort). The problem is that while it is, therefore, beyond doubt that there was a fort in the area, we cannot be sure of the exact site. We can be confident that this is NOT a reference to Oldlord fort because the water course next to it was called the Glassie. On balance my view is that the "enclosed settlement" was indeed a fort, perhaps hastily and inadequately built when the Caledonians stormed Cupar. On the other hand Canmore says:

> "There is the potential that some of the landforms (breaks of slope) to the immediate north of the distinct enclosure may constitute outer earthworks to the core site. This enclosure could encompass an area 120m by 60m with

> the well-defined site on the western side of the larger enclosure. The validity of the larger enclosure could not be confidently determined through the survey."

So actually it is more likely that this was a major site dating to an earlier period, reoccupied when Cupar was lost. At some stage this was a very significant feature, meaning that the water course now called the Craigrothie Burn was simply called the Rothie ("the burn by the fort"). The settlement name Craigrothie would then appear to refer to an outcrop of rock nearby – perhaps now quarried away. [There is a parallel place name in Strathspey: the Craiggowrie Burn. The names started of as the Gowr-ie – the goats' burn. The Crag was the Craig by the Gowrie – Craiggowrie. But this was only readily understandable to Pictish speaking people. Thus later the English word "burn" was added and the Gowrie became Craiggowrie Burn.]

For the Caledonians the clever thing to do was not to try a frontal assault. So the strategy was to focus effort on the East Neuk.

Group C: The East Neuk was far less intensely defended. Perhaps the local population was too sparsely spread, perhaps it was a judgement made by the Falcons that there would not be an attack in such an out-of-the-way place. If so it was a crucial misjudgement. The Caledonians saw this as the way of bypassing many of the forts we have discussed so far. Starting at Denork (which looked north over Strathkinness, the Caledonians overwhelmed it – and it looks as if they then established a fort which was later superceded by the broch (the grey dot of Group C) on Drumcarrow Craig a few hundreds of yards to the south – with the crucial advantage that it had line of sight not only back into Strathkinness but also south and east to the valley of the

Cameron Burn. Such defenders as there were at Blebo Hole were surrounded – there was no point in fighting on.

The time we are talking about is at the very end of the normal age of Broch building and it was neither Caledonians nor Falcons who had this technology – but it is an excellent site so it is likely that the Falcons had constructed a fort here. We might suppose that the fact that the Caledonians would go to the effort of building this broch substantially later (post 300) suggests that even then they felt their grip of the area was still somewhat tenuous.

Group D: Having successfully outflanked the Falcons, the Caledonian army was able to split up. A small force would be needed to 'mop up' the East Neuk proper, while two armies pushed forward, with one driving west to establish a fort at Oldlord, while the other drove nearly south to set up at Dunnicher Law. Meantime the fleeing Falcons set up their last ditch resistance in the area at Craig Rock (the black dot).

From Oldlord the Northern Front division were able to push on establishing a forward base at Down Law, right behind the Falcons' forts in group B. Thus surrounded, the garrisons in the Falcons' forts had no choice but to surrender – and Craig Rock would fall before long.

Again it is feasible that the Falcons had Down Law and Oldlord – perhaps even Dunicher – as their normal infrastructure before creating their new front line when confronted. If so then again it is simply the case of the Caledonians using these key sites as their bases for further advance.

Phase 3 result: The Caledonians had gained control of the whole of what used to be North East Fife district.

Phase 4: Pushing on into Kirkcaldy District

Group E: The Caledonians were now in a position where they could intensify their forces again over the more narrow front represented by the forts in Group E. West to East these are Newton of Balbirnie, Duniface, Mount Fleurie and Blacketyside. We may be confident of our general understanding of these because the entrances to them are from the South.

It is most likely that the Caledonians' tactic was to pick off these Group E forts and then lay siege to Falkland Hill. Given its location and, especially, the lack of water up there (depending on how tightly the siege was laid), it is unlikely that such a siege would have lasted long. However we can be more specific. In Chapter one I noted that Dunipace in the Falkirk Council area means "fort of death". Of the forts in Group E there is Duniface. Duniface is simply a Gaelic version of Dunipace – in Gaelic the descriptor needs to be in the genitive case – so 'pace' becomes 'phace' which can, of course, be spelled 'face' (so this change of pronunciation will have post dated the coming of the Scots – see Chapter 12). This then allows us to understand that the Caledonians picked off these forts from East to West and that the Falcons, only too aware of what was going on, decided to go 'all in' (as poker parlance has it) at Duniface.

Unfortunately I cannot have any confidence that any of the names we see in the local area can be attributed to before the date of the battle, so the best we can do is to refer to the "Battle of Duniface". The battle seems to have been decisive one – giving the Caledonians free rein to lay siege to Falkland Hill (East Lomond).

Maiden Castle, the key: This siege was no foregone conclusion – and this is where we return to Maiden Castle. As suggested, Purin and Nether Drums were a bit of a pushover, but East Lomond

Fort was another proposition. The archaeological details can be seen on the Canmore site [29936]. Let us start at the end:

(i) "...the site as a whole has the appearance of being an unfinished fort." This is not just the appearance, the archaeologists' instincts are correct.

(ii) "...there is a well-defined entrance at the W end." Again this is correct.

If one does not understand this fort then it is stupid. You cannot see to the north – because there is a higher ridge close by. You cannot see to the south for the same reason. So setting the steepness of the slopes to one side, this fort is open to surprise attack from either direction. There is a view to the west – but that is only to West Lomond Hill not far away but again far higher than is needed to block any vista.

So we can see that the only clear view from this fort is to East Lomond, directly to the east with a narrow vista down to Falkland, but in such a way that such a line of sight has no defensive value. And we noted above that the entrance was to the west. Although the archaeologists note the "suggestion" of an entrance to the east, this can be discounted due to the fort being unfinished. This eastern entrance was part of the building works and would have been sealed in the course of the completion of the project (see photograph in the colour plate section).

Conclusion: This fort was being built by the Caledonians – NOT by the Falcons!

Having secured Hilton Hill to the east, Leslie to the south and the north side of the Lomond Hills, the Caledonians came up the Maspie Den to complete the encirclement of East Lomond and prevent any organised escape of the Falcons towards eg

Auchmuirbridge whether into Kinross or for a possible link up with the Maeatae at Navitie Hill just 3 miles further on. They started building a massive fort (the name "Maiden" is a corruption of what in modern Welsh is Mawr Dyn – meaning "big fort") in full sight of the Falcons. The very size of it must have been intimidating, not to mention the numbers engaged in the construction.

The result is that even before "Maiden Castle" was completed the Falcons could see that the game really was up and so they capitulated without a fight before the fort could be completed. Once these forts had fallen, the Caledonians were free to occupy the whole of Kirkcaldy district at leisure.

Keeping in mind that both the area between Loch Leven and Auchmuirbridge and the area between Navity Hill and Kinglassie were all but impassable, the Caledonians could drive down over quite a narrow front, establishing a new forward base which, to make sure that no-one was in any doubt, they called Caer y Caledy – "the fort of the Caledonians": Kirkcaldy! This meant "We are the new masters here. Don't doubt it!"

From Kirkcaldy, outposts were established at (i) Goatmilk Hill, Glenrothes, (ii) Raith Hill by Auchtertool and (iii) Druimmuilionn (just off the Invertiel road).

Phase 4 result: The Caledonians had now annexed the old Kirkcaldy District

Phase 5: Annexing Kinross

The campaign to secure Kinross was a prospect very different from that of taking the whole of North East 'Fife'. From their base at Carmore it was a matter of just four miles to Loch Leven and only eight to Crook of Devon. Such an attack would bypass completely the line of Falcon forts facing west on the Ochils. My guess is that the best time to have done this was after the Caledonians had established their base at Kirkcaldy as that is the way to have kept the defenders as stretched as possible.

Once they had completed the fighting they established their western forward command headquarters at the Falcons' main site at Down Hill (see below) overlooking the Devon river – with an outlier fortified control point roughly where Tullibole Castle is today.

PHASE 6: SETTLING THE SOUTHERN BOUNDARY OF "FIFE"
The Maeatae (the dominant tribe in the kingdom of Manau) had reason to be wary of Caledonian intentions as soon as the forts in Group E were attacked – even more so by the time Kirkcaldy had been established. Although this was not actually 'their' land they did rather consider it as client territory (rather as the Caledonians had viewed the animal tribes and the Venicones before Agricola invaded). This is illustrated by the coin evidence (see next chapter below) So there was still some 'unfinished business'.

So we may now consider the "front line" between the two.

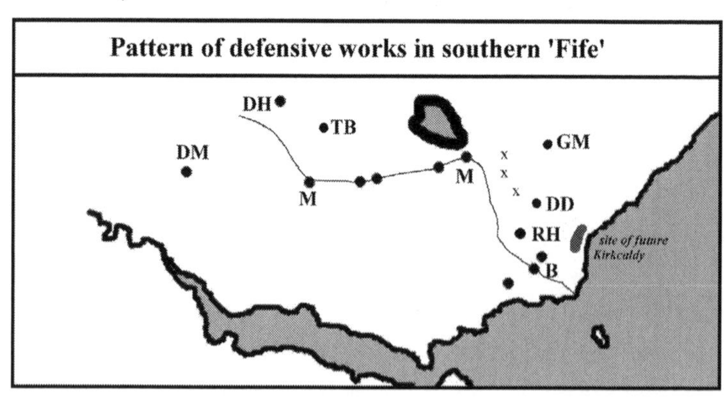

[The thin line represents the Maeatan frontier.]

DH: This is Down Hill in general terms it overlooks Crook of Devon and faces South, however it is a little too deep into the Ochils to serve the Kinross plain well – its specific job seems to have been to guard the road to Dunning from Crook of Devon. This is clearly a position designed to defend against attack from the south – ie against the Maeatae.

TB: Tullibole castle itself is relatively modern, but it is built on a much older defensive site. It would make sense for the Caledonians – and even the Falcons before them – to have had at least a guard there as an outpost from Down Hill to control the road north from Clackmannan.

Both of these probably belonged to the Falcons before being taken by the Caledonians.

DM: Dumyat, above Menstrie was one of the main bases of the Maeatae (it is generally agreed that 'myat' (say "dum EYE at") derives from the name 'Maeatae').

M…M: This line of forts, Drumglow, Dummiefarline, Benarty Hill and Dunmore on Navitie Hill behind Ballingry faces North – ie they are defending the south and so we may suppose them to be the northern border of the Maeatae. Four forts in six miles is an intensity of fortification close to the sort we have seen above!

xxx: Although there are no forts between Navitie Hill and Stoneyhall, this is probably because, as we have noted, this land was pretty well impassable due to its being boggy. Nevertheless the 'x's indicate what I interpret as boundary markers: (i) Devil's Stone at Capeldrae, (ii) Harelaw Cairn, Pitcairn and (iii) at Lochend Farm on the Eastern shore of Loch Gelly.

B: We may observe a 'front-line stand-off' situation where just 650 metres apart are Druimmuilionn fort (to the north) and Stoneyhall Hill fort (to the South) across a relatively deep valley. [Just another 500 metres south east of Stoneyhall are more standing stones (on Glassmount Farm).] Particularly given the standing stones so close by, I suspect that these forts represent an active front line between the Caledonians and the Maeatae.

DE: Standing somewhat back from the front line is Dunearn Fort.

DF: Although the clue is in the name "Dun-", no relevant archaeological evidence of just where the fort of Dunfermline may have been has come to light. At 6 miles from the "M" forts it was well placed to serve as an HQ and service centre for them – as well as Dunearn. As such Dunfermline will have performed a function almost exactly parallel to Kirkcaldy except that it was within 'home' territory rather than being an outpost of occupiers.

The remaining sites – on the Falcons' side – are shown in grey. This is because I suspect that they were not there before the Caledonians invaded.

RH: Raith Hill is not recognised by the Canmore website etc., but the clue is in the name "Raith" – from Pictish "Roth" – meaning 'fort on a mound/hill' (the Gaelic cognate 'rath' is applied rather more loosely to include fortified enclosures whether or not on a hill). [It is this "Raith" which gave its name to the Raith Estate – whence Raith House and the modern Raith Estate housing complex in Kirkcaldy.] It is next to the old Walton Farm and is most easily approached from the East and North, making it Southward facing. So this was a southern defence for the Falcons' against the Maeatae. Raith Hill is well disposed to control the

Auchtertool road (B925) just as Druimmuilionn is to control the Inverteil one (B9157). [The Site of Castle Hill also just West of Auchtertool suggests that Raith Hill was abandoned at quite an early date.]

DD: Looking further north we may note the name Dundonald. Unfortunately this area has been disturbed so substantially first by coal working and then by forestry that it is unlikely that any evidence will remain on the ground. There is a further problem in that "Donald" is an Anglic corruption of a Gaelic name and as such that part of the word belongs to a period after 850. However there is no problem with a Donald having his name attached to a pre-existing 'dun' or hill fort (from Brythonic/Welsh 'Dyn').

GM: So too with the Goat Milk Hills (now the site of Glenrothes Airport and golf course). According to local lore recorded in the New Statistical Account this was supposed to have been a "Danish" camp – ie dating from Viking times. Whether or not this was actually true we may set to one side, but we should note that a good defensive position tends to remain so through time – so the scope for an earlier base is not excluded and it is very curious that Goat Milk estate was held by Kirkcaldy into mediaeval times (appearing in Burgh records as late as 1583 and 1591).

These two defensive positions were well away from the border (marked by the standing stones and cairns) but were as close as they could be, within reason, given the lie of the land.

KY: The site of Kirkcaldy will be discussed separately later.

As implied by the comment above, the main problem with these sites is that of dating. However:

- we have established that at the time of Severus' invasion, the Maeatae could not have occupied the whole of "Fife", so they will have needed a border somewhere;
- remembering that the southern shore of the Firth of Forth opposite Inchcolm was very firmly within Gododdin territory, and noting that the old name of Inchcolm was Emona/Aemonia suggesting a connection to Manau – which would have been difficult to sustain if the Fife coast so close by had been hostile – we may be confident that the Maeatae did control the Fife coast as far as Kinghorn (see below).

So I think we are reasonably safe in assuming the M…M line of forts belong to this time. They will have needed some sort of presence further east – and Dunearn is well suited to have filled that role.

Note on the Shore Boundary: The boundary between the Falcons and the Maeatae is likely to have been the same as had existed between the Caledonians and the Maeatae before the arrival of the 'animal' tribes.

The only element of the line which I have not specified as yet is exactly where it reached the shore. The answer is the **Hoch-ma-toch** rocks 500m north along the coast from Kinghorn Parish Church (see picture in colour plates section). This can be seen as still marking the boundary of Kinghorn Parish on older OS maps. The meaning of Hoch-ma-toch remains a complete mystery – not least because even which language it derives from remains unclear. A genuine case of "time immemorial".

Phase 7: South 'Fife': One bridge too far

On the one hand the Maeatae were traditional friends and ancient comrades of the Caledonians – but they had proved unreliable in the face of Roman attack, so all things considered, it is reasonable to ask the question why the Caledonians would not push on south. Perhaps the heartland of the Maeatae (Clackmannanshire) would be a bit cheeky, but surely the south of 'Fife' – to Dunfermline and Charlestown would be a good idea. Amongst other things, it would have given the Caledonians firm control of the coastline – thereby further inhibiting another Roman intrusion.

The answer is that they did try – but they failed.

The key to understanding this lies in the place name Dunfermline. The 'received' understanding of the name is set out in PNF 443. In essence the meaning of the name has remained a mystery for over 1,000 years. The problem in recent times has been the assumption that the name is Gaelic in origin. If the name had been Gaelic then the explanations normally offered would not be possible because of the stress pattern – it would be dunferMELan rather than dunFERmelan – which is no doubt a substantial part of why all but the "dun-" is described as "problematical"!

Actually the name is barely changed at all from its Pictish original and it can be explained. The oldest spelling we have dates to 1128 – Dunfermelin. I say this should be parsed Dun-fer-melin.

Dun is the same as the old Pictish/Brythonnic "dyn" and means "fort" (usually hill fort);

Fer is the same as the modern Welsh "ffêr" which can be an adjective or a noun and means "brave" (compare this with "fierce" and French "fier");

Melin is a variant of the modern Welsh "melan" which means "steel" or something made of steel.

So Dunfermline is "the fort of the brave steel" – or, allowing for the metaphor, "The fort of the steel-hard heroes".

The closest to an accurate original spelling I can offer is "Dynyffêrmelan" – which is also a bit closer to how the name is actually pronounced by local people (the "y"s are hardly pronounced and are like "uh"). Because the original name was Pictish rather than Gaelic we can be sure that the name (and hence the town) was founded a long time before 850AD.

But why would it have that name? I suggest that when the Caledonians attempted to push forward to the southern shores of the Firth of Forth, they were seen off by the garrison at, let us say, Pittencrieff. The local people were delighted that they had beaten the Caledonians – the self-styled "hard men" – and so they crowed "You think you're hard? Our men are not just hard – they're steel hard!". Thus was the name Dunfermline born.

DISCUSSION

The huge losses sustained by the Romans left them unwilling or unable to pour in the resources necessary to sustain their position along the Highland Line, never mind push into the mountains themselves, but this came at a nearly equally huge cost to the Caledonians. Even a generation and more later the Caledonians were still weakened by the severity of these massacres carried out by Severus and Caracalla. They had other problems at this time also for, with "Scottish" support from their Cruithin cousins in northern Ireland, the Epidii were resisting them in Argyll and even beginning to push them back (See my book ALLE p54-62). So in short they needed a Strategic Defence Review to assess what was within their capabilities.

The distribution of hill forts in 'Fife' – some identified by archaeology, others by placename – and particularly their orientation (ie which way they were facing and where the entrances were) allows us to understand their function; as we have seen above this makes possible an understanding of the way the Caledonians set about the annexation of 'Fife'. However we should be clear that this is a hypothesis – a proposition – it is by no means proved.

The Maeatae had already been a confederation of very considerable strength; they recovered from the Roman attacks at about the same sort of rate. To take them on again would imply trying to conquer their whole kingdom – and every general should learn (as they still fail to learn today) that while you do need a plan of how to beat the enemy, perhaps more important is a plan for how to manage the enemy and the newly acquired territory after you have won!

The Caledonians and Maeatae had cooperated in joint ventures many times previously. As we have seen, the Caledonians had learned to their cost that the Maeatae were not willing to roll over and give up their own core territory – eg the Dunfermline area. To invade them again would be to make more permanent enemies of them and preclude future cooperation of this sort. Instead bridges needed to be built.

Chapter Conclusion

Halting at Kirkcaldy represented "job done".

(i) They had punished the Falcons for having been, in their eyes, too acquiescent in the face of Roman occupation, and
(ii) not only had they precluded any Roman reoccupation of Carpow, they had forestalled any potential Roman

beachhead at Kirkcaldy or Leven – so they would have more time and space to mobilise should the Romans attempt to mount another expedition into their territory.

(iii) With the Romans relying on even longer lines of supply and communication, the opportunity for the Caledonians to deploy what had in fact been a successful, though costly, strategy of melting away and staging guerrilla-style attacks would stand an even better chance of success.

So we may now understand that when the Caledonians annexed "Fife" they established two southern border strongholds with Kirkcaldy their Eastern Command HQ and Down Hill Fort its Western counterpart. [North of Auchterarder there was no need for a serious defence as by now this too was already their own territory.]

Outcome: The Cost borne by the Caledonians

The decision to annexe Fife was taken out of desperation. The Caledonians were utterly determined not to allow the Romans (or anyone else) an easy opportunity to establish a bridgehead close enough to be able to inflict the sort of damage wrought on them by Severus. They felt the need to do this while still seriously weakened by the encounters with the Romans. This fear was coupled with fury against the Fifers for having welcomed the Romans. This led to the Caledonians acting precipitously – rashly – and this can be seen from the hard slog the annexation became and the other collateral damage they incurred as a result.

The Caledonians had few if any friends.

1. Their aggressive nature had led the Epidii (living in what is now Argyll) to seek military support from their cousins

in Ulster who would become the "Scots" – and with that support during the 200s CE they were able to push the Caledonians back from the head of Loch Fyne and up Glen Falloch to Crianlarich.

2. Along the west bank of the Spey, the tribe Ptolemy had called the Vacomagi had built a line of forts facing the river – whose purpose can only have been to resist any oncoming threat from the Caledonians to the east.

3. But the most clear demonstration of the resentment caused by the Caledonians is the subject of ongoing archaeological exploration by Aberdeen University at Tap O'Noth near Rhynie in Strathbogie (see https://www.abdn.ac.uk/news/14019/). Here a vast hill fort, with some 800 dwellings now identified, faced south and east. It dates to as early as before 300AD.

My interpretation of this is that the because the Caledonians' efforts were focussed in the south, the locals, led by the Verturiones (Cruithin imported to bolster their strength), took the opportunity to drive the Caledonians back from Buchan, Formartine and The Garioch, establishing Tap O' Noth as their forward command headquarters. Before too long the Caledonians had been forced to concede yet more ground – the valleys of the Don and the Dee – back to their original borders before the arrival of the animal tribes.

The Caledonians may have seen this as a worthwhile exchange – gaining more and better land further to the south, which had been their own before the arrival of the Animal Tribes and which had the added advantage of facilitating plundering raids south of the river Forth. But it was nevertheless a serious set back in the power politics of the emerging land of the Picts – and as a result 'Caledu' definitely became the junior partner.

Timescale

My view about the timescale for all this has wavered. Clearly it could not have started before 210. Any end date needs to take into account Constantius' expedition against the Picts in 305. This would not have happened had there not been consistent raiding over a significant period of time and this raiding was only feasible if the raiding party's contingents were broadly at peace. It was certainly not over in a year or two. Not only was time required for fort building (hill forts are not the same as Roman marching camps) and you would not go to the expense of time and effort in shaping, carving and erecting the Collessie Spearman standing stone if you expected to move on in a matter of weeks.

Lossio Veda again!

And so it is that we return yet again to Lossio Veda and his plaque. With the analysis in the last chapter, we can say that the annexation of Fife was complete by 235 at the latest – and possibly as early as 222 or even earlier. Because he was proud of his Falcon heritage it seems highly unlikely that Lossio Veda would have taken service with Rome before the annexation of Fife was complete. But on the other hand he needed to have accomplished whatever it was he did for which the plaque became appropriate.

So all in all I would still take the view that a ten to twenty year campaign – with obvious 'fighting seasons' would be sufficient and allow plenty of scope for fort building. So this book heralds the 1,800th anniversary of the completion of the annexation!

4. Managing Caledonian 'Fife'

When the Caledonians annexed Donside, Angus, the Mearns and Gowrie etc. in the years following Agricola's recall to Rome, they were dealing with neighbours; they already had a line of forts on their previous borders overlooking their new lands and the tribes they conquered were already used to a loose overlordship. We may imagine that for the ordinary residents an air of resignation may have been combined with a relief that they were not going to be attacked any more. If there was any lingering doubt, the slaughter undertaken later by Severus would have been enough to convince them that integrating with the Caledonians was not the worst option.

Taking control of Fife – clearly a population resentful of the Caledonians' aggression – was another matter altogether. There were other problems as well:

(a) Fife is considerably further away from their base
(b) whereas for the people in Angus etc. the only option was retreat into the sea, Fifers had the option of appealing to the Maeatae for support.

1. The Caledonians' Headquarters

We should dismiss also loose talk of Abernethy (Aber-neth-ig: the mouth of the shining/pure burn) as "the" or even "a" 'Capital' of "The Picts". Those who try to press this claim have first to explain why not too much later (shortly after 565 CE) in order to visit the King of the Picts, St Columba went not to Abernethy but to Inverness. We should add to this the competing claims of many other locations (Forfar, Dunkeld etc.) including two very close by: Forteviot and Scone.

Actually in those days and for several centuries thereafter (as also in France, for example) there was no one 'capital' as such. Kings and their courts were largely peripatetic – imposing themselves on their principal subjects (the later Mormaers) as they toured their realms dispensing justice etc. The same would surely have applied on a smaller scale in the case of the Mormaers themselves.

Nevertheless there is a case to be made for Abernethy being an administrative centre – and careful authors make no greater claim than this. The principal evidence is the sanctuary marked by "MacDuff's Cross", just two miles away. The problem was that local "justice" was summary and arbitrary, so it is understandable that many people would want to have the opportunity of something like a "fair trial". To do this they needed to plead their case to their 'king' (or the mormaer). So sanctuaries were set up where the fleeing accused person could find safety from the local boss and his henchmen. Reaching the sanctuary meant that you were guaranteed a proper hearing in front of someone keen to dispense justice rather than condemnation based on spite or ill will. [A similar situation persists today where some people accused of some crimes which could be tried in a magistrates' court can demand the right to be tried in a higher court in front of a jury.] For this system to work the asylum seeker needed to be reasonably confident that the ruler would be in the vicinity reasonably soon.

In the early stages of the occupation of Fife by the Caledonians it was also desirable for the administrative centre to be as close as reasonable to 'home territory'. On the one hand it made for the quickest transmission of intelligence and orders between Caledonia proper and Fife and it also means that the ruling cadre there had the best means of escape, should the Fifers organise and rebel! So I am confident that Abernethy will have served as the principal administrative centre for the new rulers of Fife.

[We shall look at the establishment of the nunnery at Abernethy in Chapter 6. Clearly we may suppose that King William I of England viewed Abernethy to be a significant place when he chose it as the site for the signing of the Treaty of Abernethy (1072 CE) when Malcolm III acknowledged William as his overlord.]

2. GARRISON DEPLOYMENT – GENERAL

At least to begin with, the Caledonians needed a substantial and distributed garrison to exercise their newly acquired overlordship. So they needed bases and lines of communication. Here I propose the pattern adopted.

CALEDONIAN "FIFE": DEPLOYMENT OF CORE OCCUPYING FORCES AND LINES OF COMMUNICATION

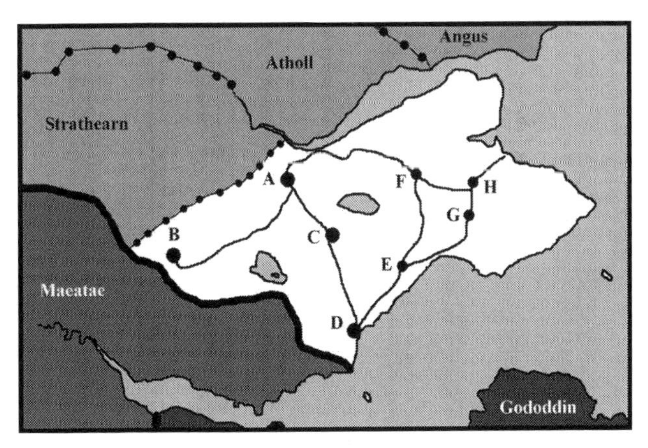

A: Castle Law, Abernethy
B: Down Hill
C: Falkland Hill, East Lomond
D: Kirkcaldy
E: Duniface, Kennoway
F: Castle Hill, Cupar
G: Dunnicher Law
H: Broch at Drumcarrow Craig

This is the 'top level' network – others, some of which were mentioned in the previous chapter, continued to be needed whether for ensuring a "good fences make good neighbours" policy *viz à viz* the Maeatae or for normal eg coastal defence against piratical raids. As can be seen, the Caledonians were able to use forts built during or prior to the annexation campaign, so there is no need to discuss them further as such – but we will need to examine the communications. This section is best read with a detailed map to hand!

The single exception is Kirkcaldy which will be discussed in some detail at the end.

Route A => C

We have noted already that the most direct route from Abernethy into the Howe of Fife is via Glentarkie to what is now Strathmiglo. From there the road goes as straight to Falkland as the terrain will allow.

Route E => F

The road from Duniface to Cupar exists today as the A916 – although the route is not the same. Originally Craigrothie was by-passed as the route ran through Chance Inn. While the road itself is not straight it does include many long straight stretches. As we have seen, Duniface was the likely location for the final defeat of the 'Fifers'; later (c1048 AD) it was the place where MacBeth attacked and killed most of the family of the Thane of Fife (see Chapter 12). So as a key central point, one would expect it to be well connected.

Route G => H

A superficial look at the map does not suggest a connection between Dunnicher Law and Drumcarrow Craig. But let us look more carefully…

Extend the road from Peat Inn to Northtown of Falfield (B941) due south and you reach Dunnicher Law precisely. Just north of Peat Inn the right fork in the road (past Wilkieston) takes you straight to Drumcarrow Craig. Continuing eastwards the road from Drumcarrow Craig has clearly been diverted north – prior to which it went right through what is now the Duke's golf course and Craigtoun Park towards St Andrews.

Route F => H

Coming out of Cupar on the Ceres road, it is clear that originally the route did not bend to Ceres Moor and Woodlands, but rather continued along the edge of Cairngreen Wood and then crossing the Ceres/Pitscottie road going on directly to Kinninmonth thereafter following the existing road to Drumcarrow Craig.

Route E => G

Seeing the connection between Drumcarrow and Dunnicher Law we should expect a continuation southwards, so it should come as no surprise to find a long stretch of the A915 from Lahill Mains to Honeysuckle Cottage pointing directly at Dunnicher Law. It is also reasonable to surmise that the road has been rerouted to go round Gilston House estate (as has happened with Balbirnie House, Markinch and, indeed Abbot's Hall in Kirkcaldy). The stretch referred to is exactly aligned with that from Peat Inn to Duncarrow Craig. This implies that the road from Duniface followed the route of A 915 to Upper Largo and on to Lahill – which is not surprising given the natural obstacle of Largo Law and the advantage in giving easier access to coastal defences.

Route A => F

There is no reason to suppose other than that the route from Abernethy to Cupar followed the general route of the current

A913 particularly given that the Earls of Fife had a castle at Lindores thought sufficiently important as to be worthy of destruction by King Edward I in 1300.

Route A => B

The A91 leads directly from the mouth of Glentarkie to Fossoway, very close to Down Hill. However a mile or two could be shaved off by using the Leden Urquhart road which crosses the Gateside/Beinn Inn road at Upper Pitlochie to meet the A91 nearly a mile west of Gateside rather than going to Strathmiglo. As there was a fort at Bein's Law the specific route from Abernethy would have passed by that – old maps show roads on either side leading to Castle Wood, Corrinzion. There is no good reason not to suppose that in general terms this was the route from Down Hill to Abernethy at that time. It is about 17 miles overall, so there would need to have been an intermediate overnight stop on some occasions – possibly in the Mawcarse area (about 2 miles along the road north east of Milnathort).

Route D =>C

From the top of The Path, the fork to the left led up Overton Road to Carberry Farm. [I invite the reader to look at a map. The upper part of Overton Road is remarkably straight, but there is a dog-leg bend around Cairns Street. If you follow the line of the lower part of this road it takes you very precisely to the junction where Mid Street meets The Path. My interpretation is that Overton Road originally ran all the way, but that the houses and factories of Mid Street, Nairn Street and Commercial Street have been built over the road, obliterating the original line.]

Carberry was an important site giving line of sight to the Lomond hills (eg for warning fire beacons which give the hills their name) which otherwise Kirkcaldy lacks – so it was a key communications relay station between Falkland Hill and Kirkcaldy. So there was a "station" there and it existed in Roman times – but it was not a Roman Station or camp (as discussed above).

From Carberry, the road went on directly (on early maps this is shown as "Hurlburn Road") fording the river Ore and on past Over Stenton Farm to the beginning of the "Rimbleton Strip" – a line of trees which remains to this day in the middle of Glenrothes just to the west of Rothes Road. However this and other parallel lines of trees are a modern imposition on the landscape. From what is now Reid Place, the road continued on its original alignment to the River Leven.

The problem of how to cross the River Leven has been largely obscured by landscaping to enhance the views from Leslie House – including the avenues of trees just referred to. There were, however, only two bridges crossing the Leven in this area: the Cow Bridge close to where the current A910 Leslie Road crosses the river and the 'Lady's Bridge' (just a little upstream from where B969 crosses the Leven (the "Bridge to Nowhere") leading on directly to Leslie House. From here the road skirted the Lothrie Burn to link up with the Leslie/Falkland road via the footpath behind the old Christ Church to reach Falkland Hill. It is a delight to the historian and geographer alike that this road remains evident in the landscape.

Route D =>E

In essence this route is the A915 Standing Stanes road to Duniface (Kennoway) and onwards. The straightness of this road is remarkable. The problem we have is how people reached this road from the top of The Path. The coin found in the Ravenscraig Street area is consistent with the route being up St

Clair Street or broadly via Normand Road and Boreland Road. However the line of the Standing Stanes Road suggests that it could have left the Carberry road at the junction with Midfield Road at the top of Mitchelson Industrial Estate.

3. The general location of Kirkcaldy as a garrison site

The question of the precise location of the "Caer y Caledy" (the Fort of the Caledonians) in Kirkcaldy will be discussed later in the chapter, but first let us see how the road network makes the case for the general location of Kirkcaldy. The road network became evident due to the pattern of finds of Roman coins in the Kirkcaldy area. So having first offered the map of where we are going, I will then begin by discussing the coins and where they lead us.

We must begin by acknowledging that it is important to be very wary of too simplistic an interpretation of the evidence: the sites where the coins are found are not necessarily where they were originally deposited/lost. So too with the time scale. The coins may have been dropped at any time – even centuries after they were put into circulation – and not necessarily by someone who was using them as coins.

In the case of Roman coins in the Kirkcaldy area I am particularly reliant upon – and hence grateful to – Ms Nicola Wilson of Kirkcaldy Museum, Dr Donal Bateson of the Hunterian Museum in Glasgow and Dr Fraser Hunter of the National Museums of Scotland for such information as I can present here.

Here is as accurate a map as I can draw to illustrate the find locations in the area. [Unmapped are a coin found "on the railway line" featuring Constans (337-350) and a coin of Antoninus Pius (138-161 CE) found "in Kirkcaldy" in 1936.]

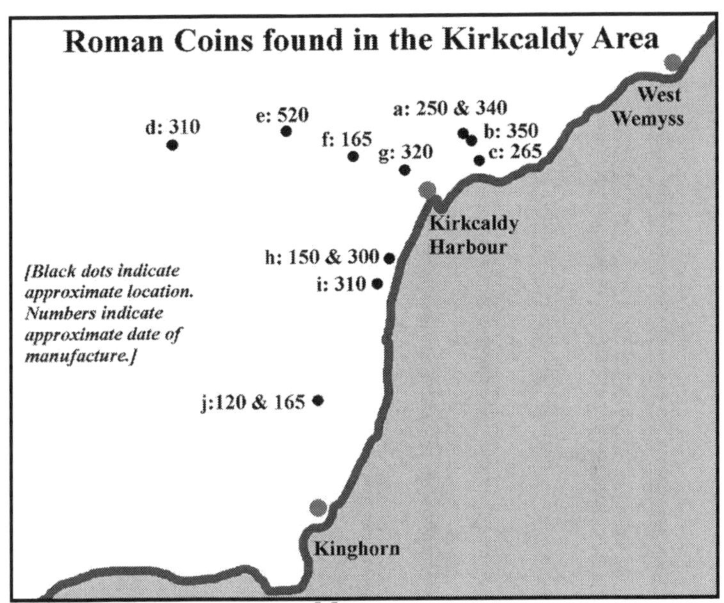

Interpretation of the Map

Coin group (i)

- **a** 2 coins found in the Overton Road area, one featuring Constantinus Gallus (c251-53 CE), the other of Constantine II as Caesar (c337-340 CE)
- **b** one coin found in Lenny's yard (now incorporated into Rejects' car park) also featuring Constantine II as Caesar.
- **c** one coin found in Ravenscraig Street.

My interpretation is that a road junction at the top of The Path dates back a very long way.

Coin Group (ii)

- **d** a coin found on Mellerstain road is thought to have been in topsoil brought from Torbain Farm. Featuring the emperor Maxentius, it dates to 306-312 CE – the immediate aftermath of the raid into Scotland by Constantius and his son Constantine.

Torbain farm is on the road variously to Auchterderran and to Lochgelly (whence possibly on to Navitie Hill fort) – very much into Maeatae territory,

Coin Group (iii)

e the coin found on Dallas Drive is the one which is very much apart from the rest, dating as it does to The emperor Justin (518-527 CE). This post-dates the final defeat of the Picts at Badon Hill by 'king' Arthur.

f the coin found in Valley Gardens featuring Lucius Verus dates to 162-169 CE – substantially before the invasion of Severus and his sons.

It is likely that these two sites were on or very near the original road from Kirkcaldy Harbour to Cluny (whence on to Kinglassie and the East end of Loch Leven).

Coin Group (iv)

g this coin was found in the area now called Smeaton Gardens and features Constantine I (hence 306-337 CE).

This site is not on the road to anywhere – but there were coal pits in the area from an early date, so the location of this find may be related to this in some way.

Coin Group (v)

h a coin was found in Marion Street; the only dating advice we have is that it is pre-321.

i two coins were found on Gas Wynd, one featuring Antoninus Pius (138-161 CE), the other Diocletian (284-305 CE).

j two coins were found at Grange Farm; one features Hadrian (117-138 CE) the other Lucius Verus (162-169 CE).We can see that both these pre-date Severus' campaign, but sandwich the building of the Antonine Wall.

My interpretation of **h, i** and **j** is that they were all on or fairly close to the route of the old road from Kirkcaldy Harbour to Kinghorn. From this we may suppose that crossing the Tiel Burn was not quite as easy as one might suppose and so the site of the current bridge has been a very long term fixture – even if it may have been no more than a ford originally. The curve on Links Street suggests (i) that this was a particularly chosen place to make the crossing (it is only 160 metres above the tidal reach) and (ii) that it may be a rather later development, with the original road running more directly from the West Port to the bridge at Invertiel via what is now Saunders Street which can be seen on very old maps ie long before the current lay out; one end of Marion Street is on Saunders Street. Between the Sauders Street / Allison Street junction and the West Port the old route has been completely erased by the subsequent developments (which themselves would have come after the development of Links Street). Beyond Invertiel I suppose that, just as with eg Carberry and Stenton (above) originally the road would have run through or immediately next to both Tyrie and Grange farms then on to Abden.

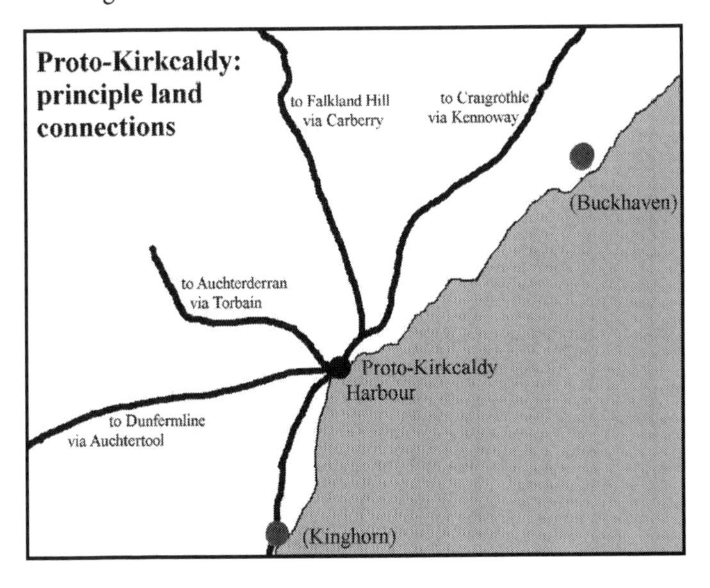

General comment about the coins

The great majority of the coins were located on or so close to roads which we may reasonably suppose to have existed at the time the coins were minted, so we can upgrade our thinking at least a bit to suppose that most if not all of the coins were found where they had been lost. It is interesting to note that the coins dating to before Severus are mostly on the roads going south from Kirkcaldy Harbour. So the coins suggest that the community at Kirkcaldy Harbour had effective working connections to the south (ie the Maeatae) before the arrival of the Caledonians; but after the establishment of the fort, the traffic flow was predominantly with the north.

Perhaps it was because the Caledonians did not have direct access to the North Sea at the time of Agricola's campaign that they failed to appreciate properly the value of the Classis Britannica – the Roman Navy. By the end of the Severan incursions they were left in no doubt and in due course the Pictish Navy was to prove to be a serious threat all along the east coast of what is now England. So by the time they were in a position to consider establishing a southern base in Fife they would be starting by considering harbour facilities. Kinghorn was almost certainly under Maeatae control. Setting the new fort back from the border had the extra advantage of its being better placed for its role regarding the second problem: internal policing.

Working backwards, the next available site would be roughly where Kirkcaldy is today. We know that the area has been populated (whether or not continuously) for a very long time. Remains dating to the period of the Beaker people have been found on Victoria Road close to the East Burn den and at the bottom of Kirk Wynd. So too bronze age artefacts (the Bronze

Age overlaps that of the Beaker people through to about 800 BCE) have been found in the Victoria Road and Oriel Road areas.

By the time we are considering – the 200s CE – I hope that this chapter will show that there was an existing settlement clustered round the old harbour at the mouth of the East Burn and hence that the fort was not built in the middle of nowhere; it was near enough to an existing harbour community not only for the supply of services locally but also to provide easy access for a nascent Caledonian Navy.

4. Kirkcaldy: The choice of the Specific Site for the fort

So big has Kirkcaldy become and so great has been the renewal even in recent years that it would be quite hard to peel away the changes away to reveal the original settlement. Even the oldest

Ordnance Survey map is not very helpful. Douglas Speirs, Fife Council Archaeologist confirms to me that there is nothing known about where the site of the fort might be. The late David Potter of Kirkcaldy Civic Society shared with me his view that the site of the Auld Kirk was likely. I agree with this so here is the explanation as to how I came to this view.

We are fortunate to have a map drawn up in 1809 by the surveyor Richard Moore. At this time the development of Kirkcaldy was still so little that old patterns can be understood. There is a copy of this map at Kirkcaldy Central Library; however The National Map Library of Scotland has done excellent work pioneering making old maps and plans available on line. This one can be seen at https://maps.nls.uk/towns/rec/448

INTERNAL ROAD CONNECTIONS: THE 'LEGACY' ROUTES

Subtleties of road alignment if properly interpreted can tell a good deal (see the map below).

(a) Abbotshall Road

Let us start at Mitchell Street and its dog leg line! The problem is that on John Wood's 1824 town plan (https://maps.nls.uk/view/74400043) we can see that between Mitchell Street and Coal Wynd there was a quarry. The layout in 1809 was quite different. My understanding of this is that originally Townsend Place continued along the first part of Mitchell Street and continued on down to the harbour roughly to the bottom of Fish Wynd and what is now the entrance to the Deas Wharf housing development (previously the main pier for the harbour). As the town developed more houses spread South and the route up to meet Townsend place got progressively steeper, becoming Coal Wynd.

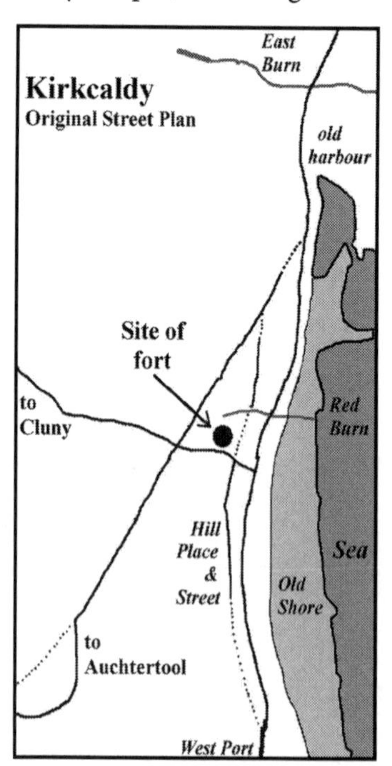

Townsend Place continued straight on through what is now the Raith Estate (previously the grounds of Abbotshall) which continues on the existing route to Auchtertool whence on to Dunfermline. [Some time after the establishment of the Abbots Hall, the road was diverted to run round the edge of the estate grounds.] At the top of what is now Kirk Wynd a fork in the road led travellers Westward, An early left fork led past Torbain Farm to Auchterderran and on to Navitie Hill; the right fork led to Cluny whence north to Kinglassie and Auchmuirbridge.

(b) The High Street

From that same point at the harbour another road ran roughly along the route of the High Street to the West Port and on (as discussed above) directly to the site of the current crossing the Tiel Burn (albeit then just a ford).

(c) The Path

While the roads above met at Kirkcaldy Harbour they did not end there. As we have seen from the coin evidence above, at the top of The Path the road forked again, with the right fork leading to Kennoway and Cupar via Craigrothie, probably via Dysart, while the left fork led to Falkland Hill.

This then is what the Caledonians had to build on when they took the area over and we may turn our attention to the streets within what would become Kirkcaldy. By the way we are using the term "road" quite loosely. There is no suggestion that any of these were actually paved. It is probably best to think in terms of the old drove roads (some of which still exist).

(d) Location of the High Street

As can be seen from Moore's map, at that time the Esplanade did not exist – the burgage plots of the seaward side of the High

Street running down to the shore. The fact that sea has continued to inundate the High Street from time to time even within living memory demonstrates how desperately short of room the local residents and shopkeepers who built these properties must have been. The High Street, particularly on the shore side, was surely not a building location of choice. At the early stage it was the main road to Kinghorn, running just high enough above the normal tideline to be passable most of the time!

(e) Nature of Hill Street

Now I invite readers to consider Hill Street (previously Hill Vennel) and Hill Place.

(i) We should note the two streets just as wide as Hill Street at right angles leading down to the High Street – one is now the footpath to the Bus Station, the other to the Postings Shopping mall, but on Moore's map they are equal to Hill Street itself.

(ii) The key lies in noticing that if you follow the line of Hill Place, it takes you directly to the junction of Hill Street and Kirk Wynd. What we see on the map is that four imposing buildings had been put up on the High Street with their burgage plots running all the way back to the land of the Old Kirk, thereby blocking the line of the road. I suggest that the development of the High Street and the connection via Oswald's Wynd was enough to allow the town elders to agree that this bit of Hill Place was surplus to requirements (and this sort of thing is still happening to this day).

(iii) At the North end, where Hill Place meets Coal Wynd, although now, as a footpath, it takes a sharp bend to meet the road at right angles, the frontages of the adjacent properties show that originally Hill Place carried on in a straight line to meet Coal Wynd at an acute angle and this is confirmed on old OS maps. Put another way, the angle of the original line of Coal Wynd/Mitchell Street (discussed above) was shallow enough to allow draft animals to bring loads up from the harbour without being exhausted by the time they got to the top (originally they would have had a long way to go afterwards). Hill Place forked off from this ascent to serve the needs of people further along its own length – there was no actual need to climb further to serve Kirkcaldy's own needs.

It is curious that at the end of the High Street is "Port Brae" – which is clearly nothing like a brae. I suggest that the original "Port Brae" was indeed the road leading from the harbour which climbed the brae to the level of what is now Hill Place and Hill Street. The burgage plots of the properties on the Port Brae still run all the way back to Hill Place – it is from their frontage on Hill Place and Coal Wynd that the name will have been derived.

(iv) Close attention to Moore's map at the Hill Place/Oswald's Wynd (then called Dishington Wynd) junction shows another point of interest. On the east side two buildings are shown parallel to Hill place (as one might expect), but behind the burgage/garden plot is quite irregular. So too Church Lane (which still exists) is clearly part of a new ordered layout. I suggest, therefore, that Hill Place may well have forked at this point – with one line going down to meet Hill Street, while the other fork went to the site of the church providing a direct route from the church to the harbour.

(v) At the other end of Hill Street, it meets Whyte's Causeway. Again the natural line of the road has been blocked by an imposing house and garden. At the west end of the High Street the road turns inland to meet the junction with the other roads about the same distance as you need to divert from the end of Hill Street on to the High Street. This is better illustrated on John Wood's 1824 map where the line runs down the back of the properties fronting on to the west end of the High Street. From this we should understand that originally Hill Street would have taken a straight line to the West Port and on to Links Street – the main road to Kinghorn. Later routes linking to this point are (a) what would become Nicol Street, leading back to the road to Auchtertool and on to Dunfermline and (b) a middle line running directly to Balwearie Castle.

Thus I suggest that what is now Hill Street and Hill Place was (a) one continuous nearly straight road running all the way from the Harbour to the Links St junction (whence on to Kinghorn) and (b) that this was Kirkcaldy's original principal civic street until the development of the "new" High Street.

(f) Redburn Wynd

"Historic Kirkcaldy" (p23) says that Redburn Wynd takes its name from Red or Reid meaning "sewage", reinforcing their case through extracts from several items of Town Council business. The Scots Dictionary confirms this. It remains quite curious, however, that this should be the case. Clearly this burn could not have been used by a very large proportion of the town in 1809, except by carrying buckets etc. quite a long way. Such arrangements can be traditional, however, ie the use remains long after the original reason for that use no longer pertains. In this context we should note that extending the line of Redburn Wynd inland takes it directly into the middle of the land of the Old Kirk roughly to where the path in from Church Place forks - ie well within 15 yards of the current building.

Summary: Why choose this site?

The Fort could have been located more or less anywhere along the bluff on which Hill Street runs, so we should perhaps ask why here and not some hundreds of yards either side? As we have seen, the road network and the coin evidence, such as it is, suggests that it is likely that there was a natural harbour more or less where the harbour is today and a community associated with it. The best site for the castle was:

- close enough to the harbour to be handy while not being on top of it.
- with ready access to a reliable supply of fresh water. There were plenty of wells in the immediate area: "Historic Kirkcaldy" (p33) refers to a "Manse well" and a "School Well" (the school was on Hill Street close to Kirk Wynd). Another well (now covered over) is in the garden of a property on the seaward side of Townsend Place.
- commanding 'foreign' traffic. The Old Kirk site sits very conveniently to oversee all roads to and from the south.
- close to a burn which could be used as a sewer.

The site of the Old Kirk meets all these criteria; the examination of Hill Place/Hill Street and the name Redburn imply that this was the site chosen.

Conclusion

The site of the Fort of the Caledonians is most likely to have been the site now occupied by the Old Kirk and its manse.

5. The Foundation of Pictland

As we have seen the Falcons were conquered by the Caledonians and became part of their "empire" and this was probably complete by 230. But in any event it was definitely done well before the establishment of the Kingdom of the Picts, into which greater Caledonia was absorbed. I have accepted the widely held assumption that Vipoig was the first recognised "King of the Picts" (approx dates 311-341) and that prior to that the tribes were not united. However this does need treating with a little caution.

1. The Verona List

I am very grateful to Dr Martin Counihan for drawing my attention to The Verona List and a rare online version of it (see http://www.arbre-celtique.com/forum/liste-de-verone-12546.htm). This list sets out all the tribes on the periphery of the Roman Empire. On this subject Wikipedia can be regarded as reliable (~/Laterculus_Veronensis).

The part relevant to us was compiled in the period 303-14. This follows immediately after Emperor Constantius and his son Constantine had conducted their punitive expedition into Scotland. Unfortunately we have no indication of where their army went but because of the closeness in time, there is reason to hope that it is accurate. For us it lists "Scoti, Picti,

Calidoni". Notice that there are Picts and they appear to be separate from the Caledonians. And this is not unproblematic because it was specifically the Caledonians who were known for their body art and hence who, if anyone, should have been identified as "Picti". We saw that Severus named the tribes north of the Antonine Wall who caused the most trouble as the Caledonians and the Maeatae – and the Maetae continued as a locally recognised group for nearly another 400 years. Could the Romans have mixed up "Maeatae" and "Picts"? Given the intimate Roman knowledge of the area, I think not. The Maeatae were no longer strong enough to be of interest and by this time were certainly not "flourishing" as the Latin implies.

So I propose that the fact that there was a people called the Picti shows that the confederated kingdom had come into existence, but, mainly because the Cruithin had little or no no direct contact with Roman Britain it was the Caledonians specifically who could still be identified as the troublesome ones and hence worthy of separate identification. Nevertheless the people referred to in the Verona List as "Picti" were what we would come to refer to as Northern Picts – led by the tribe referred to in Latin as "Verturiones", while the Caledoni and their vassals became the Southern Picts.

We saw earlier that using the Welsh equivalents it is likely that what we would call Caledonia, the natives would have called "Caledu" (say "Caledy"); the name means "the hard men". By extension the Roman Verturiones would probably have called their land Urturiu (later to be corrupted by Gaels to Fortriu and later represented by Symeon of Durham (referring to the year 934) as Wertermoras). Working out what the name might mean is problematic.

The best of the traditional efforts towards explanation suggest that the root of the name lies in the Welsh "tŵr" (Gaelic "tùr") referring to "fortress" or "stronghold" (Welsh "twr" means "heap"). While the Caledonians took advantage of their highland landscape to build hill forts, the Verturiones were largely based in lower lying areas needed to build strongholds on low land – at places like Ruthven Barracks, Rothiemurchus and even Turriff. There are problems with this explanation. The "obvious" tower builders in Pictland are responsible for the brochs – but these are overwhelmingly in Caithness and Orkney – and they were already in decline as an architectural form some time before this. Not only that, but etymologically this is unsatisfactory as it overlooks the "i" in "-turiones" and it makes Simeon's "Werter-" too far a stretch. So can we do better?

Cassius Dio states specifically that the Caledonians had no tilled fields. In a sense we should not be too surprised as they lived mostly in mountainous country. By contrast the Verturiones lived in fertile lowland regions. The modern Welsh verb "Turio" means to burrow or to root up (and the cognate word "troi" means specifically to plough). [A linguistic comparison may be seen in the Welsh "bwrdio" which means "to mock". Someone who does this is a "bwrdiwr" – so we might expect "Turio" and "Turiwr" ("turio" and "gwr") – what I am proposing here is no more than the reversal of the two elements in the word to gwr-turio – and we already know that the Pictish equivalent of a Welsh word would normally lose the initial "g".] Even in Gaelic "treabh" means "to plough". So my best guess is that "Verturiones" really means "the ploughmen"/ farmers.

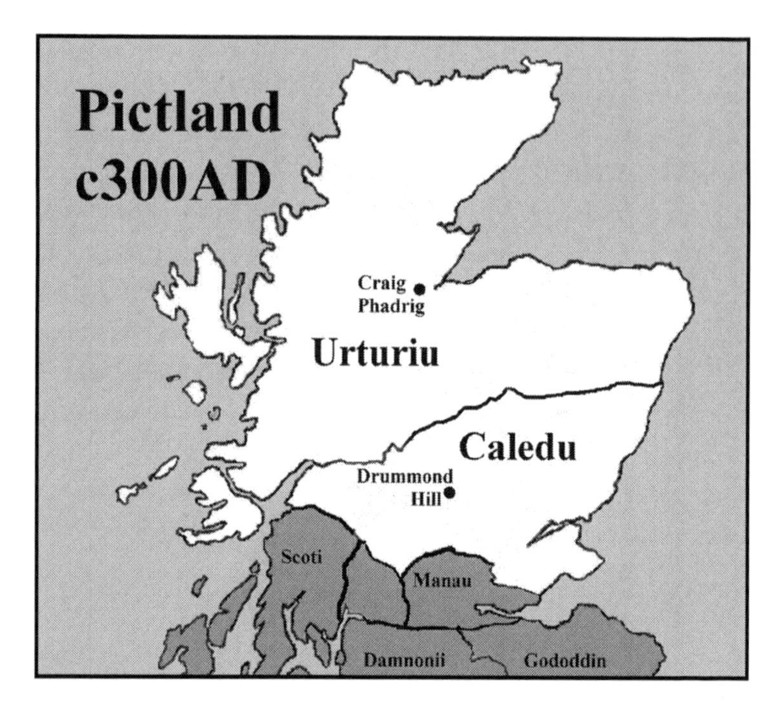

A Federal Kingdom: Given his long reign and that fact that it started at almost exactly the same time as the list was compiled, we may infer, at least as a working hypothesis, that Vipoig was indeed the first to rule the united kingdom. Indeed it is possible that it was he, as king of the Northern Picts, who had lain the Caledonians under subjection, taking so much of their territory from them, possibly taking advantage of any weakening of the Caledonians inflicted by Constantius and Constantine. Thus we should also suppose that the real power lay with the Verturiones – leaving the Caledonians as the driving force for any Pictish raiding to the south and doing so largely on their own initiative rather than because the Northern Picts told them to.

So why the name Pictland? We know it was not a name they gave themselves – and now we have a fairly clear idea of how they did 'self-identify'. Surely, however, they will have been well aware of how the Romans talked of them. So we may suppose also that adopting the name the Romans used was a good way of resolving the problem of what name to give the federal kingdom without having to get into the sort of mouthful to be found in 'Bosnia-Herzegovina' (as was), 'Former Yugoslav Republic of Macedonia' (as was) etc.

Nevertheless it would be fair to understand the Verturiones as the senior partners in the confederacy.

The place of 'Fife'

Southern Pictland comprised core Caledonia – from whom the kings were drawn – and three federated states which we would now recognise as (i) Fife, then known as Uuip, (ii) Angus and the Mearns, then known as Cwrcyn and (iii) Strathearn, whose name I am a lot less confident about, but may have been something like "hyddu".

2. Matrilineal Descent

The "well known fact" tradition is that the Pictish succession was matrilinear – in other words the next king was the person chosen to marry the crown princess. We have seen the legendary explanation for this custom to which we may add that the Caledonians gave short shrift to matrimony altogether. In modern times it has become fashionable to cast doubt on the idea that this was ever actually practiced, but the revisionists have never offered any evidence.

However there is considerable evidence to support the idea:

(i) Even a cursory look at the Pictish king list shows that it was extremely rare for successive kings to be father and son. Clearly there was some infighting from time to time, but the overwhelming preponderance is supportive of this matrilinear succession concept.

(ii) Cassius Dio writing about the Caledonians around the time of Severus' campaign said:

> *There are two principal races of the Britons, the Caledonians and the Maeatae, and the names of the others have been merged in these two. The Maeatae live next to the cross-wall which cuts the island in half, and the Caledonians are beyond them. Both tribes inhabit wild and waterless mountains and desolate and swampy plains, and possess neither walls, cities, nor tilled fields, but live on their flocks, wild game, and certain fruits; for they do not touch the fish which are there found in immense and inexhaustible quantities. They dwell in tents, naked and unshod, possess their women in common, and in common rear all the offspring. Their form of rule is democratic for the most part, and they are very fond of plundering; consequently they choose their boldest men as rulers.*
> [http://penelope.uchicago.edu/Thayer/E/Roman/Texts/Cassius_Dio/77*.html]

Until the very recent development of DNA profiling there was the truism that "it's a wise man that kens his faither". That modern profiling has forced many ancestor tracers to come to terms with "extramarital events" – ie their fathers were not who it was alleged they were. So too the Na people in southern China have a culture not far apart from that described above – and their language does not even have a word for "father"!

So all in all this is conducive with the idea that the king was chosen and then married the previous king's daughter.

3. ALTERNATING KINGSHIP

(a) A false steer: One of the more popular "well known facts" which have come down to us about early Scottish kings is the idea of the "alternating kingship". The "evidence" usually brought forward in support of this alternating kingship comes from the descendants of Kenneth MacAlpine to Malcolm II. The following list of kings is often advanced to illustrate this (I have added to this the dates and circumstances of their "leaving office"):

(Constantine II mac Aedh	abdicated 942)
Malcolm I mac Donald	killed 954 – by Moraymen
Indulf mac Constantine	killed 962 – by the Danes
Dubh mac Malcolm I	killed 967 – by Moraymen supporting Culen
Culen mac Indulf	killed 971 – in battle against Rhydderch of Strathclyde
Kenneth II mac Malcolm I	killed 995 – murdered by Constantine III
Constantine III mac Culen	killed 997 – murdered by Kenneth III
Kenneth III mac Dubh	killed 1005 – in battle by Malcolm II
Malcolm II mac Kenneth II	

But the way in which the kingship of Scots failed to progress from father to son from the reign of Kenneth mac Alpin to Malcolm II is no evidence for this sort of institutionalised alternation, for (a) it did not extend beyond the seed of Kenneth Mac Alpin and (b) all but one of these kings met untimely ends by means of foul play. So we should think of this not as an orderly system of alternation, but rather as rival mafia dons killing each other off and usurping the place of the predecessor they had just murdered (kings replaced mafia-style are shown in bold). But this is typical of the way in which Gallomaniacs – those Scottish historians who seek to attribute everything to the Scots – steal a tradition which has nothing to do with them and claim it for their own.

(b) An Excess of Pictish Kings: Pictish king lists appear excessively long – so much so that some authorities have insisted that an alternative explanation has to be sought. On close examination I have been able to divide it into several different sections. For a detailed discussion see my paper on "The Legendary Kings of the Picts". There is a mythical section, but all of it can be understood within a realistic timeframe. Disappointingly, we cannot identify any of the kings or Brudes who ruled 'Fife' with any certainty.

The principal seat of the king of the Northern Picts was at the Craig Phadrig hill fort just west of Inverness, but clearly the fort at Tap O'Noth was also very important indeed. For the Southern Picts, the fort on Drummond Hill just north of Taymouth Castle probably remained very important, but no doubt they would have spent considerable time at Abernethy in 'Fife', at Forfar or Brechin in Cwrcyn and at Dundurn when in Strathearn.

Conclusion

The kingdom of the Picts was a confederation of two kingdoms which were themselves confederations. The Picts chose their next leaders and these leaders' positions were formalised by their marriage to the daughter of the existing/previous king. The High Kingship of the Picts alternated between the Northern Picts and the Southern Picts.

This does not mean that the process was always smooth or adhered to rigidly – sometimes for practical reasons, emergencies etc. and sometimes because the throne was usurped.

Fife seems to have been out of these loops.

6. c507 CE – "King" Arthur Attacks Abernethy Garrison

As we have seen, Pictish raids into the Hen Ogledd (the 'Old North' of Roman Britain) continued even after Constantius' expedition in 306 and even more so after the Roman Legions were withdrawn in the early 400s, so much so that the Britons felt the need to co-opt the Angles and Saxons, who themselves had been fellow raiders of Britannia, as mercenary forces to bolster their defences against the Picts and Scots.

Even this was not immediately successful by itself so the Britons of the Old North decided that they would have to get themselves properly organised and take the fight to 'the enemy', as the historian St. Gildas described the Picts and Scots (NB most historians have not understood this).

The person chosen to be the Pendragon (which means 'Commander in Chief') of the coalition forces was Arthur, second son of Masgwid Gloff, king of Elmet (the area around Leeds and Sheffield). All the twelve battles for which he is famous were part of this campaign and so took place in what is now Scotland. For a full discussion of this see my "Arthur: Legend Logic & Evidence" (2017). [As I write this, a revised and extended edition of this book covering the whole of "king" Arthur's life is in preparation.]

Arthur's first battle was at Comrie (c495), after which he singled out the Scots, beating them four times before signing a peace treaty with them (498). [One clause of this treaty was that Fergus Mor mac Earca would take the throne of Scottish Dalriata.] After this, Arthur had only one front to fight on. Battles between Arthur and the Picts (with their allies, the Maeatae) flowed back and forth. It was the 7th battle which saw Arthur's forces drive deep into Pictish territory, fighting near Birnam Wood (near Dunkeld). After the Picts had counter-attacked at Bearsden, once again (probably sometime in the period c507x509AD) Arthur pushed deep into Pictland. This time his target was Abernethy: "The City of the Legion" so called because of the old Roman Fort at Carpow.

In my book on Arthur I had been reluctant to specify Abernethy as the precise site of this battle – but this was before I had understood the Caledonian take over of Fife or the way Abernethy was such a key site in the Pictland of those days.

This battle at Abernethy was, in effect, in the middle of a 20 year war; two subsequent battles took place fairly nearby – one near Auchterarder and one just north of Stirling.

At this stage we cannot be precise about the exact site of the battlefield, but one site does recommend itself over the others: the area around Netherton Farm east of the Fargie (River Farg as it is now called) recommends itself because it is an area of flat land without any watercourses getting in the way. Not only that but the Picts had two lines of escape: up Glenfarg or into the Abernethy Glen. The Picts would probably have taken the view that if Arthur had the Farg behind him this would hinder his troops' escape had the Picts won the day. The distance between the Farg and the foothills of Castle Law is rather over a mile, while the space between the Farg and the Carey Stank, at just over 1000 yards, tight but manageable for a front line. Arthur may have taken the view that the River Earn from 0 to 1,500 yards to his rear would be a positive advantage to him as it would make any reinforcement from or attack to his rear more or less impossible. Such speculation needs to be treated with some circumspection, however, not least because the lie of the land today may bear little resemblance to how it was just over 1,500 years ago.

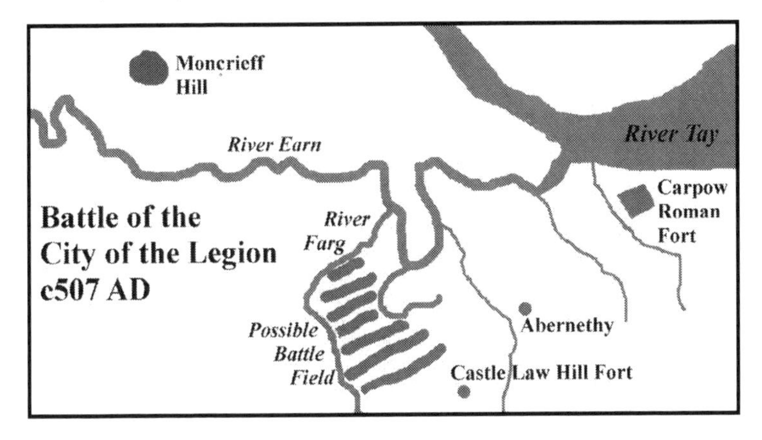

Arthur's forces, including, as we must suppose, many Anglian troops, won this engagement and after Badon Hill (517 CE) there was a whole generation or more of peace between the Picts and the Ancient Britons.
Please note that this is a "possible" site. On a practical basis it may have been too waterlogged when Arthur arrived.

One of Arthur's principal lieutenants was St Kessog (see more in the next chapter). Of Arthur's twelve battles in Scotland, Kessog's presence has left its legacy. He preached

(i) at Comrie where to this day there is Tom Chasaig,
(ii) at Callander where there is Tom ma Chisaig and

(iii) at Auchterarder where there are the ruins of St Mackessog's Church.

But this is only three out of twelve and it is not necessarily the case that Kessog was in the army when it came to Fife.

Nevertheless while there is no doubt that the battle took place in this general area and in the general time frame indicated, what would help us to pin down a specific site would be a place name suggestive of St Kessog preaching in the area. So far no such place name has come to light.

7. The Arrival of Christianity in Fife

Introduction

In this book there are various items regarding Christianity in Fife which need to be addressed; they interlock with each other so much that trying to deal with them in a time line context is particularly difficult. Christianity in Fife was first Columban/ Celtic then Catholic then Celtic again then Catholic again until the Reformation in 1560 – which is beyond the scope of this book. These different phases will be addressed separately in the relevant chapters.

Good sources for seeing the problem can be found at:

https://web.archive.org/web/20130916085046/
http:// www.nas.gov.uk/about/051124.asp

The underlying problem for anyone trying to understand it properly is that since the 1200s, if not before, it has been put about that around 345 CE the Bishop of Patras, called St Regulus, fearing that the emperor Constantine was about to remove the bones of St Andrew which were buried there, rescued them and then went on an epic voyage which ended up in Scotland. Sadly there are still too many people who swallow the very poorly constructed impossible fiction. I will deconstruct this systematically in Chapter 10. It seems that it was the famous Historiographer Royal for Scotland William F Skene (1809-1892) who first questioned this myth.

Background: How 'Christianity' came to Scotland

We should start by noting that there is a difference between Christianity and Chrestianity. But it seems that both were "churches" with priests, bishops etc. "Chrestos" means "Good Man", while "Christos" means "Anointed Man". Chrestians have been around since the 200s BC, but their purposes and even their beliefs did change considerably over time. On the other hand Christianity as we know it today really only came to the fore after the Council of Nicea in 325. One school which emerged were the Culdees who were more of a philosophical school than a religion even if they shared significant common roots. Note also that

- the French given name is "Chrétien" *rather than* "Chri(s)tian".
- St Palladius was sent to Ireland in 432 to bring the Culdees there into obedience to Rome.
- St Augustine was sent to Britain in 597 because the British were not "properly" Christian (there were also Culdees in what is now England and Wales at that time).

Despite this, for the purposes of this book I am going to lump them all together and refer to them as Christian only noting differences where this becomes relevant.

(a) The first person to evangelise in what is now Scotland was St Ninian. He was based at Candida Casa ("The White House") at Whithorn on the Solway Firth and worked in the general period 380x420. It seems likely that he was Chrestian rather than Christian.

Ninian's main targets for conversion were the Novantes and the Selgovae – the people of the Southern Uplands of Galloway and the Borders. He did not manage to secure the new faith, however, for after his death they quickly reverted to their old ways. This is why St Patrick (c420-493) was able to refer to them as "apostate Picts". [NB We have noted above that the Novantae were Cruithin, so Patrick's reference to them as "Picts" was wholly appropriate even if they were not part of the Kingdom of the Picts.]

Ninian clearly also converted the kingdom of Strathclyde – for if he had not, there would have been no basis for St Patrick to complain about their enslaving Irish Christians. [Patrick was born at Gretna, and most of his work was done in Ireland, but it is very likely that he did found a church at Old Kilpatrick on the Clyde.]

(b) The first person to evangelise north of the Antonine Wall was St Kessog, son of Oengus mac Nad Froich (King of Cashel in Southern Ireland). The family had been converted by St Patrick who may have brought Kessog to Strathclyde personally (which would be the occasion for the founding of Old Kilpatrick). Kessog played a highly significant part in 'king' Arthur's army – and as we have seen in the previous chapter we know that he preached to the defeated Pictish forces at Comrie and Auchterarder (the war took place in the period 495 to 517). It looks likely that Kessog visited the king of the Picts at Inverness soon after 517, but we cannot specify which king it was as there were three different kings of the Picts before Kessog was killed on the shores of Loch Lomond (probably in 530). [See ALLE]

(c) The first person to evangelise in Dalriata was Kessog's brother St Fáelán (Anglicised as 'Fillan') nicknamed variously 'the Leper', 'the Dumb' and 'the Stammerer'. He is also associated with (ie he also evangelised in) Strathearn: St Fillan's is named after him).

(d) In 565 St Columba arrived from Ireland. He went to see King Bridei mac Maelchon in Inverness and convinced him to allow Columba and his team of supporters to evangelise throughout Pictland. We should note that this was two generations after St Fillan in Strathearn and a whole generation before St Augustine came to Canterbury (597), so there is no basis for supposing any Roman Catholic influence at this stage.

Columba was based on the island of Iona – and there is dispute as to who gave it to him. Most Scots claim that it was their king – Conall mac Comgaill – who gave Columba his base. My own belief is that this is yet another part of Scottish mythologising – an attempt by Scots to claim the credit for anything that happened in Scotland. This was soon abetted by the Community on Iona itself to keep in with their new masters. I prefer the Pictish version of the story which says that it was Bridei who gave him the island, which had been a Druidic centre. James E Fraser ("From Caledonia to Pictland" p123) concurs. This is supported by Bede (Bk 3 Ch 3) who says:

> That island belongs to Britain, being divided from it by a small arm of the sea, but had been long since given by the Picts, who inhabit those parts of Britain, to the Scottish monks, because they had received the faith of Christ through their preaching.

It is most likely that it was the Scottish Dalriatan king Conall mac Comgall who expanded his realm in 570, hoovering up some of the Inner Hebrides – including Mull and Iona. [Indeed Bridei may have given Iona to St Columba because he could see trouble brewing and that in any case he would not be able to hold onto it.]

Had the Scottish version been true one should expect that the Druids would already have been expelled at the behest of St Fillan the Leper. Not only that, but had it been so important to Dalriata then why was no Dalriatan king buried there before Kenneth mac Alpine (858), 300 years after Columba arrived? Before him, Brude mac Beli, King of the Picts was buried there in 693. Clearly it would be otherwise a totally bizarre idea for a Pictish king to be buried on Dalriatan territory! So too, Ecgfrith, king of the Northumbrians was buried there after being killed in battle in Badenoch against the Northern Picts in 685... Early Irish kings buried there had first abdicated to become monks. See also

http://www.cushnieent.force9.co.uk/CelticEra/burials.htm

'Christianity' come to Fife

c580 CE St Rule establishes a church at St Andrews

One of Columba's main lieutenants was St Kenneth of Aghaboe (which is about half way between Dublin and Limerick). Kenneth brought with him St Riaghail, abbot of Muicinis (now the island of Illaunmore in the Lough Derg on the River Shannon). He is also sometimes referred to as Riaghail of Benchor. This probably means that he did his training at Bangor. While Kenneth eventually returned to Ireland (dying in 600), Riagail stayed on, based at St Andrews, and as "St Rule" (as we know him today) he founded several churches in eastern Pictland, including at St Andrews, or Cennrighmonaid as it was then known.

(see https://saintsplaces.gla.ac.uk/saint.php?id=541).

It is normally claimed that the name "Riaghail" (variants include "Riagail" and "Riaguil") is the Gaelicisation of the Latin name "Regulus" (see for example Skene "Celtic Scotland" Book II p268). But this is not true. Riagail is a Gaelic rendition of the name of the Archangel "Raguel" which is Hebrew and means "God shall pasture" (like a shepherd looking after his flock). The equivalent modern name is Reuel. The name is also to be found – in its pure form – at Crossraguel near Maybole in Ayrshire where, later, an abbey was built (in 1244) and dedicated by the Cluniac monks to the Virgin Mary. But this was on the already ancient site of the Cross of St Riaghail.

Archangel Raguel's specific duty was to mete out punishment to those angels and demons who had transgressed God's laws. He is not mentioned in the Bible but he does appear in Jewish lore and in The Book of Enoch (an apocryphal work excluded from the official Bible at the Council of Nicea in 325). What this demonstrates is that by his name alone we can see that St Riaghail – and hence St Columba himself – was indeed drawing on traditions older than and separate from those of the Roman Catholic church.

St Columba died in 597 and we may be confident that the church at St Andrews had been established well before that. The wide window is 565x597, but it is likely that it was before 580.

From St Andrews the word spread out, including, particularly, a hermitage at Dysart (the name coming from "desert" – where the "desert fathers" retired to contemplate in isolation). Here was set up a cell of… Culdees.

595X616 CE: THE FOUNDATION OF THE NUNNERY AT ABERNETHY

1. The fake story: Regarding the Pictish king Nechtan grandson of Uerb, AO Anderson (*Early Sources*, pp. cxx–cxxi) quotes Skene's *Chronicles of the Picts & Scots.* regarding the foundation of Abernethy (in Fife):

> "So Nectonius the Great, Uuirp's son, the king of all the provinces of the Picts, offered to Saint Brigid, to the day of judgement, Abernethy, with its territories ... Now the cause of the offering was this: Nectonius, living in a life of exile, when his brother Drest expelled him to Ireland, begged Saint Brigid to beseech God for him. And she prayed for him, and said: "If thou reach thy country, the Lord will have pity on thee. Thou shalt possess in peace the kingdom of the Picts."

The local legend is, furthermore that Der Lugdach, the Abbess of Kildare who followed St Brigit directly came over in person to establish the site.

The Nechtan (son of Uuirp) to whom this appears to apply is generally credited with the dates 456-480 – when Brigit herself was very much alive (indeed it is not clear that she had even founded the monastery at Kildare by this time), so there is no room here for Der Lugdach. Moreover this is a time 100 years before Columba and when the conversion of Ireland itself had barely started. Had this Nechtan embraced Christianity in the way implied, Scotland would have been a very different place; the mission of St Columba would have been unnecessary and would have taken a very different course. So we may discount this first King Nechtan.

2. Another Nechtan to ignore: We should also notice that the reign of Nechtan son of Der-Ilei, covers the period 706 – 729 CE. Given his other activities it is possible to conceive that it was he who was responsible. There is no doubt, however, that we do have the names of the relevant abbesses of Kildare for this period, so we can be confident in ruling out any connection with Der Lugdach. Moreover Nechtan son of Der-Ilei was very much trying to support Roman practices and thinking – indeed it was he who expelled all the Columban Christian priests in favour of Catholic ones in 717 (see chapter 9 below). So we may definitely discount this King Nechtan also.

3. The real story: And so we are left with the remaining Nechtan (son of Cano, grandson of Uerb). It is not seriously questioned that St Brigit died in the 520s, while this Nechtan's reign covers the period 595-616. It is clearly not feasible that the next abbess would still be in post and capable of such long distance travel (from Kildare to Abernethy) – at least 70, probably considerably more, years later. However if we look at the list of Abbesses of Kildare (see Wikipedia) we find some 25 of them following Brigit covering the period to 1171. Of these the first 5 are:

- Brigit ingen Dubthaig, d. either 521, 524, or 526. Abbesses of unknown death year alleged to have followed Brigit
    - Der Lugdach, commemorated 1 February
    - Comnat, commemorated 1 January
    - Tuilclath, commemorated 6 January
- Gnáthnat (or Gnáthat), d. 690
- Sébdann ingen Cuirc, d. 732

If we consider the abbesses from Gnáthnat onwards, we find that they served an average of about 23 years each in post. If we take the whole period from 526 (the latest date for Brigit's death) to 690 (the death of Gnáthnat) we have 164 years – so by applying the average, we should expect there to have been seven abbesses in between – but only four are named. Clearly there are variations (we see that that Sébdann ingen Cuirc served for 42 years) but we may be confident that there are missing names. If, then, we assume that the missing abbesses are those immediately following Brigit and if we apply the 23 year average to the ones we do have names for then we find that it is likely that Der Lugdach died sometime in the period 615x20. Thus

- She could have been a contemporary of Pope Boniface IV (in office 608-615).
- She could indeed have been broadly contemporaneous with this third King Nechtan;
- This Nechtan's reign follows the period of St Columba who spent time in this Tayside area of Pictland;
- The Bridei who accepted Columba was Nechtan's predecessor-but-one and had died a decade before Nechtan came to power, so we should have every reason to suppose that this Nechtan would have some positive connection with Christianity even if he had not spent time in Ireland

While it is true that even today people in crisis ask friends and even prelates to pray for them, if we understand the reference in the chronicle to mean that Nechtan sought the intercession of St Brigit, it would have been more likely that this would have occurred after her death, as with most saints. And this could easily have occurred with the assistance of Der Lugdach.

Objections considered

(a) We should also note the phraseology of the day. Thus under the year 854 The Annals of Ulster note the death of "Columcille's successor" - and no-one should take this to imply that there were not many other "successors" in between.

(b) There was a king of Strathclyde also called Nechtan and the eras of their reigns do overlap. The modern fashion is to suppose that these two were one and the same person. This analysis shows this idea to be false – if only on the basis that there would have been no need to go to Ireland at all when he was forced into exile from Strathclyde. [There are other political objections which need not concern us here.]

(c) Today many people may be tempted to assume that an

abbess would be busy running her nunnery – too busy to be making such a long journey eg to Abernethy. However such an objection is easily set aside when one considers the life and activities of other abbots such as Columba, Cuthbert, not to mention Kenneth and Riagail already discussed.

To summarise

It is reasonable to suppose that it was the king Nechtan who was contemporary with Pope Boniface IV who was responsible for the foundation of Abernethy; there is no strong basis for discounting the influence of Der Lugdach, Abbess of Kildare. On the contrary, what this analysis suggests is that it is the list of Abbesses of Kildare which is deficient, particularly with regard to Brigit's immediate successors, of which there are likely to be 2, 3 or 4 missing. It seems clear that, when he was busy scribing, the Pictish Chronicler had the wrong Nechtan in his mind.

Conclusions

- Christianity arrived in Fife around 580 CE, brought by St Kenneth who installed St Rule at St Andrews.
- The nunnery at Abernethy was founded in the period 595-616 CE at the behest of King Nechtan map Cano.
- The name Riaghail is not a Gaelicisation of Regulus – on the contrary Regulus is a Latinisation of Riaghail.
- The name Rule is an Anglicisation of Riaghail, not of Regulus
- The name Raguel in the place name Crossraguel is not a corruption of the Gaelic Riaghail, rather it is the pure form of the Hebrew original Raguel.
- St Riaghail took his name from that of the Archangel Raguel when he took holy orders.

Footnote: The Culdees

The 'normal' understanding of the term "Culdee" is *Céilí Dé*, which is supposed to mean "Spouses of God". This understanding has developed because it has supposed that they originated in Ireland – but as we have seen this is not correct, so there is no basis whatsoever for assuming a Q-Celtic etymology. The name has even been represented as "Kaledei", so we can see just how easy it was for people not knowing any better to associate this with Kirkcaldy!

Let us consult Dwelly, who offers us a veritable smörgåsbord of possible origins:

"**ceile-de**": this means "Preserver of the Fires" as well as Culdee (though he describes this as "fanciful word") and hardly "spouses of God"! On the contrary this might be taken to imply a connection to Zoroastrianism or at the very least a pagan Irish tradition (cf the names Aeth and Aedan).

"Culdich": is often offered Dwelly says of "**Cùldaich**": see "Cuilteach" – which means "retired", "set apart", "obscure" which is certainly appropriate given their hermit tendencies.

"**Céilidh**": which means "wise" – again appropriate particularly given the way they were able to rub along satisfactorily with the Druids.

While it is possible to see how any of these words which sound so close to Culdee do apply to them, they all presuppose that the name "Culdee" was Q-Celtic (as was spoken in Ireland). But this is definitely not the case – we know there were Culdees in what are now England and Wales from a date so early that we may be confident that they did not come from Ireland. I am of the minority view that the name derives from the fact that they came from Chaldea. As we shall see, however, the precise meaning is not in itself of crucial importance.

We saw above the distinction between Christian and Chrestian. Only gradually did these turn into religions. What we recognise as Christianity started off as a philosophy – the Gospel of Thomas is not a gospel as we would understand it but rather a collection of sayings attributed to "IS" rather than to Jesus by name. Many different sects existed with very different ideas. Among them were the Chrestians who became a revolutionary organisation due to revolutionaries deliberately joining them ('entryism') to make the organisation one to suit their purposes. They then caused a lot of trouble eg to the Roman Emperor Nero. It was really only after the Council of Nicea in 325 CE, brought together by the Emperor Constantine, that Christianity began to take the form we would recognise today. Two major decisions taken at Nicea were

- Which books to include in "The Bible"
- To expel the "Gnostics" and other sects deemed heretical.

As we have seen, the Book of Enoch was one of those excluded from the Bible – so we know that the Culdees or Chrestians or both and their embracing of Archangel Raguel must go back to before that date and come from a separate, expelled, sect. As long ago as 1886 François Bonifas ("Histoire des Dogmes de l'Église Chrétienne") suggested that the Culdees go back to the 2nd Century. There are others who accept the story of Jesus' immediate family – even Jesus himself – visiting eg Glastonbury and so make the direct connection to the Culdees this way.

The Culdees operated in groups – communities, if you will – and spent a lot of time in isolation as hermits. At least initially, they did not have "priests" or "bishops" or indeed churches as such. Whereas (Catholic) Christian monks had a tonsure which resembles male-pattern baldness, Culdees shaved the front of their head from ear to ear.

So we can see that St Ninian and St Patrick were not themselves Culdees. Their belief systems were a good deal closer to what became Catholic Christianity, but they were not subject to Rome. Patrick was able to form a good working relationship with the Culdees. The primary object of Palladius' mission to Ireland in 432 had been to bring them under Roman control – and it was not successful. Celtic Christianity became a hybrid of the Patrician and Culdee schools. But, with relentless pressure from expanding Catholicism, gradually the practices and beliefs and even the structures fell increasingly into line – particularly after the Synod of Whitby in 664.

However we can now see what the leaders of the Scottish Reformation (the pivotal date is 1560) meant when they claimed that they were rejecting Catholicism to embrace an older and purer heritage. Unfortunately so much hybridisation had taken place that although this should have been true, much of the original teaching which had made the traditions separate had already been lost. [Thus, for example they never reverted to the Pre-Catholic way of calculating the date of Easter.] Such Culdees as had remained in Scotland after the arrival proper of Catholicism under King Malcolm III and his 2nd queen St Margaret had long since been incorporated into the Catholic Church as chapters of lay canons and the teachings of the reformed Church of Scotland bore little or no resemblance to those of the original Culdees.

Although we can allude to some of the difference in rites between Catholic and what emerged as the amalgamation of

Chrestian and Culdee, so great has been the attrition that we no longer have access to the genuine differences in teachings and spiritual understandings. I will not attempt to reconstruct them, because if I did, I would be mainly offering my own prejudices and preferences!

[See also "Celt, Druid and Culdee" by Isobel Hill Elder (1938).]

PEREGRINE FALCON - "VIP"

Photo taken by the author, with thanks to handler Roxanne and courtesy of Elite Falconry, Cluny KY2 6QU

Please visit www.elitefalconry.com

BALBIRNIE STONE CIRCLE

BALFARG REPLICA EXCARNATION SITE

Photos taken by the author

The Collessie Standing Stone

The author at the stone; warrior image enhanced digitally later.
Photo taken by the author.
Thanks to the Barr family for facilitating the visit.

EAST LOMOND HILL FORT - FROM MAIDEN CASTLE

Photo taken by the author

Caledonian Warrior

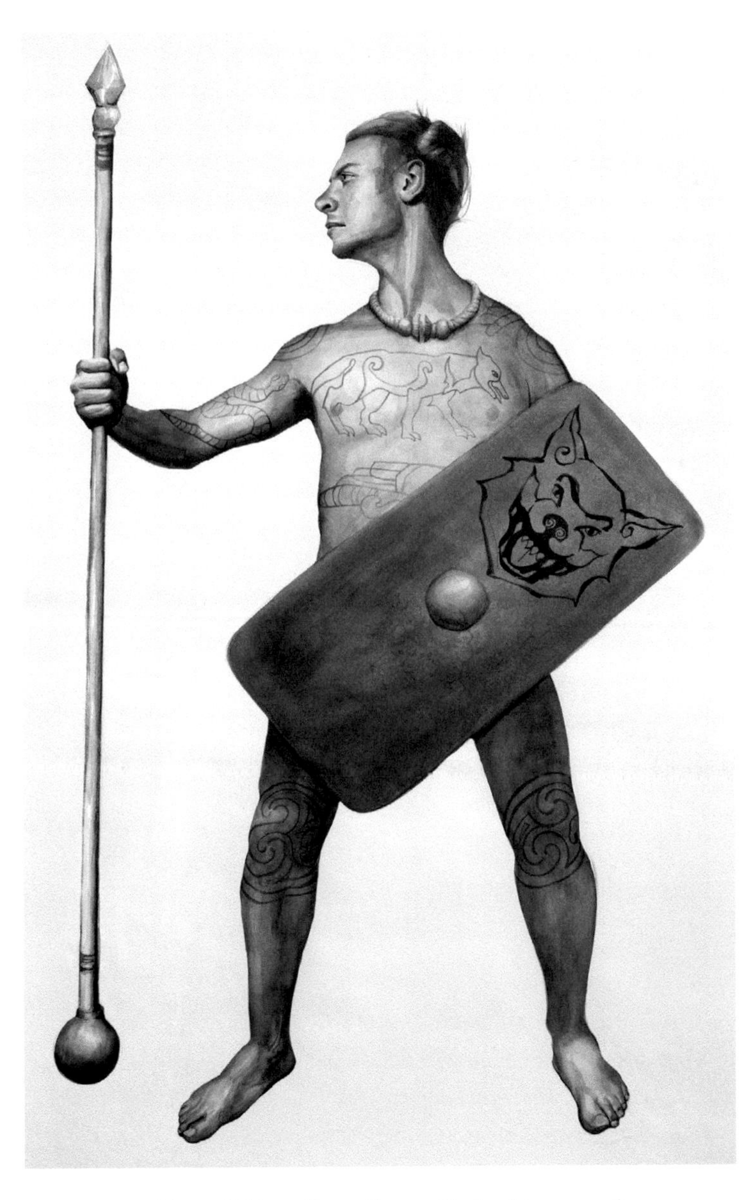

©Kirsty Whiten (https://www.kirstywhiten.com/)
see "Notes on the Front Cover illustration"

Hoch ma toch (from the south)

Photo taken by the author

Silver denarius 137 CE

Photo taken by the author with thanks to staff at Fife Council Archives.
Obverse: Hadrian bare headed "Hadrianus Augustus"
Reverse: (Juno) Moneta standing holding scales and Cornucopia.
Real diameter: 1.5cm
[see further https:/./www.baldwin.co.uk/.product/hadrian-silver-denarius-63]

Red Whortleberry - "Fib"

Photo © Ray Woods

Photo © Deborah Long

Images courtesy of Plantlife (in Scotland Charity SC038951)
Please visit www.plantlife.org.uk

GOSHAWK [=> FALKLAND]

Photo taken by the author, with thanks to handler Roxanne and courtesy of Elite Falconry, Cluny KY2 6QU

Please visit www.elitefalconry.com

COATS OF ARMS

Wemyss

Wemyss (formerly Earls of Fife)
The Lion Rampant Undifferenced

Abernethy

Abernethy (cadets of the Earls)
The Lion Rampant Differenced by a Ribbon Sable

Kings of Scots

Kings of Scots (from Alexander II)
The Lion Rampant surrounded by a double Tressure

Earls of Strathearn

Earls of Strathearn (Celtic line)
Gules a double chevron or

Chief of Grant

Gules three ancient crowns or

Balfour

Argent, on a chevron sable, an otter's head erased of the field

Images courtesy of the late Eddie Geoghegan

Kirkcaldy Town Seal [Obverse]

"Kirkaldie: Azure an abbey of three pyramids, the central taller than the lateral argent each ensigned with a crosspattée or. Round the shield: Sigillum civitatis Kirkaldie."

Motto: Vigilando Munio

Illustration by Glenrothes Art Club member Margaret West, Milton of Balgonie

Kirkcaldy Town Seal (Reverse)

"In a field azure St Bryce vested in long garments with a mitre on his head. all proper standing in the porch of the church argent which is ensigned on the top with a cross pattée of the third; his dexter hand holds a fleur-de-lis or, and his sinister hand is laid upon his breast; the whole between a decrescent and a star in fesse of the last.

Round the shield: Sigillum civitatis Kirkaldie."

Illustration by Glenrothes Art Club member Margaret West, Milton of Balgonie

DUNFERMLINE ABBEY [WEST DOOR]

Photo taken by the author

8. The so-called Battle of Raith

There are several "well known" battles in Scotland which are in fact wholly fictitious. One such is the so-called Battle of Barry which is supposed to have taken place between the Scots and the Vikings. The origin of this myth is unclear (see the relevant Wikipedia page ~/Battle_of_Barry).

Sadly the so-called Battle of Raith is another such supposed battle which did not take place, but fortunately we can get a complete and firm handle on how this myth was created – and in this case we can see that there was no intention to mislead.

The notion of the "Battle of Raith" was first proposed by Edward Nicholson, who was in charge of the Bodleian Library at Oxford University in the early 1900s. He published his proposition in *The Celtic Review* Volume. 6, No. 23 (Jan., 1910), on pages 214-236. This can be read in many academic libraries and is also available online at https://www.jstor.org/

The basis of Nicholson's article is that he was aware of the poem Y Gododdin, written by the bard Aneurin about a battle which took place at "Cathraeth" around the year 600. He was frustrated that no-one had identified the location – and he knew that in Gaelic "Cath" means "battle". So he thought "Ah! Maybe the battle did not take place at Cathraeth, but was the 'cath' at 'raeth'!" And then he remembered that there was a place in

Scotland called Raith! So he proposed that the battle which was the subject of the poem took place on the outskirts of Kirkcaldy.

Well… it was a brave attempt but he was wrong on very many counts. This is not the place to exhaust the reader with all the erroneous linguistic gymnastics he undertook (in his paper generally, not just with Cathraeth specifically). However three considerations should suffice:

1. We may recall from earlier in this book that at the time in question the place name "Raith" applied not to the Raith estate area in Kirkcaldy, but rather to Raith Hill – beyond Auchtertool.

It would be a really stupid general who would establish a beachhead at a well defended place like Kirkcaldy and then march his troops into the middle of nowhere only to encounter a vast army on the shores of Loch Gelly! Where did the army think it was going? Its only objective could have been Dunfermline – and if that is where you were going there are far better landing places than Invertiel!

2. Taliesin was a very famous bard in the 500s and many of the poems and songs he composed and performed remain available to us. He served Urien, King of Rheged who was born about 480 and was assassinated shortly before 550. Urien's power base was in Cumberland, but he was also overlord of Galloway and had influence as far south as Leeds. In one of his poems Taliesin describes Urien as "**the ruler of Cathraeth**". (The poem is in Llyfr Taliesin XXXVII in "Four Ancient Books of Wales"; see online at http://www.ancienttexts.org/library/celtic/ctexts/t37.html).

This tells us first of all about the general whereabouts of the place; second that the place was already called Cathraeth during Urien's reign (roughly 510<550 – 50 years before the battle to which the poem Y Gododdin refers) and third that Cathraeth was a place special enough to be worth mentioning in a praise poem. Today Cathraeth is generally understood to be Catterick. It was one of the Roman cities of Britain mentioned by Ptolemy (so it already had a name c120 CE) which Ptolemy understood as Κατουρακτονιον ("Catouractonion") and which the Romans normally called Cataractonium. These Greek and Roman names are understood to be a corruption of the original Brythonnic name which we would normally render as Cathraeth (see Wikipedia ~/Catterick,_North_Yorkshire). Even though this was a disastrous loss for the British the heroism of those who took part was celebrated by the Bard Aneirin in the very famous poem Y Gododdin, translations of which can be found at:

https://www.maryjones.us/ctexts/a01a.html

https://www.maryjones.us/ctexts/a01b.html

and the original here:

https://www.gutenberg.org/files/9842/9842-h/9842-h.htm

Modern opinion is that Nicholson's parsing of the place name Cathraeth was correct – it does contain the elements "cath" (battle) and "rath" (defensive fortifications).

3. Meanwhile, as we have seen, at the time in question both Kirkcaldy and Raith Hill were part of the Pictish Kingdom on whose southern border lay Manau, the kingdom of the Maeatae – nothing to do with Urien. There can be no doubt that Cathraeth was and is nowhere near Kirkcaldy.

Postscript

Edward Nicholson was a serious scholar, but he lacked the

opportunities afforded to us by the ready access we have to such a vast amount of information via the internet and, indeed, by the explosion in the development of scholarship generally which has occurred especially since the end of World War II.

His paper and hence the idea of the battle of Raith would have remained of minor interest to a small *côterie* of academics had it not been for the enthusiasm of Lachlan Macbean (1853-1931) who wrote a very short *précis* of Nicholson's paper which was printed in "Kirkcaldy Burgh and Schyre" (1924). This book is readily available in Fife Libraries where readers can see exactly what Macbean wrote but the extract is also online:
https://www.electricscotland.com/history/articles/raith.htm.

I updated the Wikipedia page to reflect this in May 2019.

Afterword

In 926 King Athelstan of England brought several other kings (including Constantine II, King of Scots) together at Eamont Bridge, near Penrith where they signed a treaty. In 934 Aethelstan invaded Scotland in 934 both with a land army and with a seaborne force (on the (probably correct) pretext that Constantine had broken the terms of the treaty). The land army took the same route as the Romans – up Strathmore as far as Stonehaven ("Dunfoeder", now Dunottar Castle) – while the naval forces raided right along the east coast even as far as Caithness. It is highly likely that one or more of these seaborne raids will have been on Kirkcaldy or somewhere close to it along the coast, but sadly and ironically the details have gone entirely unrecorded. (see "A history of the kings of England" by Symeon of Durham).

9. Along Came the Angles

Introductory Background

Even in Roman times there had been a system of coastal defences along the East coast of what is now England to protect against raiders from across the North Sea (or German Ocean as it was called previously), territories now in Denmark and Germany. The raids were led by the Angles, the Saxons and the Jutes – and as the chapter title implies our interest will be in the Angles, who lived broadly in the area covered by Schelswig, their core home (shown in black below) being Angeln.

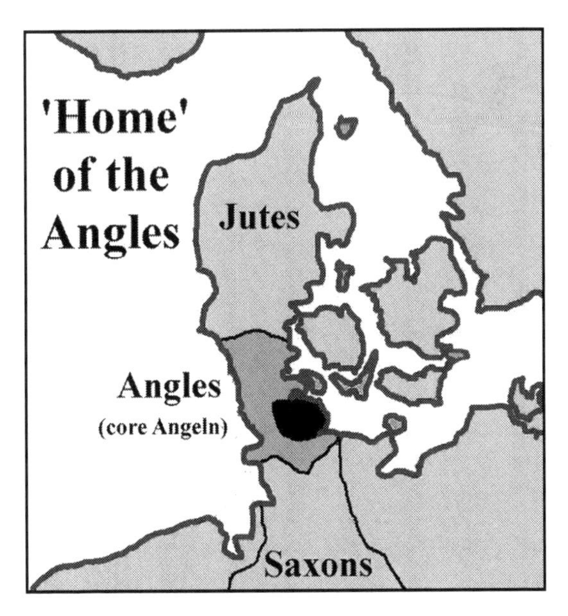

The people in what is now England has suffered from predatory raids from the Picts and the Scots as well, but when the Roman legions left the Britons did not have the resources to defend themselves, so they turned to the Germanic raiders for help against these raids. The Anglo-Saxon Chronicle suggests that Vortigern, the High King of Britain, invited Hengist and Horsa to the shores of what is now southern England, allowing them to set up their own enclave in Kent (from which they later expanded their control south of the Thames).

After the death of Old King Cole around 420 his kingdom (the Old North mentioned before whose southern boundary broadly lay between the Humber and the Mersey) was split amongst his sons and a generation later there was further Balkanisation. There remained two kingdoms of particular importance to this narrative: Bryneich and Ebrauc. The kings here did the same sort of thing as Vortigernt – importing Angles to help with their defence (around the year 450).
The kings allocated two enclaves for these Angles:

- In Ebrauc (based in York) the Anglians were allocated their own enclave which was called Deira. Its boundaries were the river Hull to the east, the river Derwent to west, the river Humber to the south and, to the north, the old road from Beverley on the River Hull to just south of Wressell on the Derwent. The Anglian 'capital' was at Brough-on-Humber, the old 'Civitas Parisiorum'.

- In Bryneich (perhaps based at Corbridge) the enclave allocated probably lay between the Tyne and the Wear and probably as far inland as the road through Wrekenton to Gateshead to the north and close to Chester-le-Street to the south with its 'capital' at South Shields. [The reasons for supposing this is that one Anglian king is noted as being born in South Shields and the establishment of the twin monasteries of Wearmouth (on the north bank of the Wear) and Jarrow (on the south bank of the Tyne).]

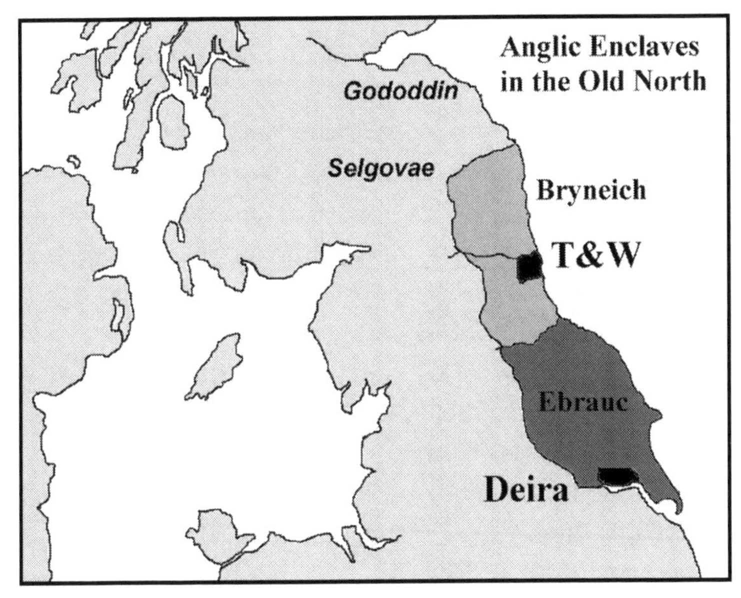

[Other groups of Angles were established, also by invitation, in East Anglia (around the same time) and in Lindsey and Mercia (starting some 70 years later), but they need not concern us. For a compete explanation of all this see my paper Penda.]

In the previous chapter we noted that 'King' Arthur was able to benefit from the support of these Anglian troops in his campaign against the Picts and the Scots.

There are historians who take a contrary view, believing that the Angles and Saxons merely barged their way in and took such land as they wanted. The problem for this proposition is that although Nennius, for example, does acknowledge that the Saxons did cause local trouble from a relatively early date, there is no hard evidence at all of any problem in the North before 547 – a century after their first arrival.

Just as there was intermarriage between the families of Vortigern and Hengist, so I am sure that there was similar intermarriage between the ruling families of the Angles and their Brythonic hosts.

The Angles arrived around 450 and were generally helpful until the death of Morcant 'Bwlch' ('the gap toothed'), king of Bryneich in 547. At this point Ida, king of the Angles in Tyne and Wear who (I am sure) was both descended through intermarriage from earlier kings of Bryneich and was himself married to a local princess, seized the throne. Morcant's son Coledog may have been killed in the coup, but in any case the remaining family fled for refuge in Strathclyde; Ida pursued them with the clear intention of destroying anyone with a rival claim to 'his' throne but he was badly beaten at the battle of Alt Clud Ford. The army of the Britons (Strathclyde and Rheged) then chased them and he and his forces ended up besieged on Lindisfarne (then called Metcault). They would have been finished off there and then had not Morcant (grandson of Morcant Bwlch) procured the assassination of Urien, King of Rheged out of personal spite and jealousy. The siege collapsed (c550 CE) and the Anglians were safe to continue in power in Bryneich, which Ida renamed Bernicia partly in honour of his wife and partly to justify 'their' reign there. Meanwhile the young Morcant and what remained of his extended family were allowed to set up a court-in-exile at Cadzow in Strathclyde. [For extra detail and explanation of this see my paper "Siege".]

The Britons were not at all happy with this situation, but they might just about have been able to live with it. But such stability as there was was thrown into turmoil one generation later, in 580, when the Angles of Deira overthrew the Kingdom of Ebrauc (York – see my paper "Caer Greu"). The two Anglian kingdoms then linked up, by marriage, by agreement and sometimes by force, making the combined unit a clear and present danger to the remaining British kingdoms of the Old North. Near continuous raiding and skirmishing on the borders (which were not natural or obvious because they had not needed to be) ensued.

The upshot of this was that a great army of Britons, led by the Gododdin (by then based in Edinburgh and at Traprain Law) launched an attack at Catterick in about the year 600 – where they were soundly beaten by the Angles. This was recorded in the poem Y Gododdin by Aneurin – and this has already been referred to in the previous chapter because this battle was misrepresented as the "Battle of Raith".

There had also been jealousy and in-fighting within the Anglian royal family of Bernicia: so much so that Hering the son and heir of his father 'Hussa' had to seek refuge – which he did with the Scots in Dalriata. In 603 when he reached the age of 21, another army, this time commanded by King Aedan mac Gabhran sought to put Hering onto the throne which he not unreasonably saw as his birthright – but they too were soundly beaten at the Battle of Degsastan (see details in my paper "Degsastan"). This was the last hurrah for the natives and the way was open for the Anglian take over of all of the Old North, including the Lothians. The Gododdin made their final stand in Edinburgh in 638 when the Anglians laid siege successfully. The Gododdin then finally vanished from history.

Perspective problems

So many historians have seen things from a supposed Anglo-

Saxon perspective that they have missed a lot of nuance. The Angles were not one amorphous, yet coherent mass of people who randomly invaded what is now England. On the one hand we have seen two, perhaps loosely related, groups who were invited in and took service under the kings of the Old North. Separately from that a party took service under the Iceni in East Anglia. Much later yet another group belonging to the line of the last king of the Angles sought refuge in the lands of the Britons. As royals we would expect them too to marry into local royalty and it is this way that we find Penda and his immediate ancestors as Kings of Mercia. Angles they may have been, but we find them fighting on the British side against the Angles of Northumbria, against the Angles of East Anglia and against the Saxons to the South. So I ask the reader not to suppose that all Angles were the same!

Anglians take active control of the Southern Picts – including 'Fife'.

Battles with their fellow Anglian neighbours in Mercia to the south did not stand in the way of the Northumbrians turning their attention northwards.

Anglian Dominion

Bede (book 2 Chapter 5) says

> "Oswy … for the most part subdued and made tributary the nations of the Picts and Scots, which possess the northern parts of Britain…"

Bede (book 3 chapter 6) says

> "King Oswald…… brought under his dominion all the nations and provinces of Britain, which are divided into four languages, viz. the Britons, the Picts, the Scots, and the English."

Oswald and Oswy (variously Oswiu) were brothers. Oswald died in battle in 642; he was king of Northumbria from 634. Oswy died in 670 having been king of Bernicia from 642 and of all Northumbria from 654.

There are no records of set piece battles which may have led to this situation. On the contrary the brothers had been exiles in Dalriata. Not only that but Talorcan, King of the Picts (653x57) was the son of Eanfrith, king of Bernicia who is reported to have married a Pictish princess while also living in exile. He was the elder half-brother of Oswald and Oswiu. [I suspect that there has been a bit of guesswork here – it would have been Talorcan who became king by marrying a Pictish princess, but with two dynasties, both could be true.]

We should pay close attention also to Bede's use of the phrase "for the most part". This I interpret as the Bernicians stopping short of the Highland line and not getting further north than Dunottar – so the Inverness-based Northern Picts retained their independence and reinforced their control of Buchan in the North East and the Grampian mountains – the old core Caledonian territory. In other words the Anglians got as far as Severus (the difference was that this time they were able to maintain their control for some decades) but not as far as Agricola.

So it would be tempting to suppose that this was a fairly friendly relationship with everyone accepting their place. But no – as will become clear.

In 671 the Picts seized the opportunity of the potential instability arising from the death of Oswy to rebel against Anglian control. But they were soundly beaten at the Battle of the Two Rivers.

The location has not been determined, but armies tend to march along roads and so we might hazard a guess at the Stirling area in general, where various confluences (Allan/Teith, Forth/Teith) where so many known battles have taken place offer themselves as a likely venue. On the other hand the confluence of the Tay and the Earn somewhere between Perth and Abernethy – another 'normal' site for a battle – should not be ruled out.

A useful indicator of how far the writ of the Northumbrians ran is the fact that around 680 Bridei mac Bili, King of the Northern Picts (based in Inverness) attacked Dunnottar (immediately to the south of Stonehaven) – clearly a key Anglian stronghold at that time. So we may be confident that the whole of what is now 'Fife' had come under Anglian control probably sometime around the year 640 and that they were still feeling oppressed by this more than 30 years later.

Fife's place under the Anglians

James E Fraser ("Caledonia to Pictland" p 200/1) suggests that at this time Fife, or a part of it, was called Niuduera, ruled for the Bernicians by one Beornhaeth. This is not at all convincing – all the more so given that Fraser concedes that Manau still existed at that time. He admits that he has no basis for linking Beornhaeth to Niuduera – and he has come to the wrong conclusion.

First let us dispose of Niuduera. The only reference to this place actually comes from the anonymous life of St Cuthbert which is reproduced at the website stcuthbertorthodoxchurch.org:

> *§15. On another occasion he travelled from Mailros with two brethren and, after sailing to the territory of the Picts, arrived without incident among the Niduari.****
>
> **** Niduari is the reading in Bede for the corrupt Mudsieralegis given by the MS. By Niduari is probably*

meant a people dwelling by the banks of the River Nith, that falls into the Solway

The footnote is the webmaster's – but it makes a good deal more sense. The river Nith runs through Dumfries. Next door Kirkcudbrightshire is named in Cuthbert's honour. "Niduari" is probably a vernacular name for the people Ptolemy called the Novantes. Fraser has fallen foul of the modern and thoroughly unreasonable fashion amongst historians to try to pretend that there were no such people as Galloway Picts. We should not overlook the slight spelling difference between Niduari and Fraser's "Niuduera Regio". From the text above we can see how Fraser could have derived such an interpretation. So the group probably travelled down the route of the A7 to Carlisle whereafter it seemed quicker, easier and safer to take ship to, say, Kirkcudbright – where a church is dedicated to… St Cuthbert! [Presumably this dedication occurred some time later.] The story is not without incident – they might have been better going overland(!) – but that need not detain us. The story seems garbled – the chances are that he actually went elsewhere first (eg Cumberland) and only then set sail for Galloway.

So now we can turn to Beornhaeth: there is no doubt that he was a local man in charge, but how far did his writ run and where was he based? The discussion of "Niduari" etc. has been conflated with an "urbs" which Bede calls "Giudi" and Nennius calls "Judeu".

One problem I have faced throughout this book is how far to stray off message for the sake of providing a complete explanation. In this case I am going to avoid providing the full proof on these pages, but the interested reader can find it online in my paper "Urbs Iudeu". Suffice it here to say that despite the doubt which has suffused academic writing, it is completely clear to me that Beornhaeth's headquarters was at Blackness Castle – on the southern shore of the Firth of Forth, facing Fife.

This is reinforced by the appointment of Trumwine to be the "Bishop of the Picts" in 681. Where did Trumwine set up his Bishopric? Not in Fife! Not in Pictland at all! He based himself just three miles from Blackness at Abercorn – making further nonsense of Fraser's suggestion that the Anglians would have ruled Southern Pictland from Fife. Had the 'Fifers' been sympathetic to the Bernicians, or even if there had been a substantial settlement of Bernicians in 'Fife', Trumwine would surely have wanted to be closer to his flock – and his king's local representative.

The 'Fifers' were not in league with the Bernicians, they were under their yoke.

The Angles put to flight

Egfrith served his father Oswy as sub-king of Deira from 664, becoming King of all Northumbria in his own right on his father's death in 670. [There are many more modern day parallels of this sort of arrangement including the position of Prince of Wales, except that in the times we are examining the title was not just ceremonial.] Perhaps it was this experience, unnoticed by the Picts, which was the basis of their underestimating him when they revolted in 671 – but it is true that they had also underestimated Beornhaeth. However perhaps Beornhaeth's military prowess gave Ecgfrith an excessive opinion of his own capabilities.

Oswy had been the acknowledged "main man" in Britain. The danger for Ecgfrith was that the only way would be downwards. While Ecgfrith did try to live up to his father's image eg with a raid on Brega in Ireland and his short term acquisition of

Linsey, what turned out to be the disastrous adventure against the Northern Picts in 685 and his own death at the Battle of Nechtansmere was not as cavalier as many paint it.

I have no idea who wrote the Wikipedia page about him (retrieved 03/20), but it is ludicrous to suggest that the result of the Battle of the Two Rivers in 671 was that he gained control of the land "between the Forth and Tweed". Not only had there been the successful siege of Edinburgh in 638 and deals done in Blackness (Iudiu) between his predecessors, but, as we noted also, Bridei attacked Dunottar in 681. This attack was not a squabble amongst Picts, this was Bridei attacking the Angles at their northern outpost.

Although Bridei, the Pictish King, had been attacked by the Scots (who, too, were a client state of the Angles at this point) not only had he seen them off, but he had raided deep into Dalriatan territory - perhaps as far as Dunadd. We do not need to look far to find Bridei's motivation. Despite being Ecgbert's cousin, he was by birth a member of the Strathclyde royal family - yet another kingdom forced to bend the knee to the Northumbrians.

These attacks by Bridei really forced Ecgbert's hand. Conquering the Northern Picts became a necessity - for otherwise Bridei would continue to attack and perhaps even gain territory from Ecgbert's client states. And even if Bridei was seen off, the ongoing trouble would sap Ecgbert's strength potentially leading to trouble in the south. So Ecgbert really did have to deal with Bridei once and for all. His decision to do this led to his own death and the rolling back of Anglian control.
In recent years there has been dispute as to the location of Nechtansmere. Until 2006 it was generally agreed that the location was in the area of Dunnichen in Angus, 3 miles

east of Forfar. But Dr Alex Woolf reviewed the evidence and proposed instead that the site was in Badenoch – at Dunachton beside Loch Insh. This makes sense on at least three grounds:

- There is no 'mere' near Dunnichen
- There are no "narrow passes in the midst of inaccessible mountains" (Bede's description) through which Ecgbert's army could have been "lured" in order to get to Dunnichen.
- Given what we have seen of Dunnottar above, Dunnichen is well within the territory already controlled by the Angles.

However in order for the Picts to do this "luring" it is clear that while the Angles controlled the kingdom of the Southern Picts, in practice their writ did not run significantly beyond the Highland Line. The fact that the Scots had attacked Bridei at Dundurn (at the east end of Loch Earn) demonstrates that the Angles had not penetrated into Pictland that deeply there either – in other words and as already suggested above, they got about as far as Severus had done 400+ years earlier.

Had Ecgbert had a free choice of military strategy it would have made far more sense to carry on with the Romans' strategy – ie advancing through Buchan complete with naval support. So we may suppose that his advance up the Tay was prompted by what at least appeared to be an imminent threat posed by the Picts, perhaps massing (at Rohallion (near Birnam) for example?) which led Ecgbert to chase them up the valley of the Tay at least as far as Blair Atholl and then over the hills and down Glen Tromie to Ruthven, just 5 miles from Dunachton. Here his worn out troops met forces fresh from Inverness. In the ensuing engagement the Anglian army was routed and Ecgbert himself was killed.

Aftermath of the Battle

The Battle of Nechtansmere had very substantial long term consequences both for Pictland as a whole and for 'Fife' in particular.

As we have noticed the Picts and the Scots had been raiding each other sporadically – and the association between the Scots and Manau meant that the Picts had to maintain far too long a front line. On the other hand it was the general weakness of Manau which had allowed the Angles far too easy a path into central Scotland offering them a choice of ways into Pictland proper.

So after the Picts had chased the Angles back 'home' a good deal of redrawing of boundaries became a very good idea.

First: the Central Valley – of the Teith and Forth – which had been part of Manau was annexed to Strathearn, and hence fully integrated into Pictish kingdom. This gave control of Stirling to the Mormaer of Strathearn and also meant that the Scots were cut off at Crianlarich – so a very short border with Dalriata. The Pictish kingdom now directly bordered the Lennox – an integral part of Strathclyde.

Second: Fife was extended to take in broadly what is now Dunfermline District. This again considerably reduced Manau – and shortened the border between Fife and Manau roughly to today's Fife/Clackmannan border.

Third: Trumwine, "Bishop of the Picts" felt so insecure and his position so untenable that even though he was based in Abercorn he felt the need to up sticks – seeking safety (and retirement) at Whitby. He was not replaced (but see next chapter).

Fourth: As a result the Kingdom of Manau was now reduced to the Falkirk area and the Clackmannanshire of today. This was so small as to be no threat at all. It seems never to have been absorbed fully into any other mormaerdom (which could really only have been Fife or Strathearn). So it probably came into the direct "ownership" of the crown, albeit managed as one or more thanages.

The precise border between the Picts and the Angles seems not to have been defined immediately.

- Ecgfrith's successor as king of the Angles was Aldfrith who had been studying on Iona. He seems to have been someone broadly acceptable to the newly independent Picts and Scots.
- Despite their victory and a friendly king in Northumbria, the Picts actually had to deal with local placemen. So they followed up their 685 victory in 698 where Ecgbert's general Berctred (variously Berht) was killed, but it is not clear just where this battle was. Most probably it was south of the Antonine Wall, but west of the river Avon. My supposition is that the Picts had reached the Antonine Wall, but were keen to press on to the Avon gorge. It was likely after this that peace was agreed.
- Aldfrith died in 704 after which infighting for the crown of Northumbria broke out.
- In 710 or 11 the Picts were in their turn defeated by the Angles "in campo Manand" (according to the Annals of Tigernach), "mag Manonn" (Annals of Ulster) – ie on the plains of Manau. [The term "mag" implies a particular sort of boggy area, so this is probably not far from Bannockburn (in those days the vast majority of the Forth/Teith Valley was boggy).] Florence of Worcester says that the Anglian force was led by Berhtfrith and he was successful. As Berhtfrith

was probably Berhtred's son, then this expedition may have been inspired by personal revenge. Whether the border was then moved as a result (back to the Antonine Wall?) is hard to say.

- 'Fife' reached its maximum territorial extent.

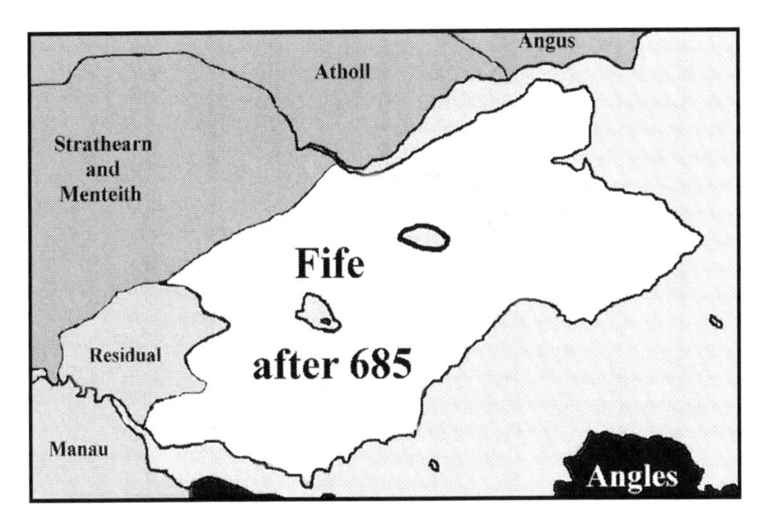

Footnote on the Edinburgh Pictish Symbol Stone

In Scotland there are just two "rogue" Pictish Symbol stones. One, mentioned already, is at Trusty's Hill, Dumfriesshire and my opinion is that this should be dated to the 180s CE and need not detain us. The other one is and was in Edinburgh (Canmore site 52135). It was found in Princes Street Gardens in the early 1800s, not in its original position. The stone was already in very poor condition when first recognised with much flaking ('lamination') having occurred – leaving us having to speculate about it. It would be too much of a diversion to enter a long discussion about the understanding of the symbols, but suffice it to say that my view is that this stone was set up and carved to mark a peace treaty, the so-called V rod actually being a "broken spear" – a symbol of peace (compare turning swords into ploughshares). I suggest that the crescent may represent the rising full moon – which may have been considered an auspicious occasion for the solemnisation of the treaty.

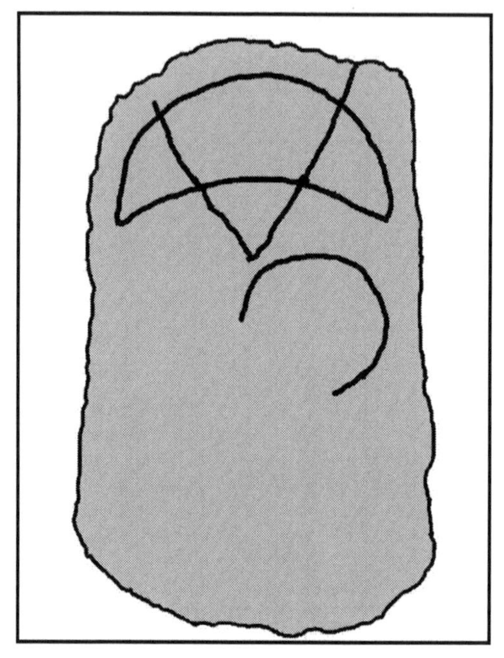

Edinburgh Pictish Stone
see https://canmore.org.uk/site/52135/edinburgh-princes-street-gardens

I suspect that when originally erected, this stone only had the Crescent and V-Rod on it.

The arc of part of a circle beneath the crescent and V rod cannot represent part of a Double Circle and Z rod as has been speculated in the past. The most likely possibility is that it was originally a mirror – which I interpret as representing the soul and hence memorialising a death – which, if this speculation is correct, may have been added in 704 to commemorate the death of Aldfrith.

The Wikipedia pages about the two principal actors here are a useful start but, as indicated above, they must be treated with considerable caution, because there are errors.

https://en.wikipedia.org/wiki/Bridei_III
https://en.wikipedia.org/wiki/Ecgfrith_of_Northumbria

Conclusions

- For nearly 50 years the Angles exercised day to day control over all of what would become Fife.
- Following the Pictish Victory at Nechtansmere in 685, the kingdom of Manau was dismembered. Fife gained the eastern portion – ie the Dunfermline area east of the Clackmannanshire border.
- At this stage the county/Mormaerdom of Fife was called "Uuip" or some such.
- There is an irony that the term "Sassenach" (meaning "Saxon") was first used by many Highlanders to refer to lowland Scots and later used by Scots generally to refer to English people generally even though the Angles and the Saxons were and are not the same!

10. St Serf and the Romanisation of Christianity in Fife

The kings of Bryneich had been Christian, but the Anglian kings who took over and renamed it Bernicia had been Pagan. St Oswald, King of Bernicia, had converted to Christianity while a teenage refugee in Dalriata (616x20), so as king it was natural that he would turn to Iona for spiritual instruction – and Lindisfarne was founded. This did not find favour with followers of Rome who had been increasing in power steadily following the arrival of St Augustine in 597.

Oswald's brother and successor Oswiu had been a fellow exile and so he too was imbued with Columban Christianity, but he was genuinely concerned by the schism, so in 664 he convened the Synod of Whitby to thrash it all out. Roman Catholicism won the day. In 681 Ecgbert pursued this approach further by facilitating the appointment of Trumwine to be the (Catholic) Bishop of the Picts – who, as we have seen, were his client people at the time. However the Angles realised that conversion would be a tough call with a lot of local opposition, so Trumwine set up his base at Abercorn, well into Bernicia and close to their strongpoint at Blackness.

Adomnan, became Abbot of Iona in 679 and from 686 had occasion to visit Northumbria on several occasions; during this time he came to adopt the Roman view. In principle he should have been able to work with Trumwine on this, but by the victory at Nechtansmere the Northern Picts had liberated their Southern brothers from Anglian overlordship and soon after that Trumwine himself had withdrawn, leaving Adomnan with the problem of how to 'correct' Pictish – and, indeed, Scottish – Christianity.

The records do not tell us exactly how it happened, but in the end Adomnan managed to convince the king of the Picts and he secured the assistance of St Serf – who must have been sent from Lindisfarne, Jarrow or Wearmouth.

1. St Serf (695x710)

Much nonsense has been written and spoken about "St Serf". Even today there are those who think he had something to do with St Kentigern and particularly today there are those who think he "came from the west" and was a Culdee! What links all these fantasists together is that they pay no attention even to the 'real' claims made about him.

His 'official' Life

The anonymously written manuscript *Vita Sancti Servani* ("The Life of St Serf") dates from the 1150s – bizarrely although it is broadly contemporaneous with the life of St Kentigern, it contradicts it! It was freshly translated by Dr Alan MacQuarrie, who published it in the *Innes Review* of the Autumn of 1993: Volume 44 No 2 pp122-152. This paper is readily available online.

As it stands it would be easy to discard it as evident rubbish. But if we are careful to sift through and if we compare the claims with what else we know of the secular history of the time, we may form quite a useful understanding of what actually went on.

We may begin by summarising the main chapters of St Serf's life leading to his arrival in Fife:

- He was born the son of the King of Canaan and named Malachi (= "my angel/messenger") as well as Serf/Servanus (evidently, therefore, a translation);
- His father died when he was seven years old;
- At the age of 13 he became a monk – leaving his brother to take the crown;
- At the age of 30 he became a priest;
- Soon (?) thereafter he became the Bishop of the Canaanites to whom he ministered for 20 years;
- He then spent 7 years as Patriarch in Jerusalem;
- Travelling, he spent three years in Constantinople before leaving for Rome;
- In Rome he was elected Pope and reigned for 7 years before abdicating to come to Scotland.

According to this story he was, therefore, about 70 years of age (or more!) when he reached the Firth of Forth. There is, of course, no reason to place any credence whatsoever on any part of this nonsense, not least because the same story is told of other saints – particularly St Boniface! [We will return to this.]

Dating the arrival

According to the Vita, at the beginning of his ministry in Fife he had discussions with Adamnan (in his role as Abbot of Iona) and Bruide map Der-Ilei as King of the Picts. So let us consider the feasibility of this:

Name	Position	Assumed office	Died
Adamnan	Abbot of Holy Isle	679	704
Bridei map Der-Ilei	King of Picts	695/7	705/6

As can be seen the dates for Bridei's reign are in minor dispute, but this is trivial. What we can see is that there is a window of time which allows Serf to have had discussions with both these important figures – broadly 695-704.

As we can see the Vita claims that immediately before his journey to Fife he was serving as Pope. There was, of course, no Pope Servanus, but now that we have a fairly precise date to work from, let us examine the roll of Popes from that era:

Pope	Date of Election	Date of Death
John V	685	686
Conon	686	687
Sergius	687	701
John VI	701	705
John VII	705	707

Immediately our attention is drawn to Sergius – born in Sicily about 650, elected as Pope aged 37 and dying aged about 51. So it is quite possible that the anonymous author conflated the arrival of Serf in Scotland with the death of Pope Sergius which he had misunderstood as resignation. If this analysis is correct, it would give us an even more precise date for Serf's arrival in Fife as 701/702, but for other reasons this seems a bit late.

My proposition is, therefore, that this "front end" of Serf's life was tacked on to explain (a) that he was a foreigner and (b) that he was already an older man when he arrived – and why, therefore, his mission is Scotland was a short one (I conclude that he was already dead by 710, see below). It may even be that Serf was about the same age as the Pope Sergius (and so early

50s on arrival and c60 when he died) – which seems more likely than the 70+ implied by his back story (above).

St Serf's activity in Scotland

MacQuarrie's translation of the *Vita* runs to just over 8 pages; of this, the section discussing his mission to Scotland is not more than four, including substantial footnoting – altogether under 1200 words.

He was met on arrival by Adamnan who assigned to him "the land of Fife, from the Hill of the Britons to the Ochil Hills". Places mentioned as having been visited by him include Kinneil, Culross, Lochleven, Dysart, Tullibody, Tillicoutry, Alva, Airthrey, and Dunning (where he died). The *Vita* is very specific in stating that Serf himself chose the site at Culross for his base and that it was virgin territory – thus rendering impossible the contortionist efforts of James E Fraser ("*From Caledonia to Pictland*" p 254 &c) to suggest that an earlier St Serf – or indeed anyone else, sainted or otherwise – had first occupied that site. [For further discussion of this see ALLE.]

Why Serf came to Culross

I was very surprised by what I came to understand as Serf's mission. For this we have to recognise the politics – both clerical and lay – of the era. In the previous two chapters we detailed the tides in politics.

Tides in Religion

Christianity was already present (albeit quite tenuously) in Strathclyde and amongst the Picts of Galloway in the time of St Patrick (ie pre-500), gaining a foothold in Lothian in the early 500s under British influence when 'king' Arthur's sister married Ljot (see ALLE). Dalriata adopted Christianity with the arrival of Fergus Mor; the kingdom of the Picts came under serious Christian influence in the time of Columba (c563-597). Starting in Inverness it spread south and east.

- Edwin of Northumbria (king c616 – c632) was converted to Christianity in 627 due to southern influences,
- but it was to Iona that his successor Oswald (king 634-642) turned very soon into his reign to establish the centre at Lindisfarne, installing Aidan as the first bishop. [This should come as no surprise as Oswald had spent his formative years in exile north of the Antonine Wall.]
- It was Oswald's brother Oswiu (king 642-670), also a previous exile, who convened the Synod of Whitby in 644. It was as a result of this synod, particularly the influence of St Wilfrid speaking there, that Oswiu turned away from Iona in favour of Canterbury and Rome.
- Bede ("Eccl. Hist." v. 15. 2 Ibid. v. 15, 21) tells us that in 688 on a visit to Aldfrith (king of Northumbria 685-704) Adamnan was convinced of the primacy of Roman rule and practices, but he was much less than generally successful in seeking thereafter to convince Christians under his aegis of this. Robert H Story ("The Church of Scotland, past and present: its history, its relation to the law and the state, its doctrine, ritual, discipline, and patrimony" 1890 (Volume 1) p205) suggests that this was before 692. [Bishop Ceolfrid of Jarrow (tenure 674-716) later reminded King Nechtan of Adamnan's views in a letter.]

So by 698 we have the situation that Adamnan is bent on Romanising Scotland. He hoped that influence would come from every quarter. With regard to south east Pictland he had been relying on Bernician influence based at Abercorn. Now that this was lost and, despite the peace treaty, with very frosty relations between the Angles and the Picts, he needed a new tactic and a new champion for his cause on the North shores of the Forth. Enter St Serf…

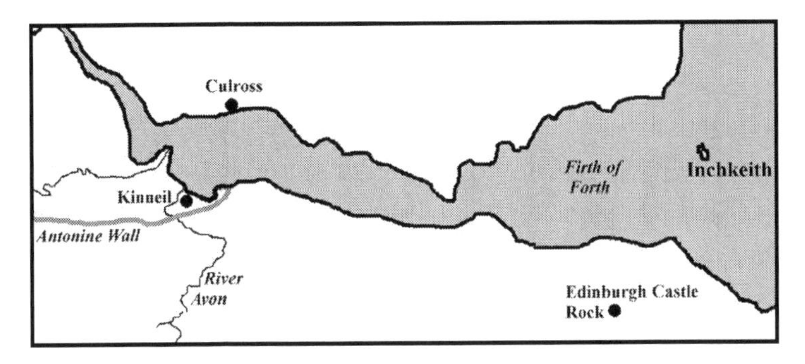

HOW SERF CAME TO AND SETTLED IN CULROSS

- The Vita tells us that Adamnan welcomed Serf to Scotland at Inchkeith.

First we should not be surprised that he and his party arrived by sea. Even hundreds of years later the seas were the highways in Britain generally – even more so throughout Scotland. Second we do not know whether the Picts or the Angles had any claim over the island but Adamnan would surely have had a free hand in either case. Like Inchmickery and Inchcolm (and especially the Bass Rock where St Baldred (d. 757) is recorded as living so nearly contemporaneously) it is far from unlikely that these were already in church hands for hermits and/or for burials. [The name Baldred is Anglic rather than Pictish.] There would have been no problem with a landfall in Lothian as the Bernicians were fully on board with Adamnan's intentions, so a whole host of harbours were potentially available. Thus we must assume that Inchkeith was a matter of choice rather than of any real necessity.

- From Inchkeith the party sailed to Kinneil.

The choice of this site was no accident. Kinneil (the name means "Wall's end" is RIGHT ON the Antonine Wall… on the northern side. Had there been any hostility it would have been a matter of running a few hundred yards and the party would have been back in Bernician territory, under Bernician protection. Given that this was not an armed group, there would have been no real pretext for any pursuit, but they landed without Pictish royal permission so it was better to be safe than sorry.

- From Kinneil Serf saw Culross and decided to settle there

The Vita said that he "cast his staff" across the water and this gives rise to derision – and yes it is nearly 3 miles. But he may well have pointed his staff; we are familiar with "casting one's eye" on something and this is never normally interpreted literally, so I recommend some pedants to get a life! When Serf reached Culross, which, we are told, was a virgin site and so needed clearing, news got to king Bridei and the wisdom of making landfall at Kinneil became clear! Bridei was not pleased and proposed to kill Serf and his team of followers. The Vita says that this was merely because he had no permission; what Bridei's real motivation was we can but guess. In the end Bridei was won round and not only was Serf allowed to carry on with Culross, he was also given the island in Loch Leven which bears his name. Macquarrie is of the view that the idea of Serf meeting with Adamnan at that island is really no more than a duplication of the anecdote about the meeting at Inchkeith, but I see no reason to assume this. Given that Serf was on a task for Adamnan the idea of plural meetings is far from having been out of order.

- Adamnan allocated Serf his territory

The fact that Serf was there to do a specific job for Adamnan is no better illustrated than by the way he was allocated an area just as sales reps are today. The Vita specifies that Serf's "patch" was "the land of Fife from the Hill of the Britons to the Ochil Hills". We can see from the places mentioned in the Vita it is clear that Serf stuck to his job, notwithstanding that it is far from clear where the "Hill of the Britons" may have been. [It probably represents the most Easterly point of Strathclyde on the Lennox/Manau border, perhaps Darrach Hill in the Kilsyth Hills.] Indeed the fact that there is no mention of anywhere North of the Lomond Hills of Fife or west or south west of Stirling reinforces the idea that Serf's ministry was short and that he was working outwards from his Culross base.

What St Serf did

It is not my purpose to replicate the Vita here. The text is readily available and it is for readers to decide for themselves what to make of the various anecdotes. What I have sought to do is to show the "when" and the "why", thereby to understand Serf's mission and to complete his dissociation from Kentigern.

However I do take this opportunity to specify one event particular to Fife. It is said that St Serf went to Dysart to argue with the Devil. In fact he went there to argue with the Culdee hermits there whose views and practices were the most divergent from Roman orthodoxy of all the Columban Christians whom he was tasked with 'converting'.

So St Serf probably came from Jarrow/Wearmouth at the behest of Adomnan as the key figure in Adomnan's plan to Romanise Pictland. He had nothing to do with Kentigern (see below).

2. "Fothrif": Funding St Serf's mission

My explanation here both about the meaning of the name Fothrif(f) and just where it was are both extremely controversial. At the time of writing the reader will not find any reputable academic who understands either properly. Here I show where it was, the meaning of the name and what it was for, but for a full explanation of why today's academics have got it so wrong, see Appendix A below about Dunfermline Abbey.

What Fothrif was for

Any 'project' needs funding. This project, the Romanising of the Pictish church, was no different in that respect, except that the project was massive and so the funding would need to be substantial to match the anticipated expenditure. This funding could only come from the revenues to be derived from land holding – and this process continued for many centuries (ie churches were sustained in this way).

Landowners tend not to be stupid people – and in that regard tend to hold on to their more valuable assets. I invite the reader to look around their local area and see how many churches and, especially, graveyards are built on land which was fit for nothing else. Many graveyards are sited near river banks on lands which are liable to flooding and so of relatively little use to agriculture. There are many others which seem to be on excellent land, but the name betrays their origin. Monymusk in Aberdeenshire is one such – the name combines "usk" which is no more than a variant of Brythonic (Usk/Esk etc.) and Gaelic ("uisg" etc) meaning "water" or 'burn'; "Mon-y" comes from Brythonic (cf Welsh 'mign', Gaelic 'moine') for "bog" – so Monymusk is Pictish and means "the river through the bog". It was only due to the importation of skilled, mostly Flemish, workers that the land, previously considered worthless, was drained, and suddenly became very valuable.

Where Fothriff was

In the case of St Serf it was a similar process. He was given land, but in this case, although largely undeveloped, it was not poor land – just as well as it was intended for income generation, not just for burial – but it was marginal in the sense that it had only just been incorporated into Pictland in general and 'Fife' in particular. It lay on the border of what remained of Manau. Parishes as we came to know them did not exist at this time, but the land he was given may now be recognised as that which was to become the parishes of Culross, Tullyallan and Kincardine. Some time later the lower (and contiguous) half of what was later still to become the parish of Saline was added. The *Vita* pretty well implies that the first of these was a donation from the King of the Picts directly. I have no definite idea when Saline was added – or by whom. Perhaps a later king, perhaps a Mormaer of 'Fife', but two possibilities regarding a date do suggest themselves: one 'obvious' possibility is 710 – with the huge number of extra clerics needing to be taken care of. 717 is also possible (see details below).

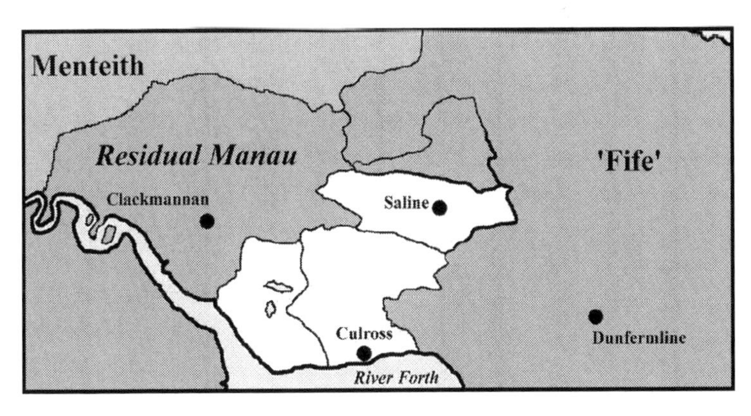

Location of Fothriff: Tullyallan and Kincardine, Culross and southern Saline parishes

Suffice it to say that in old charters Fothrif is described variously as a "shire" and as a "parish" and neither of these fits with the nonsense the recognised academics will tell you.

MEANING OF THE NAME FOTHRIFF

In a talk to Kirkcaldy Civic Society (2019) the 'normal' (ie Gaelic-based) understanding of Fothrif was rehearsed as being a combination of "fother" = beside and "-if" = "Fife" (the first 'f' being lost by normal genitive lenition). It is useful to know what you are up against and it is not impossible that this is how, much later, Gaels understood it – even if what they understand by Fothriff does not at all accord with this explanation (again see Appendix A). Not only is this explanation nonsense; those who propound it do not acknowledge that they are denying the views of WJ Watson (Celtic Placenames of Scotland pp 114) who says:

> The name is a Gaelic form of O. British Vo-treb-, 'sub-settlement,' in modern Welsh godref, 'small town, lodgement'; Godre Fynydd, 'small town of the hill,' is at Aberllefeny in Merioneth; Godre Dewi, 'St. David's Godref,' is in Caermarthen, south of Newcastle Emlyn.

As usual the reason that modern historians have got it entirely wrong is that the name is NOT Gaelic, it is Pictish – and they would have done well not to be so dismissive of Watson's direction. This land was given to Serf 150 years before the Gaels even had a look in and at a time when the Celtic church was being suppressed in the effort to make everyone conform to the Roman Catholic faith. Watson is right to prefer Brythonic to Gaelic, but his explanation could be better. In fact "Godre" means "bottom edge of the foot" and the problem with Godref is that Fothriff was not a small town.

So just as with the names of Dunfermline and Kirkcaldy which we have considered above, we must join Watson in looking to Pictish/Brythonic and modern Welsh for the original meaning and see if we can do better – which we can now that we realise he was promoting Catholicism.

In modern Welsh we have "ffydd" meaning "faith" and "Rhufeinog" meaning "Roman". So Fothriff as it has come down to us, is a mangling by Gaels of "ffyddyrhuf(einog)" meaning "Roman Faith" and refers to the fact that this land was given to the Catholic church for the purpose of providing a revenue base for their further proselytising.

Saline

T&M [PNF 820] struggle with the name Saline – and no wonder, for they seek a Gaelic answer. However in modern Welsh there is the readily available "sâl" meaning "payment/benefit/gift". The accent makes the pronunciation much closer of the "sawl-" of early spellings and "-in" being added by the Scots, meaning "place" (the Gaels did the same to the name Kirkcaldy from time to time). So "Saline" is "the gifted lands".

And so it was that St Serf was funded to enable him to recruit, build and to travel freely. So too this land, so recently added to 'Fife' was alienated from it again. [This arrangement, however, came to an end just 150 years later when the Catholics were thrown out by the incoming Scots.]

3. St Boniface

Adomnan died before Serf; Serf died substantially before the work was complete. So too King Bridei map Der-Ilei was soon dead. But his successor (his brother Nechtan) was keen that the work should continue.

Nechtan map Der-Ilei	King of Picts	706-724 & 728-729

We noted above that the back story (including being Pope) attributed to St Serf is also attributed to "St Boniface" (see Story Vol. 1 pp 210/1). In that version of the legend, Serf is just one of Boniface's retinue.

[The nickname/soubriquet (or adopted name) "Boniface" does not imply any pleasing appearance ("bonny face"), but rather implies the intention to "do good deeds" (from the Latin *bonus* and *facere*).]

The tales of Boniface's claim too belong to the era of king Bruide's brother. We should consider also, therefore, the eras of various Popes called Boniface:

Pope	**Date of Election**	**Death**
St Boniface I	418	422
Boniface II	530	532
Boniface III	607	607
St Boniface IV	608	615
Boniface V	619	625
Boniface VI	896	896
Boniface VII	974 & 984	985
Boniface VIII	1294	1303

As we can see there is no Pope Boniface who could possibly "fit the bill" – far less the sainted ones. The good news is that this paradox can be resolved.

In 710 Nechtan sent word to Jarrow to ask for guidance in religious matters; the conclusion I draw is that Serf had died, so Nechtan needed someone to take his leading place in the project.

Story also alludes to another version of the "Boniface" legend where the protagonist is really called Albanus Kiritanus (St Curetan). This story is not without its problems either, as www.catholic.org gives the date of his death as 660 – even before the synod of Whitby! www.celticsaints.org says that despite dying in 630 he was active in the 700s! It also claims he was born in Italy. The idea that Curetan could have been the leader of a mission from Jarrow to king Nechtan in 710 can be ruled out completely when we appreciate that he was already abbot/bishop of Ross, based in Rosemarkie on the Black Isle, in 697 (whence/when he attended the Synod of Birr). So we can conclude that Nechtan sent Curetan/Boniface TO Jarrow to get the advice needed first hand – and he returned with a large retinue including at least some of those mentioned in the fabulous stories.

While Adomnan was having his own difficulties securing the agreement of his monks on Iona and was the dynamic figure generating change in Pictland, it was Curetan/Boniface, who is described as "bishop" who essentially had the principal rank within the church in Pictland.

Thus when Serf arrived, although he was the flagbearer for Roman ways, he came to serve in Curetan's team which means that we can resolve the dichotomy – Serf did not arrive in Pictland WITH 'Boniface', but he did serve "under" him.
This also provides the basis for understanding yet another conflation, for it was, as we have seen, a different Nechtan (map Der-Ilei) who had dealings with a different Boniface (not a pope

but St Curetan) which then provided the opportunity for the hagiographer to get his story all mixed up.

4. 717 Columban Expulsion

Curetan/Boniface was so bolstered by the phalanx of clerics he brought back with him that Nechtan was in a position to expel all Columban clerics – including all the Culdees – in 717.

In this way Pictland in general and Fife in particular became fully Romanised.

Footnote on St Kentigern
As we have seen we can date St Serf's arrival in Fife to some time very shortly before 700 and his death to about 710.

There has been a lot of dispute about St Kentigern's dates. The Catholic Church tended to insist that he was born in 518 and so he died c603. Others insisted that died c614 and so was not born until c528. I worked out that the reason for this was that neither party was willing to try to claim that he was more than 85 when he died. In ALLE I explained why I came to the conclusion that he really did live to 95 – so the Catholics were right to claim he was born c518 and everyone else was right that he died c614. Since my book was published, this new understanding has been gaining ground.

The details of the argument are irrelevant here – the general point is that Kentigern died aged about 95 in c614 and St Serf did not arrive in Pictland until c695 – 80 years after Kentigern's death and 175 years after his birth. So the supposed connection between the two is pure fiction. The Catholic Church wanted to make up this story because in the early 1100s they wanted to claim that it was "their" St Serf who had introduced Kentigern to Christianity.

What they latched onto was that after Kentigern was born his mother St Thaney (often spelled Theneu) married a prince of Strathclyde whose name ("Serguan" and variants, a Brythonic name probably deriving from the Roman name Sergius which although it can mean "servant" here carries the loftier idea "guardian") could be translated roughly as "Serf". [In her turn, St Thaney became a victim of the cancel culture of the Scottish Reformation of the 1560s when the reformers turned her into "St Enoch".]

The story about St Kentigern and his mother being cast adrift at sea and miraculously ending up at Culross is ridiculous on several counts which need not detain us (see ALLE) but was a cut-and-paste job by the Catholic Church as the same story had been told about St Dubricius more than a century earlier and, in its turn, this story too had been lifted from antiquity.

Footnote on St Triduana

There is no direct connection between St Triduana and Fife (she is commemorated in the chapel dedicated to her in Restalrig, Edinburgh), but she is was an integral part of the influx of Catholic proselytisers of this period. While King Nechtan may (or may not) have been entranced particularly by the beauty of her eyes, the story that she plucked them out and sent them to him is apocryphal – this was a story lifted in the first instance from the legend of St Lucia of Syracuse. This too in turn is likely to be a copy-and-paste job from antiquity.

In short we can see a systematic generation of lies not just about St Serf and St Boniface but also about St Kentigern and

St Triduana (just two examples) to impose a new narrative to bolster the new Catholic religious rule at the intended expense of the Columban church. As we shall see in the next chapter, the same approach was applied to the bones of St Andrew.

Postscript on St Serf's name

If the reader were to surf the internet, churches apparently dedicated to St Serf are to be found in Brittany:

- Saint-Servan-sur-Mer near (and now merged with) St Malo in Brittany who adopted St Serf some time after 1235.
- Saint-Servant-sur-Oust a commune in the Morbihan Department, also in Brittany.
- There are actually others as well (eg represented as Saint Servais)

I am grateful to Maureen in the St Malo tourist office for correcting the internet (including catholic.org, June 2023). The "Servant" venerated here is actually a reference to St Servatius of Tongeren who is generally understood to have died at Maastricht in 384.

Such is the widespread respect in which St Servatius seems to have been held we should not exclude the possibility that "our" St Serf chose that name in honour of and/or respect for St. Servatius when he took holy orders. On the other hand Pope St Gregory I (in office 590 – 604) was the first to assume the title "Servus Servorum Dei" – so this is another possibility for the basis of St Serf's name.

11. The "Bones of St Andrew" arrive in 'Fife' [732 CE]

It is usual to describe as "legend" the various stories surrounding the association of St Andrews with St Andrew. In general terms this is a euphemism for "tissue of lies". In this case some of the untruth is due to ignorance (in my view a wilful ignorance based on an unwillingness to consider the facts clearly), but beyond ignorance some of the corpus of untruth is deliberate fabrication – done for nefarious purpose.

Deciding how to set this out has been problematic; ultimately I have chosen first to tell the correct story and then to itemise and explain the stupidity and the deliberate obfuscation of the legend. This enlarges upon and partially corrects the outline provided in ALLE and my paper Bones.

The bones of St Andrew in question

- three fingers of the right hand,
- a part of one arm,
- one kneecap and
- one tooth.

There are at least 206 bones in an adult human body, so straight away we can see that these (maximum 12) bones represent a very small fraction (less than 6%) of a single body – hardly "the" bones of St Andrew, more "a handful" of such bones, even supposing that they were authentic. The reader is invited to look at the "Relics" section of the Wikipedia page about St Andrew for a summary of where other, perhaps more important, alleged parts of St Andrew's skeleton are and have been located.

1. The real journey of the bones to St Andrews

Although brought up in a Columban Christian environment in Northumbria, St Wilfrid (c633 – 709/10) became convinced of the superiority of Roman Catholicism. Wilfrid became particularly devoted to St Peter to whom he dedicated the Abbey at Ripon which he founded and led for some time. He played a key part at the Synod of Whitby (664) whereby Oswiu became convinced of the superiority of Roman doctrine and observance; following this he was made Bishop of Northumbria (the political niceties need not detain us). He made several visits to Rome which is the most likely place where, amongst other things, he acquired some bones reputedly of St Andrew, his second favourite apostle, to whom he had already dedicated the Abbey at Hexham which he founded in 674. He invested Hexham with these bones.

It is possible that St Acca (c660-740/2), had accompanied Wilfrid to Rome on at least one occasion. He took over from St Wilfrid in 709 as abbot and bishop of Hexham, thereby becoming the guardian of the bones.

[The Wikipedia authors of the page on St Andrew suggest that the bones may have come to Britain in 597 with St Augustine. If so there are two 'obvious' occasions when such a gift might have been made: (a) on the successful conclusion of the Synod of Whitby (664) when Catholicism finally triumphed over Celtic Christianity in Northumbria and (b) when Archbishop Theodore restored Wilfrid to the Bishopric of Northumbria in 668. Different dates would apply if Wilfrid acquired the relics in Rome – which seems more likely.]

In 732, immediately after the restoration of Ceolwulf to the Kingdom of Northumbria (the names of those who usurped him briefly have not come down to us) Acca felt the need to flee Hexham. It is surmised that Acca had sided with Ceolwulf's opponents. [Ceolwulf abdicated in 737/8, became a monk on Lindisfarne and died in 765.] It is not clear whether Acca had a particular destination in mind when he decided to flee, but he took the bones with him, took to sea and ended up shipwrecked at Mucros close to Boarhills on the 'Fife' coast just a couple of miles from St Andrews. [For a full explanation of my identification of this site see below.] Bearing in mind that Bernicia still included the Lothians, Fife was actually the nearest place to head for, and given that he must have boarded his boat at Alnmouth or further south, then Fife Ness was really the nearest landfall. Under these circumstances it would make sense to head for St Andrews. So my view is that in general terms Acca was on his intended course.

St Acca was welcomed to Kilrule at Cennrimonaid and may even have served in an Abbot/Bishop-type capacity for the remainder of his life there, helping to reinforce the Roman rule which, as we have seen, had been instituted exclusively just 15 years earlier.

In "Saints Cults in the Celtic World" James E Fraser suggests that, in the general times we are considering, Catholicism in England generally favoured the St Peter and St Andrew duo – so that in any kingdom which had two bishoprics, one would be dedicated to each. He goes on to propose that the same happened in Pictland where St Curetan had dedicated his see to St Peter. If so it is possible that a dedication to St Andrew could have followed on from Catholicisation in 717. I consider this vanishingly unlikely, not least because St Andrews was not at all a convenient central place from which to govern the whole of the Southern Pictish church (compare this with Fortrose so close to Inverness). Brechin, Forfar, Dunkeld, even Perth would have been far better places in that regard. So I say that St Andrews got its name and rose to extreme prominence because of the bones and not vice versa.

[The Pictish king of the day was the first of two kings called (the Pictish original of) Angus mac Fergus who was continuing Nechtan's policy of Romanisation. Acca was buried back in Hexham; his successor, Tuathalan (d. 747), is the first Abbot on 'official' record.]

Despite the way the legend remains in the popular memory and is still believed by so many, the true 732/Acca explanation is supported on the websites of St Mary's Catholic Cathedral in Edinburgh and Historic Environment Scotland as evidenced on their scran.ac.uk site.

2. Examining the Legend

The essence of the legend, which became current only in the 12th century, is well summarised at

https://webarchive.nrscotland.gov.uk/20170106025652
http://www.nas.gov.uk/about/051124.asp

> The bishop of Patras (Saint Regulus) removed the relics about AD345, sailed beyond the Mediterranean and was shipwrecked at Kilrymont, where he founded

> a church… Saint Andrew appeared in a vision to the Pictish king (Hungus or Angus), who was about to fight a major battle against the Saxon king (Athelstan), and promised victory to the Picts. The grateful king welcomed Regulus and the relics and endowed the fledgling church with the lands around the bay where the saint had landed.

The reason given for this is that he, Regulus, feared that the Emperor Constantine was about to remove the bones of St Andrew buried there. However there are many problems associated with this claim:

1: Emperor Constantine actually died in 337 and his son, Constantine II died in 340 so here is the first impossibility. However "most" of the relics were indeed transferred to Constantinople c357 CE on the orders of the Emperor Constantius II.

2: The threat was that the bones would be removed to Constantinople and the solution was… to remove the bones even farther away!!

3: There was no bishop of Patras at the time proposed. Until 733 Patras was part of the See of Corinth which was not yet an Archbishopric.

4: Only the Scottish tradition mentions Regulus.

5: Regulus' concern could only have been due to a deep concern for/love of Patras. But Patras is in Greece. The name Regulus implies that Regulus was NOT Greek, never mind being from Patras, but rather that he was Roman – his name is that of a Roman gens and the meaning "Little King" clearly shows that it would not have been adopted when he took holy orders. Given that he was Roman there is no reason why he would have been at Patras and even if he had been he would have had no good reason to be concerned about the removal of Andrew's bones.

6: If the story were true Regulus was a thoroughly incompetent. What happened to the other 200 bones of Andrew's skeleton?? We must consider that "St Regulus" had done a pretty rubbish job!

There is also a basis for genuine confusion:

A: The Pictish King who welcomed Acca (732) was Angus mac Fergus I (729-761). The Pictish king who won the battle of Athelstaneford (832) and made St Andrew the Patron Saint of Pictland as Angus mac Fergus II (820x34). This was a simple sophomore error – the monk who wrote this did not know enough about Scottish history and so conflated the two kings.

B: In 832 the king of the Northumbrians was Eanred. There was an Ecgbert who was the king of Wessex and the king of Mercia was Wiglaf. There was a king Athelstan in 832 – but he was king of East Anglia, so it is not feasible that he would have been the king opposing Angus mac Fergus II. [Of course it is still possible that the leader of the army opposing Angus may have been called Athelstan.]

C: St Rhiagail was Abbot of Muicinis (the sows' island). St Acca was shipwrecked off Mucros (the sows' headland).

D: Another version of the legend casts Regulus as the leader of the army of clerics, including St. Triduana, which we have previously seen attached to St Boniface and St Serf. This appears to have been genuine confusion (but given that the name "Triduana" has nothing to do with "three days", but is Germanic (composed of *þrȳð* = 'strength' (Old English) and wunna = 'blissfulness'

(Old High German)) and given that she was contemporaneous with King Nechtan, we know that she belongs not to the time of the bones, but rather to the cohort who returned with Curetan. However given that these people arrived in 710 and the bones only 20 years later and that both came from Northumbria it is easy to see how these might have been conflated in a writer's mind by carelessness.

Reasons for the legend

The legend was concocted as an integral part of the Catholicisation of Scotland. Although this process had been going on in earnest since 1070, it took time to find opportunities to replace incumbent Celtic Christians without causing excessive civic unrest.

- There was no St Regulus whether as Bishop or Monk at Patras: he was deliberately invented to be the 'same' as St Riaghail to create the idea in parishioners' minds that it was a Catholic who had brought Christianity to Scotland and to erase the name of the Archangel Raguel. St Acca was collateral damage. We have seen that the name "Regulus" means "little king" – this is a ridiculous name for a monk to adopt as it represents the opposite of the sort of humility expected. [And because as a Roman name it is that of a Gens, or family, it would not be one used by a monk or bishop if it had been a birth name.]
- The date was invented to predate any other non-Catholic Christian (eg St Ninian and the others discussed in Chapter 6).

The idea that the legend could have been created in the earlier period of Catholic hegemony (717-850) is really not feasible. It would not be possible to concoct such a legend until all those who knew St Acca – not just those who remembered his landing

– were dead. This would bring us to after 800 and Catholicism was extirpated again around 850, so there is no time for such a legend to take root. However by the time Malcolm III gained the throne of at least this part of Scotland (c1055) there had been well over 150 years of renewed Columban Christianity. So between the two contrasting periods the way was well open to invent something new because no-one could remember the facts.

CONCLUSIONS ABOUT THE BONES

Whether or not the bones are/were actually those of St Andrew is open to conjecture, overall the number of bones of saints hugely outnumber all that there could be. St Anne appears to have had five heads!
[See Henry Foulis "The history of Romish treasons and usurpations : together with a particular account of many gross corruptions and impostures in the Church of Rome, highly dishonourable and injurious to Christian religion : to which is prefixt a large preface to the Romanists" 1671]

The main reason that the legend was deliberately fabricated was an ill thought through attempt to promote disdain for the Columban church and to strengthen the authority of the Catholic church.

POSTSCRIPT ABOUT THE BONES

We noted above that Jerome records that the bulk of St Andrew's bones were indeed removed from Patras to Constantinople in 357 at the behest of Emperor Constantius II. At the time of the Catholic/Orthodox schism (1054) they were moved again from Constantinople to Amalfi in Italy, with the head later being moved to St Peter's in Rome, then returned to Patras in 1964 at the behest of Pope Paul VI.

The Scran page about St Andrew explains that on 14th June 1559 John Knox and his followers entered the St Andrews Cathedral, removing anything of "value". At this point the bones of St Andrew were "lost".

Had these bones been secreted by a Catholic they would surely have come to light by now (St Mary's Edinburgh has since been given two different bones). Had they been held by a reformer again surely by now there would be no reason for them not to have come to light. So sadly we should count them as irretrievably lost.

Appendix: Locating "Mucros"

Readers happy to accept my proposition can pass over this section, but it is necessary to include it to counter widely available misinformation (detailed below).

As usual with many placenames we have been and will be considering, confusion arises because the wrong language has been assumed – the tendency of far too many people in Scotland to assume that a word is Gaelic in origin. They thereby ignore Pictish and Old Norse, not to mention Anglic. Very many Pictish and Gaelic place names in Scotland refer to the farming practice in the area.

The Howe of Fife pig names justaposition: Along the north rim of the Howe of Fife we find the juxtaposition of four pig-based names:

(i) Bannety with the core word "banna" meaning "wild boar"; One of the forts on Hadrians Wall was called Banna, garrisoned for a while by the "Venatores Bannienses" – the Boar hunters. With the subsequent invasions of people speaking different languages – and the extermination of wild boar, this word has been relegated so that now the modern Welsh word "Banw" means "piglet"; in Gaelic there is "Banbh" which is a generic word for a pig. However in Fife in the 700s I am reasonably confident that Banna still meant "Wild Boar".

(ii) Glentarkie with the core word – "twrch" in Welsh ("turc" in Gaelic) meaning "castrated boar";

(iii) Auchtermuchty with the core word "muc" (in Gaelic) meaning "sow". There is still the Welsh word "mwc" meaning "muck", so we may be confident that this used to mean "sow" in Welsh even though this meaning is no longer recognised. This is where the words "muck(y)" come from!

From the presence of wild boar we may deduce that the area in question was a good one for pig farming. From the two separate names we can understand that the castrated boars were separated from the sows and each were reared in separate but neighbouring valleys – with the burns being where they drank.

Ros(s): We need also to consider the element "ross". On the one hand we get a general understanding of the word from places like the Ross of Mull. In Gaelic ("ros") it is generally understood as "headland" – a bit of land sticking out into the sea. Unfortunately we have lost many "ross"es as they have been replaced by "ness" – meaning the same but coming to us from Anglic or Old Norse.

However in modern Welsh the word "rhos" has lost this shade of meaning, now referring specifically to: "upland moor" or heathland. We need not be concerned about this, as in SCLLE I detailed other parallel examples of words where the meaning has evolved substantially (notably "van"/"fan"). In discussing Rosyth [PNF 529] T&M cite the earliest extant reference as "Rossiue", dating to 1162x4 and they try to claim that this means "headland of Fife" (where the second element is "Fiobha" (which is not how it was at that time) and they go on to suggest that the *ros* "most probably refers to the neighbouring headland of North Queensferry". This is unlikely to be correct as the parishes of Rosyth and Inverkeithing were united in 1636 and the Queensferry promontory is far closer to Inverkeithing than it was to Rosyth Parish Church, so it is highly unlikely that Rosyth included the headland on which North Queensferry stands. However the Welsh dictionary give the plural of "rhos" as "rhosydd" - ahem... rosyth!! So Rosyth means "the headlands" - referring not North Queensferry, but to lesser promontories - some of which are now incorporated into the extensive docks there (see also Chapter 13).

Meaning of Mucros: So, bearing in mind that the timeframe we are considering is more than 100 years before the Scots conquered Pictland, so that the working language was NOT Gaelic, we may start by understanding not just that Mucros means "the sows' headland", but also that even though it works well in Gaelic, the name is actually Pictish in origin (probably "mwcrhos" or some such).

Locating Mucros: I was first attracted to the site I believe to be correct because of the neighbouring settlement Boarhills [PNF 2174]. This name is doubly problematic: not only are there no recognisable "hills" in the area, but also the earliest extant reference there is to "Byrehill" - an English language name - in the late 1400s. Here T&M say "The change to Boarhills probably came about through antiquarian awareness of the Boar's Raik." and this I can accept. Not least because of the proximity of the farm "Bannafield" (see map below).

The Boars' Raik ("Cursus Apri" in Latin) was a large tract of land given to the church at St Andrews to yield an income for the church's upkeep. However we do not know how old the first grant was or how far it extended – so what was later understood as the Boars' Raik was not necessarily exactly the same as eg an original grant given when the bones first arrived.

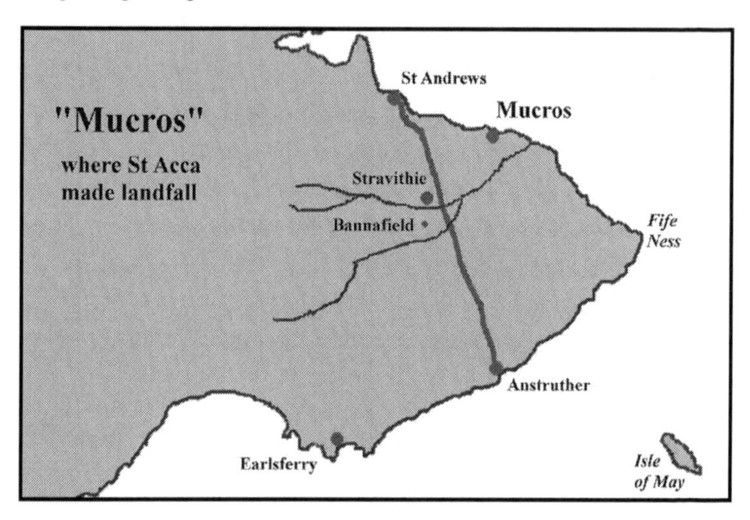

We noted above that many places which were probably called "ross" have been renamed "ness" under the influence of Angles or Norsemen. So too we have a problem with river names. The river shown on the map above is now called the Pitmilly Burn for its last stretch to the sea, but the southern of the two main tributaries is the Wakefield burn [PNF 1990]. Wakefield is 'obviously' English and leaves no hint as to what its previous name may have been. However the place name Stravithie [PNF 1985] may help. T&M again hamper themselves by not looking beyond Gaelic for an answer.

Stravithie

We may start by noting two of the earliest written forms available to us: "Struuithin" (1140) and "Strufithin" (1172x8).

T&M suggest that the first element is Gaelic (variously srúb(h) or sruth) meaning "burn" – and this I accept. The comparators are with places such as Stirling ("Striveling" is an early form). However there are many examples (see especially the next chapter) where a place name is a mishmash of a Pictish element and a Gaelic element.

So, especially given the "fithin" example, I propose that the second part is "fithie" representing "ffydd" and "ig" – just as in Fothriff in the previous chapter. It means "the faith burn". In addition to the prefix srúb(h) the Gaels added the suffix "-in" meaning "place".

Now let us notice how amazingly straight the B9131 road from Anstruther to St Andrews is! Anyone would think it was Roman (it wasn't). Why would anyone build such a road? St Andrews wasn't even a place until St Raguel built his church there around 600. It would make sense for this road to have been built soon after the bones of St Andrew were installed at St Andrews. It would have been in constant use from as soon as it was built after 732 at least until the Catholic clergy were finally expelled (see next chapter), but given that the bones do not seem to have been removed and given that business is business there is little reason to suppose that Columban clergy would have disdained the income from the tourism which Pilgrimage represented and some Catholic monks may even have been allowed to stay on to look after both the bones and the pilgrims.

So although the use of charters is in essence introduced by King David I and although the Boars' Raik as now understood may date from this time, what we should understand also is that just as Fothriff was given to St Serf to provide him with an income for his work, so too a proto-Boars' Raik was given to the church in St Andrews almost as soon as the bones were installed – with what is now the Wakefield Burn as its southern limit, this burn becoming known as the Faith Burn or Ffyddig. The road to Anstruther was built more or less immediately. Anstruther was handy as the destination on the south coast of the East Neuk not only because it was an existing harbour but also was convenient both for North Berwick and for the Isle of May, already a religious centre. When the Scots invaded (see next chapter) they did not understand "ffyddig" nor did they care to seek to understand and in any case they were anti-Catholic. But they knew it was the name of a burn – so they stuck "srúb(h)" on the front.

And so to Mucros

If we look along the coastline south of St Andrews, we see that most "ross"es have names: Kinkell Ness, Buddo Ness, Bobbet Ness and Fife Ness. There is one ross which is now nameless – south of Buddo Ness but north of the mouth of the Pitmillie burn. This is the location which I propose was called Mucross. Not only that but on its north side a "boat harbour" is shown on old maps. This whole strip of coastline has no beach for a boat to run onto, however. It is seriously hazardous to shipping as it is rocky – so one false move and you are likely to run aground – perhaps even break up.

We know from the records that there was a 'Mucros' – so we can be sure that pig farming was taking place in the area. On this basis we should expect a "turk" place for the castrated boars nearby – but it seems that no trace is left. It is less than a mile from Mucross to Kittock's Den [PNF 2235]. T&M say

> Sc *Kittock* is a hypocorism (pet form) of Katherine, but was also used as a common noun to refer to 'a woman or girl of low rank or character; wench; mistress, concubine' (*DOST*).

However Gaelic "Ci" means "beast". [In modern Welsh "Ci" is reserved for dogs, but "cïaidd" means brutal or inhuman – so it looks as if there is a more generic quality lying behind Ci in Welsh – and this nuance fits the pattern we have seen.]

So might "-tock" be a corruption of "turk"? It requires no leap of imagination to suppose that the sows were watered in the Pitmilly burn (variously the Kenly Water) and the boars in the Kittock's Den burn – which rises very close to the Boarhills settlement. I think the pattern is complete and as it should be. The only real problem is that there is no natural barrier keeping the boys and the girls apart.

In the Howe of Fife comparator places I cited, the place names stuck because they were inhabited. The same is true of the farm Bannafield. But in the cases of Mucros and Citwrch (if that indeed is what it is) the problem is that there was no reason for the place name to stick once the farming practices moved on (in these cases the land being given over to arable use). This adds power to the Citwrch proposal precisely because the den could not be put to an alternative use and so there was no reason to change the name. However no-one could relate to the meaning of the name because there ceased to be a reality underlying it – and so the corruption to Kittock became all too natural. However the reader can see that this is a stretch even if the name Kittock is exactly as T&M suggest, this does not mean that the boars were not kept there at the time in question!

Disposing of what others have said

1. Robert Sibbald ("History of Fife" (1803)) claims that Muckross was the old name of Fife Ness. There is no evidence of this and on the contrary Fife Ness is a good

descriptor, so is likely to be of old standing, even if it was previously eg Rhos y Uuipy or some such.

2. Fife Council makes this lamentable claim about St Andrews (June 2023) at https://www.fife.gov.uk/kb/docs/articles/community-life2/gaelic-language:

The town was first called Muckross (boar-wood), then Kilrymont (church on the royal mount), then Kilrule (church of St Regulus) and finally St Andrews after the church of St Andrews

We may now note:

- Muck does not mean boar
- Ross does not mean wood
- Before there was a church (kil) there, it was actually Ceannrimonaid (actually it may well have been Penrimonaid)
- Mont here does not mean "mount"
- Kilrule was the church of St Riaghail/Raguel – not St Regulus

Conclusion

If St Acca genuinely had been shipwrecked then it would indeed have been a miracle for the relics to have survived. However given the nature of the coastline, and assuming there was bad weather, then Acca may well have been forced to seek the shelter of the "boat haven" at Mucros rather than sailing on to what became St Andrews and given the nature of the harbour he may well have run onto the rocks, with the ship's company forced to scramble ashore as the boat began to break up.

Summary

1. St Acca fled with the bones of St Andrew and landed in Fife just short of his intended place (now St Andrews) in 732
2. Not only did these relics need housing appropriately but they immediately attracted the interest of pilgrims.
3. A substantial tract of land was given to the church at St Andrews to fund its new responsibilities – this land was the core of what would be known as the Boars' Raik. The southern boundary of this land shoring up the new faith was what is now the Wakefield Burn which became known as the Ffyddig.
4. A new road was built from St Andrews to Anstruther to cater for the pilgrims attracted to the relics.
5. When the Catholics were relegated in importance by the Scots c850 and then finally expelled in 900 the pilgrimage business did not stop completely and it may well be that a small phalanx of monks of a Catholic persuasion were allowed to stay on to guard the relics but were not allowed to perform any priestly office in public.
6. When Catholicism was reintroduced (from 1055) while the road could still handle the hugely increased traffic, the ports could not – so new routes replaced it via Queensferry and Earlsferry (for which see Chapter 13 below).

12. Along came the Scots 845x50 CE

Background

When we left our story in 732 there was an opportunity for stability. There was a basis of mutual respect between the Picts and the Angles – with ever closer mutual understanding based on their now shared Roman Catholic religious practice enhanced by the arrival of St Andrew's bones in Fife. There was a clear cultural divide between the Picts and the Scots based on their differences of faith which could have served as a basis for guarded mutual respect. We should also note that in 637 following the battle of Magh Rath in County Down, Scottish Dalriata had gained full independence from their notional Irish overlords – so they were a law unto themselves. In practice there was more or less incessant bickering and skirmishing, with the Picts periodically gaining an ascendancy over the Scots – but the details need not detain us.

While it is fairly easy to identify some of the triggers of instability, it is harder to assign any rank order as to which may have been key to what happened next.

Let us start with the deeper underlying considerations: the Picts (and the Scots) had been over-breeding (ie beyond the carrying capacity of the land) for centuries. The Caledonians had been the worst, particularly because they refused to farm, but also, at least before Christianity arrived, because, as we have seen, they did not pay any serious attention to "the family". Whenever the land could not support the people, it was necessary for the young men to raid abroad. Either they would die in the process – and the number of mouths to feed would reduce to what they could produce – or they would succeed and the booty they were able to bring home would ensure the resources to feed them… until the next time. The choice raids had mostly been into Roman and then post-Roman Britannia. On the other hand one of their favourite soft targets – for practice if you will – were the Orkney Islands, which should come as a surprise if only because the Cruithin had arrived in Scotland from Orkney, so they were raiding their own cousins.

The Scots too were in expansionist mood and having been largely staunched in the west by a powerful Strathclyde their attentions turned to the softer and nearer parts of Pictland – so raiding back and forth became endemic, with one side and then the other gaining hegemony.

A parallel process had been going on in Scandinavia. Inter-tribal raiding was beginning to run its course – but population pressure was relentless and so they were beginning to need to look farther afield.

Orkney was a "soft target" for the Picts, but the Orcadians were a proud society who had even signed a peace treaty with the Romans at the time of the first invasion of Britannia, so we may be sure that they had had distant trading links over many centuries.

When the Picts attacked the Britons, the Britons turned to the Anglo-Saxons for support – and the Anglo-Saxons ended up taking over. The same thing had happened 200 years earlier in what is now Argyll: the Epidii turned to the Scots for support for their defence against the Caledonians – and the Scots ended up taking over.

So my interpretation of events is that the Orcadians turned to the Vikings (specifically the Hordalanders from the area round Stavanger) for support in their endless defence against Pict and Scot and Irish – and all too soon the self-same Vikings had taken over. This taste of success quickly turned to a taste for expansion – and, given their culture, it was a bloody one.

The Picts and the Scots were now in a quandary. Mutual hostility had become their habitual stance, yet now both realised that they had to combine to face the common enemy who were the Vikings. Following the raid on Iona in 795 the Vikings even set up their own Kingdom of the Isles – ousting some of the Scots' ruling classes from what had become their traditional homes.

Alpin

The way kings were chosen differed between the Picts and the Scots. For the Scots it was the Derbhfine: all those descended in 5 or fewer generations from a king met together to decide who the next king would be from amongst their number. Sometimes this would be done before the existing king died, in which case the appointed next in line (the "crown prince") was known as the 'Tanist'. In Pictland the nobles would choose who should marry the crown princess and so become king. [At least in both cases that is how it was supposed to work! Too often in practice kings were murdered and the murderer seized power.]

And so we may turn out attention to Alpin. Very little is known for sure about him, the father of the famous Kenneth. He appears to have been a member of the Dalriatan royal family. He appears to have married a Pictish princess and increasingly it is supposed that he may have become the (sub-) king of the Northern Picts. However he later became the King of the Scots of Dalriata. He clearly had a view about trying to unite people to fight off the Vikings. He married one of his daughters to the king of Strathclyde and he died near Cairnryan. The usual explanation is that he was fighting against the Picts of Galloway, but I wonder whether he may not have been seeking some sort of unity with Galloway and may have been assisting in the fighting off of a Viking – or even an Irish – raid. Other stories about the death of Alpin – to his head being stuck on a pole and any connection to Abernethy are apocryphal and are explained in my book SCLLE – these stories are NOT actually about Alpin.

His early death is frustrating to us now, particularly because we are left with no idea as to what his plans might have been for unifying Scotland – but it seems to have been one based on persuasion.

Kenneth mac Alpin

So far we have been considering general tides in history but we should not overlook the influence of a powerful individual, whether driven by greed or ambition of even a messianic sense of purpose. Kenneth mac Alpin had no difficulty becoming king of the Scots – for which he was well qualified – but the kingdom of the Picts was another matter. As the son of a Pictish princess he may have considered himself qualified for this job also – but the descendants of the old Pictish 'Brudes' had other ideas. Kenneth decided to take Pictland by force – but he realised that, even with the full cooperation of his Dalriatan subjects, he simply lacked the strength in numbers for the mission.

Below the king in Dalriata were the "Mormaers". This has always been understood to mean "great stewards", but there has always been a problem with this because, as has been suggested to me years ago in another context, if this were the case then the title should really be "Maermor". There are occasions, especially where a 'Gaelic' word is actually Pictish where the order of the elements can be reversed, but in this case the problem persisted. Kenneth's plan was to rule Scotland by dividing it up and putting each part under a "Mormaer".

In March 2023, Neil Macgregor, one of the foremost Gaelic experts of our day, suggested to me that in this case "mor" may not mean "great" but "sea". This is a brilliant insight. The Scots, outcasts in Ireland, had survived by piracy. The key commanders would have been the Commodores (admirals if you will) of the fleets which went out to conduct this piracy. Not only that but the successful pirates would become immensely rich and hence buy land. So they would end up as the major lairds. Not only that but it is clear that throughout the west coast and the isles military forces were thought of in terms of numbers of boats. Thus "Mormaer" really means "sea lord".

This insight into the meaning of the title also gives us a very clear understanding of the powers they were to exercise. Until very recent times a captain of a ship at sea had powers more or less equivalent to a king – albeit he may have to answer for his decisions when he came back to dry land. Only modern technology has allowed "normal" authorities to take back some of the powers delegated to the captain. Even on land – at a time when travel was not easy – the king and any central judicial system could not exercise day to day control, so the mormaers would need to be trusted to get on with things for themselves on a day to day basis.

There were four principle leading families in Dalriata:

- The **Cenel Loarn** descended from Loarn – the direct descendant of the original ruling family who had been sidelined by the treaty with Arthur in 498, but several of whose representatives had been king in the subsequent 340 years
- The **Cenel Gabran** was Kenneth's own branch – descending from Fergus mor mac Earca through Gabran mac Domnangirt.
- The **Cenel Angus** – a cadet branch of the Cenel Gabran. Their main stomping ground had been the isles – they had been based on Islay – but since being expelled by the Vikings they had been at something of a loose end.
- The **Cenel Conall** another cadet branch from Gabran. They may have given their name to the Cowal peninsula (although there is at least one alternative explanation for that name).

Argyll

With all his regiments of fighting men (who would normally keeping order in Dalriata) needed to effect the conquest of Pictland, Kenneth was concerned that a power vacuum might emerge in Dalriata. Kenneth devised a plan as is recorded in the Annals of the Four Masters. [As we can see the date to which this is assigned is in error, but the scribes own doubt is readily seen – and the real date was 845.]

> *835.15 Gofraidh, son of Fearghus, chief of Oirghialla, went to Alba, to strengthen the Dal Riada, at the request of Cinaeth, son of Ailpin. DCCCXXXV DCCCXLV*

Years ago I had seen that "Oirghialla" was the same name as "Argyll", but as 'Oirghialla' means 'the lands from which hostages are required', I was content to assume that this was the meaning too of Argyll – it would have been quite reasonable for Dalriata in Ireland to require hostages of the semi-independent Dalriata in Scotland.

However ask any academic and you will be told that it means "borderland of the Gael". This is nonsense, but we can see where it comes from. Fife Council Archaeologist Douglas Speirs has the expertise here – for when new towns were built, especially in the reign of David I, they were exclusively for foreigners, often Flemish. Native Scots were excluded from them. So just outside these towns townships of Scots developed – and these were 'Argyle's, like a vicus beside a Roman fort or a Bantu township in South Africa during the apartheid era. A good example is in St Andrews where Argyle Street comes away directly from the West Port. [Argyle Street in Glasgow is an exception to this explanation, dating from a much later time.]

So the etymology of the name of the county "Argyll" does not lie with "the Borderland of the Gael"; it was the area of land given to the Oirghialla from which to exercise control of Lorne. They had been given this task because the leadership of the Cenel Loarn had departed for Pictland. It is only too easy to see, however, how the names "Argyll" and "Argyle" have been conflated in people's minds (and the Argyle Street in Glasgow proves the confusion as it was named in honour of a Duke of Argyll).

My proposition here is supported by the Senchus Fer n'Alban which says:

> *The expeditionary force of the Cenel Loairnd, seven hundred men, but the seventh hundred is from the Airgialla.*

Wikipedia tells us that Oirghialla (alternatively Airgialla) was rendered "Ergallia" in Latin – and it is interesting to note that in early Scottish charters Argyll was rendered "Ergadia" (the difference probably being a compounded scribal error).

The core of Oirghialla is now County Oriel in Northern Ireland and my understanding is that this too was an area where Cruithin were confined after the bulk had been expelled – and, as the annal we have noted says, hostages were required. So Kenneth was calling on/inviting more Cruithin to join his cause. This would make sense to both sides. Kenneth needed the men, the men did not like the constraints they were living under.

Genocide

(a) **The Chronicle of the Picts and Scots** (Skene p203) says:

> *...the Scots contrived a conspiracy, and at a general council were privately armed, and in the council house slew the aforementioned king and all the great lords of the Picts, who did not think of evil. They sent afterwards for such others as they wished and slew them as they came...*

Note here the parallel with the way the Jews were sent to Auchwitz and so many murdered "as they came".

(b) **The Chronicle of the Kings of Alba** says:

> *Pictland was named after the Picts, whom, as we have said, Kenneth destroyed; for God deigned to make them alien from, and void of, their heritage, by reason of their wickedness; because they not only spurned the Lord's mass and precept, but also refused to be held equal to others in the law of justice.*

We should note the irony here: not only does the reference "as we have said" not refer to anything (any such text must have been edited out and we are left to speculate as to why – but we may assume that it was not considered, shall we say, complimentary by King Malcolm II or his close advisors) but also it was the Picts who had embraced Catholicism – not the Scots!

[To be fair it was compiled before the year 1000, a era when Catholicism had no part of Scottish life. So this does tell us exactly what the Scots of that time thought of Rome!]

(c) **Gerald of Wales** says:

> *The Scots betook themselves to their customary and, as it were, innate treacheries, in which they excel all other nations. They brought together as to a banquet all the nobles of the Picts, and taking advantage of their excessive drunkenness and gluttony, they noted their opportunity and drew out the bolts which held up the boards; and the Picts fell into the hollows of the benches on which they were sitting, caught up in a strange trap up to the knees, so that they could not get up; and the Scots immediately slaughtered them all.*

The detail of Gerald's tale we can dismiss as this story is taken from antiquity (perhaps the story of Ixion and Eioneus is the original) and has been copied into several folklores – for example The Russian Primary Chronicle, Laurentian Text. But Gerald was illustrating a point.

Elsewhere it is claimed that Kenneth beat the Picts in battle seven times in one day. The number 7 is suspicious – given also that there were 7 kingdoms in Pictland. 7 battles in one day is itself odd – why would they not count as one? Seven waves perhaps or does this represent beating all the seven sub-kingdoms?

What I find amazing and extremely disappointing is the way in which today's academics seek to whitewash this event. Irrespective of the exact detail, it is clear that the Pictish ruling class was indeed exterminated and that skullduggery of one sort or another was involved. This was indeed a genocide.

Reorganising the Ruling Structure

Scots and some other Irish mercenary supporters were put in the places now vacated.

- The **Cenel Loarn** were given control of Strathearn (including Menteith) and of Moray (including Ross)
- The **Cenel Gabrain** was given control of Atholl (now including Gowrie) and Marr and Buchan.
- The **Cenel Angus** was given control of Angus (including the Mearns).
- Control of Fife (Kinross was still an integral part and the Dunfermline district had been added, as noted above) is not entirely clear. On the one hand the Book of Ballymote (written c1390) says that the Mormaers came from a **Cenel Conall** (a junior branch of the Cenel Gabrain), but there are easily identifiable mistakes in that Book and I think that this is one because there was a particularly close relationship with the **Cenel Angus.** As we shall see below, whenever there was a leadership problem it was to the Mormaers of Angus that the kings turned for a locum.
- Clackmannan and the Forth Valley seems to have been held directly from the crown.

The Book of Ballymote also refers to a kindred in Gowrie, a cadet branch of the Cenel Gabran (which is logical) even though there was not a separate Mormaerdom here at this time. We will return to this too.

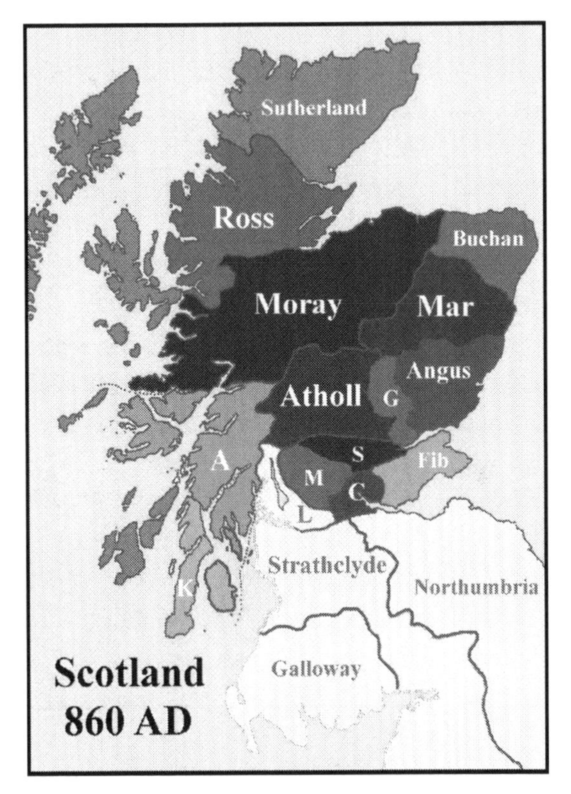

The new kingdom of Alba

Map Legend

1. (i) Moray & Ross and (ii) S: Strathearn & M: Menteith were allocated to chieftains from the Cenel Loarn
2. (i) Atholl & G: Gowrie and (ii) Mar & Buchan were allocated to chieftains from the Cenel Gabrain
3. (i) Angus and (ii) Fife ('Fib'), including Fothriff were allocated to chieftains from the Cenel Angus
4. (i) A: Lorne and (ii) K: Kintyre (the old Dalriata) was allocated to the Airgialla
5. (i) C: Clackmannanshire – with or without (ii) the Falkirk area were not allocated in this way – probably remaining directly under the crown

Clearly Caithness and Sutherland were considered part of Alba, but Kenneth mac Alpin's writ did not run that far – this land was controlled by the Vikings.

Also not part of Alba were Strathclyde (including L: Lennox), Northumbria and Galloway.

The pedigrees of the two Cenel Loarn lines have come down to us reasonably intact – ie sense can be made of them (see my paper Fortriu). The Cenel Gabrain is represented by the royal line – but we lack any detail of its precise relationship with the Mormaers of Mar and Buchan. It is not surprising that the landless Cenel Angus would try to assert themselves by giving their name to their territory (though even in Shakespeare it was still known by its old Pictish name 'Circinn'). Sadly no lore remains of the Mormaers of Fife (see also in the next chapter (13)) and the line of the Mormaers of Angus is very far from complete (see Appendix B).

The Effects of the conquest and genocide on Fife

(a) A new Language

A change of language may not seem like the most important effect, but because other effects are best examined though an understanding of the change from Pictish to Gaelic we need to examine this first.

These incoming new masters and their henchmen retained their own Gaelic tongue and anyone who wanted to do business with them had no option but to learn to speak Gaelic. Just as with the rest of Pictland the pressure of necessity meant that Pictish was redundant in no time – and, because the Picts had no tradition of writing, all too soon much of the language was extinct.

(i) Introduction

A significant part of our legacy of this lies in place names. When I first started looking at this I was constantly told that in Gaelic words had a "locative case". Strictly speaking this is not true, but the way it works comes to have this effect. The difference is small but, as we shall see, significant. There is a Gaelic word "aid" which means 'piece' or 'portion' and hence by allusion 'of land'. It was widely used as a suffix to mean "piece of land". This needs to be coupled with the problem that the Gaels did not understand that "ie" meant 'burn'. [This despite that Dwelly does recognise 'igh' meaning burn in some parts of Scotland.] With a good dose of arrogance the Gaels assumed that they both meant the same and did not bother to check.

Thus in the highlands the Pictish 'Craigelachie' – Craig-elach-ie , 'the crag of the burn where you can cross (the river) dry-shod (ie on stepping stones)' – became Craigelach-aidh, the 'Craigelach place'.

There is another Gaelic word "in" meaning 'country' or 'island' and hence by allusion 'place'. This too was used as a suffix by Gaels to signify a place name. Thus, in Glenrothes, Caskiebarran comes from 'Gasg', 'barr' and 'in' – "the place on the slope below the ridge", which is an accurate identifying description.

In Pictland many estates started with "Pit" – so much so that it was "borrowed" into Gaelic. Dwelly says simply that it means a farm or a portion. There are three Welsh words which may hint at its origins: "pitw" means small, "pwt" means a small amount and "pedair"/"Pedwar" means four ("pedwerydd" means fourth or quarter). So this suggests that "pit" was a small division of a larger unit of land. In Gaelic the word "baile" means village or farm or home. So when the Gaels took over many existing places had a "bal-" put in front of their name.

The Gaels could not cope with words beginning with "u" or "w" or "gw" – and they stuck an "f" on the beginning. Thus the personal name was "Fergus" in Gaelic replacing "Uurguist" in Pictish.

(ii) The name Fife

Fife had the Fergus problem! Its name was "Uip" meaning Falcon. But the Gaels could not cope with that so with complete disdain to our history they imposed the nearest name they could think of from their own vocabulary: "Fib" – which means Red Whortleberry (now more often referred to as the Lingonberry). We know that this is right for two reasons:

- "Fib" remains in some written records from not long afterwards and
- the Red Whortleberry is the plant badge of the MacDuffs.

The connection to the Falcons was lost for 1150 years and only now with the publication of this book is it rediscovered.

Worse still would happen later, but for this see Appendix C "The End of the Earldom"

(iii) Falkland too…

The incomers did a similar job on Falkland. Just as most students of French need to be taught that "librarie" means 'bookshop' and NOT 'library' it is with some smugness and glee that place name people will tell you that Falkland does not mean "falcon land" – and they are correct. However we can be one step ahead of them. We can all agree that "land" is a minor corruption of (Pictish/Welsh) "llan" meaning "enclosure", but if we remember that the Welsh (and residual British who had not been overwhelmed by the Anglo-Saxons) only started putting an initial "g" on many words (so that 'wen' became 'gwen') well after 500AD we can take the "f" off Falkland and substitute "gw" and we end up with "gwalch" – the Pictish/Brythonic word for... Hawk!

Just as the Peregrine Falcon is the archetypal falcon, so the Goshawk is the biggest and best of the Hawks (and so called because it was used to take down geese – no small endeavour). From very early times Falkland was a hunting lodge and we may now understand that hawking was one of the hunting practices they indulged in.

Footnote on Freuchie

Freuchie [PNF 1108], next door to Falkland is another Pictish-Gaelic hybrid, but in this case it **is** a translation – of the Pictish Grugie. It is most likely a name transferred from Loch Freuchie (Glen Quaich was called Glen Freuchie until 1098). [Although the name means "burn in the heather" this was probably actually a reference to King Grig (hence Grig's burn and Grig's glen – he is often misrepresented as Giric or as Gregory the Great) who, although he was primarily a member of the Strathclyde royal family, was king of Scots (having been elected by the Derbhfine) in the period 878-889.] Fife's Freuchie was probably the base of the proto-Grants (ie before the surname was adopted) in the period 1130-50 (see Chapter 15 below).

(iv) Pittencrieff

There are several places in what was Pictland where the name now includes the element "crieff" which is an Anglicisation of the Gaelic word "craoibh" meaning "tree". However T&M [PNF 2700] identify the earliest spelling still available to us (from 1294) as "Petincreher". This makes no sense at all in Gaelic, but even modern Welsh still has "crehyr" meaning "heron". So the "proper" name really means "the farm/estate of the heronry"

– and I am pleased to be advised by the rangers at Pittencrieff Park that herons are to be seen there to this day! The fact that "creher" survived for as long as it did shows that it was not the original Gaels in 850 who neither knew nor cared and so corrupted the name to mean something else entirely, but a much later generation. There are some other placenames which also include the element 'crieff' but whose correct explanations do not include a tree – and these become obvious as soon as they are examined properly.

(v) Pitlessie

On the other hand there are placenames which have been almost entirely left alone, but which are now misinterpreted by those who assume that the name must be Gaelic. Pitlessie is a case in point. One recently published "history" book makes the ludicrous claim that

> "Pitlessie was the portion of land of – perhaps Lossio or a Pictish personal name like it."

This is a case of simply making it up and not even bothering to do any research. There are "Pit-" placenames where the next bit is a personal name, but they are a small proportion. T&M [PNF 1055] clearly show that the earlier examples still available to us are of the form "Petglassin". But here again we can see another danger of Gaelo-centrism. We can agree that Pit/Pet broadly means Farm, but what to do with "glas"?

I deal with this in detail in SCLLE. This word started off meaning blue/grey/green (like the greasy Limpopo!). In Ireland, however, once the Cruithin had been expelled it came, by allusion, to mean river. Thus flowing into Loch Lomond from the west are two rivers called the Fin(g)las and the Duglas; this was a heavily

Gaelicised area and so we may translate these as the Whitburn and the Blackburn. On the other hand, now built over by the Southfield Industrial Estate in Glenrothes was Finglassie: Fin + glas + ie – The sunny side (fin = white) of the blue/green burn.

The original place name for Pitlessie is Pictish: "Pit" + "glas" + "ie" – 'the farm on the green burn'. The only original corruption the Gaels did was to add their "in" on the end. Sadly T&M take the Gaelic line and so tie themselves in knots, despite the fact that it may be that the burn was described as green because it flowed through eg particularly lush grassland.

(vi) Kirkcaldy

I embarked on this research project because I was incensed by "Cair Chaladain" the ersatz Gaelic name for Kirkcaldy on the signs at the railway station (the "c" or "k" in the middle has ALWAYS been hard – not lenited as this spelling insists). As T&M [PNF 726] have shown, the earliest versions of the name Kirkcaldy that we have include "Kircalethyn", "Kircaladin" and "Kercaladint" in charters dating to the 1100s – the time when Gaelic was at its zenith in Fife.

We can now understand this very well: The Gaels stuck one of their "in"s on the end to signify that this was a place (So Kirkcaladin). Then one of the scribes ended the word with a flourish which a later copyist has interpreted as a "t" (whence Kercaladint). [Geoffrey of Monmouth did a very similar thing with Urien King of Rheged. He (or the scribe whose work he was reading) saw the flourish at the end of "Urien" and interpreted this as an "s" – so he wrote 'Uriens'.]

There was absolutely no need for a *faux* reinvention of the wheel. It would have been easy – and far more authentic – to revert to the Pictish original: "Caer y Caledy". Failing this the real original Gaelic version would have been "Kircaledin".

(b) Genocide of the Ruling Class

The first effect on Fife was the destruction of the ruling class and its replacement by a new alien one. At the top of this élite the Brudes were replaced by Kenneth's Mormaers – and for Fife sadly we do not know any of the names of the Brudes any more than the Mormaers. At the next level down we can see that almost all of the major existing land holders were replaced, whether by Scots or – as in several places – by Irish mercenaries now being given their reward by a grateful Kenneth MacAlpine for their part in the genocide:

Rathillet: The Rath of the Ulsterman
Ramornie: Morgan's Rath
Pitoutie: yes, the "pit" is Pictish but "Ultan" is also 'The Ulsterman'
Bal-: There are huge numbers of places with Pictish names but with "Bal-" stuck on the front.

First we note "rath" which is the Irish counterpart of the Pictish "roth" – but there is a real difference. While the Pictish "roths" normally stood proud on a raised piece of land, the Irish "rath" really meant no more than a fortified farmstead (many English placenames end in "-worth", which has a broadly similar meaning).

Second, Neil Macgregor advises me that very many of the "Pit-" placenames are followed by a Gaelic name – so this is a Gael usurping the place of a Pictish laird.

Third – and opposite to the note above – the "Bal-" element is Gaelic, but usually what follows is Pictish. This too represents a

Gael ousting a Pict – but in this case most of the Pictish elements are not personal names, rather they describe the land or where the farm is.

These are pre-existing Pictish estates which then passed into Scottish or Irish hands.

The reader is invited to consult T&M's "Place Names of Fife". It runs to several hard copy volumes as well as the online version referred to in this book. While, as has been seen already, I do not agree with the interpretation of every entry, the hunt for and documentation of old forms of the names has been a stupendous effort and is presented in such a form which is very helpful even to anyone who might take issue with individual explanations.

(c) Religion

Perhaps a far bigger shock for ordinary Fifers was the re-imposition of Columban Christianity and the return of the Culdees. Fifers had been forced to adhere to the Catholic church for over 130 years (ie far longer than anyone's lifetime, so no-one could remember any different) and this had been reinforced by the bones of St Andrew being housed in St Andrews. As we have seen two major estates (Fothriff and the Boars' Raik) had been allocated to support this work.

Entry 26 in the Chronicle of the Kings of Alba says:

> *And in his 6th year [905/6] king Constantine and bishop Cellach, on the Hill of Belief near the royal city of Scone, pledged themselves that the laws and disciplines of the faith, and the laws of churches and gospels, should be kept in conformity with the Scoti. From that day on the hill has deserved its name, that is, the Hill of Belief.*

First we should note in passing how the location of the Hill of Belief at Scone illustrates my point in the previous chapter about St Andrews not being a convenient central religious location at that time.

The entry does not say that re-Columbanisation had not been pursued energetically from the start, but this entry is for 50 years after the conquest and the genocide. Thus two generations elapsed before the Catholics were given their final marching orders, so we can acknowledge that this at least was a generous adjustment period.

That is the headline change, but just as the Culdees were a pale reflection of their former selves, having absorbed so much Roman teaching that the differences were very much more of form than substance, so too all the Roman practices could not be simply swept aside. One good example of this was church dedication.

In the days before St Serf, churches in Scotland acquired a dedication mostly by 'osmosis' – they were associated with the person who had evangelised the area and set up the church. The 'dedication' was more a statement of historical fact than an honorific or trying to invoke the intercession of the saint in question. This was true also for some churches founded by St Serf. But the general Roman practice was very different – using the dedication of the church to focus the attention of the congregation on the qualities of the saint (whether real or supposed) to whom the dedication was made.

Kirkcaldy Old Kirk: A good example of this is Kirkcaldy Old Kirk which was dedicated to St Patrick and St Bryce. The St Bryce dedication we can date to the Catholic consecration of 1224, but this leaves the matter of St Patrick.

- Patrick never visited Kirkcaldy, so that cannot be the reason; it also rules out the period before 717 when the Columban clergy were expelled.
- It would have been unthinkable for the Catholics of that time to dedicate a church to St Patrick (we have seen the extreme enmity between the two traditions in the Chronicle of Alba extract cited above).

And so it is that we may be confident that the Old Kirk was not established until after 850. But the Catholic Church had left its mark – whereas in the old days the church might have acquired an association with its founder, now, instead, St Patrick, forefather of the Columban church, was chosen as the dedicatee.

The Caer – the stone built fort – had been surplus to requirements from the time the Falcons had annexed Dunfermline (immediately after 685); what use may have been made of the building or the stones (think of the way the stones of Hadrian's Wall were "robbed out" to make nearby buildings) or for how long the building may have remained derelict I cannot say, but surely one should have in mind the possibility that much of the old fort may have been used to construct the original Old Kirk, especially given that it was built on the same site.

Note on the Kirkcaldy Town Seal (see image in the Colour Plates section): Kirkcaldy was created a Royal Burgh in 1644 and was first granted arms in 1673. So really they were not used as "arms" as such, but rather as a seal. In his Encyclopaedia Heraldica (1828) William Berry defined the seal in this way:

Kirkaldie: Azure an abbey of three pyramids, the central taller than the lateral argent each ensigned with a cross pattée or.

> On the reverse of the seal is insculpted, in a field azure St Bryce vested in long garments with a mitre on his head, all proper standing in the porch of the church argent which is ensigned on the top with a cross pattée of the third; his dexter hand holds a fleur-de-lis or, and his sinister hand is laid upon his breast; the whole between a decrescent and a star in fesse of the last.

Motto: Vigilando Munio.

> Round the shields on each side of the seal these words: "*Sigillum civitatis Kirkaldie.*"

The Abbey represents Dunfermline Abbey before the collapse of the central spire and is an allusion to the town being the "property" of the Abbey until the reformation. Depite the registration date above, we should assume that the design was established and was in use after 1244 but long before 1560. Further details can be found at https://www.heraldry-wiki.com/heraldrywiki/index.php?title=Kirkcaldy

Culross and Fothriff: So too the Culdees were able to enjoy the advantages made available by the forced evacuation of the Catholics from Fothriff. So much did Culross become associated with the Culdees for the rest of their independent existence that there are still people who think St Serf was a Culdee!

Conclusions

Readers may – and no doubt will – draw their own conclusions about Kenneth mac Alpin's motives for what he did. Clearly there was an emergency – Scotland HAD to be united in the face of the Viking threat and, given people's reluctance to accept this, it did require a strongman to take the issue by the horns and drive it forward, however undemocratic this may have been. But surely here we see a prime example of the proverb: "All power corrupts, absolute power corrupts absolutely". Heady with success it is all too easy to reward your pals irrespective of the cost to the incumbents.

So what were Kenneth's motives? How much was messianic mission? How much was he affronted by being, as he saw it, unjustly overlooked for the Kingship of the Picts? How much was the baser lust for power and the trappings that surround Kingship? This is for you, the reader, to judge.

For Fife: Through all this, Fife was no more than collateral damage. Fife posed no threat to the overall direction of Scottish politics; Fifers were happy 'doing away' as the saying goes. Perhaps for this reason it was easy to trash the old order and offer easy pickings to minor supporters. And yet the many "raths" we find make clear how much ordinary Fife folk resented these uninvited incomers. Had these been welcomed there would have been no need for such defensive structures.

End note

The Scots not only destroyed Fife's ruling class, but our history and culture as well; it has been a very hard task to reconstruct even a hint of what went before.

13. Enter the Vikings

There is something of a hiatus in our story after Kenneth mac Alpin's takeover, largely because the period is so poorly documented. However there was plenty of Scottish history during that period. On the one hand too many of the kings of Scots behaved like mafia dons, murdering each other and usurping the throne. On the other hand life was a fairly continuous matter of resisting Viking depredation.

This chapter proposes some radical and completely new history of Fife – weaving a body of narrative round only a few fixed points so it is a matter of speculation. We have seen the dangers of this in chapter 8 – the false history of the so-called Battle of Raith. So I ask the reader to be careful. Because this analysis is so new it should not be the last word on the matter. Nevertheless I would not advance it here if I did not believe it to be very substantially correct.

Vikings leave their mark on the landscape:

(a) **Ness:** In Chapter 11 we noted the large number of "ness"es along the north east coast of Fife – but actually there are several other nesses on the shores of the Forth – all will be explained below.

(b) **Dunshelt** [PNF 2439]: Understanding Dunshelt goes a long way to unlocking far more general understanding of the area – and I am grateful to Dunshelt local historian Steve

McHardy for his time and the excellent collation of historical material he has done on the Dunshelt Community website.

I agree with T&M that the first element is Dun – meaning a fort (and there are earthworks there validating this). Close to the earthwork a beaker of the sort made by the beaker people has been found – showing that occupation of that site, whether or not continuous, goes back a VERY long way!

I also agree that the second element is innis/inch – island. So just as we have Markinch so we have Duninch – the island by the fort. There is part of the village round Chapel road whose title deeds predate the draining of the Rossie Loch, while in the northern part of the village it is still common for people to be wading around in water from time to time. So whether the surrounding area was bogland (witness neighbouring "Myres" Castle) for some of the year, it seems that the water level rose enough for Dunshelt to be an island at least for a significant part of the time. The straight road from Falkland was clearly laid out after the draining of the loch and we can see from early maps that before that time, the main road from Falkand to Auchtermuchty lay along the current minor road past Nether Myres and Cash Mill. Such a detour shows where the reliable solid ground lay.

For the last element of the name, T&M suggest Gaelic "ealt or ealta" meaning a flock of birds. They go on to say:

> "The form Dunshalt, which appears on several local sign-posts, is due to a piece of local place-name lore dating from at least the late eighteenth century (*OSA*, 62), which states that the name is actually *Danes' Halt*, since the Danes halted here on a raid up the Eden."

First of all we should note that T&M have not looked farther than Gaelic for an explanation. But both Dun (W Dyn) and Inis (W Ynys) work equally well in Welsh. So there is no problem with supposing that the original name dates to Pictish times – in fact it is much more likely that it does.

When considering this third element, however, my mind turned first to Elterwater in the southern Lake District. Diana Whaley ("Dictionary of Lake District Place Names") tells us that "elt" comes from Old Norse "elptr" or "alptr" meaning swan. Wikipedia tells us that whooper swans still winter on that lake. The reader may imagine my delight, therefore, to see a picture of whooper swans at Dunshelt posted on Flickr by the late Brian Forbes, latterly of Kinross. [As this whole chapter and what flows from it was really triggered by this photograph, the reader may imagine how relieved I was that this cache of photos remain on line so long after his sad passing (2020). His Fickr 'handle' is B4bees.] This suggests to me that the "elt" element in Dunshelt should be understood as referring specifically to these swans and so I propose that the name does include an element from Old Norse and means "the island beside the fort where the swans come".

The converse of this is that Dunshelt does NOT mean "the Danes' Halt". However elements of the lore which gave rise to the idea of the "Danes' Halt" are true – but not in the way a normal person might suppose. This will be explained in full in this chapter – for the very first time in history. The reason this has been suppressed will also become clear.

(c) **Kettle** (Kingskettle [PNF 1297]): It seems therefore, that 'Vikings' did penetrate the area not just to raid but also to settle for long enough for their name for swans to stick – and this is supported by the element "kettle" in Kingskettle – which is essentially an Old Norse name – Ketil – meaning "vessel"; while it could and can be used on its own it was more normally used as part of a compound name eg Thorkettle (which has come down to us as Torquil) – meaning "vessel for (the spirit of the god) Thor" and Ulfketil (Ulf = "wolf").

(d) Ormiston [PNF 24094]: Although I accept T&M's proposition regarding the person called Orm (an Old Norse name Ormr means "Snake") that there was an Orm son of Aeth/ Hugh of Abernethy this begs the question of why Aeth would have given the name Orm to his son. A likely explanation is that Aeth married the daughter of a local man called Orm, so it is quite likely that the names for Ormiston farm and the accompanying Ormiston Hill originally belonged to an earlier Orm.

(e) Rivers ending "-o": Notwithstanding T&M's interpretation it is likely that ending river-based place name with "-o" is Old Norse (as with Thurso) – the o meaning "river/ burn". This would include Cambo [PNF 2113], Dunino [PNF 1977], Balmerino [PNF 2481] etc.. Even Dura [PNF 1169] may fit this pattern (there is no need to invoke Gaelic 'dobhar' when there is the perfectly normal Welsh (for Pictish) 'dŵr'). What has happened here is that the Vikings stuck the o on the end of a Pictish or Gaelic name to make it clear to them that they were taking about the water course. It should come as no surprise that further corruption has taken place in the very long time since the Viking influence dissipated. [Exception: The modern name Blebo [PNF 1159] is not derived this way.]

Other rivers worthy of a rethink include the Kemback burn [PNF 1172]. "Burn" is obviously Scots – so much more recent

– but one of the earliest forms we have includes the spelling "-beck" which is Norse. The earliest form of the first part is given as "kene" which could be taken to imply Kin – ie, itself a Gaelic hybrid corruption of the Pictish Pen – ie the burn of the headland, which would fit the lie of the land.

I do not want to be too assertive here. The general point is that because the Norse influence has not been considered properly there are many place names which need to be reviewed in the light of the new understanding. Wormit [PNF 2884] and Buddo [PNF 2181] are just two of these. In short it is clear that Norse speaking people had a substantial influence on North East Fife specifically – so we should try to understand how, why and when this occurred.

1. When and Why

If this settlement by Vikings had been hostile, it would have been unlikely to have occurred (i) before the year 900 when King Donald II was killed at Dunnottar during an attack by Vikings or even (ii) before 934 when king Athelstan attacked up the eastern seaboard of Scotland widely after King Constantine broke the terms of the Treaty of Eamont Bridge (927) (for which see my papers on Brunanburh and White Hill). On the other hand the occupation must have been for quite a long time if the placenames were to embed themselves enough to survive – which means well before 1000 (see next chapter).

This brings us to a period in Scottish history – from 954 to 977 – which is chaotic to say the least.

To try to understand this we need to go back to king Constantine II ("Causantin mac Aeda") who was king in the period 900-943 when he abdicated to become a monk in St Andrews, dying in 952.

We must now reprise part of Chapter 5 but with a slightly different gloss. After Constantine II, the kings were these:

Malcolm I	943 – 954	son of Donald II
Indulf	954 – 962	son of Constantine II
Dub	962 – 967	son of Malcolm I
Culen	967 – 971	son of Indulf
Amlaib (Olaf)	973 – 977	son of Indulf
Kenneth II	971 – 995	son of Malcolm I

The overlap in dates (971-977) of Amlaib and Kenneth II will, I hope, unlock our understanding.

Note on "Tanistry"

We have discussed Tanistry and its relationship with the Derbhfine above. It was only Kenneth II who would initiate the move to try to replace this by primogeniture (where the eldest son succeeds automatically). And even then, as we may imagine, the nobles did not like the idea of their power to choose their king being taken away from them, so he was not successful!

Way Points

Wikipedia (June 2023) says of King Indulf:

> Indulf's death is reported by the Chronicon Scotorum in 962, the Chronicle of the Kings of Alba adding that he was killed fighting Vikings near Cullen, at the Battle of Bauds. The Prophecy of Berchán, however, claims that he died "in the house of the same holy apostle, where his father [died]", that is at the céli dé monastery of St Andrews. He was buried on Iona.

Wisely Wikipedia avoids some editorialising (although, oops, the reference to the "céli dé" is indeed editorialising (see below) – however it is not impossible that he was wounded in battle and the wounds proved fatal even if he did not actually die until he had been taken back to St Andrews. The Viking raiders he confronted are likely to have been led by one or more of the sons of Erik Bloodaxe as this sort of thing was routine for them and they had had experience of raiding in Scotland.

At this point we need to introduce two paradoxes – but I think they can be resolved.

1. As we can see above, Indulf's son Culen became king in 967. This means he must have been born before 946. This in turn means that Indulf himself must have been born before 921 – and these are "latest" dates. More likely Culen was born in the early 940s and so Indulf most likely around 916. On the other hand it is reported that he was baptised in 927 at the behest of Athelstan (at the time the Treaty of Eamont Bridge was being signed) – and Dr Alex Woolf has speculated that his name may be associated with that occasion. Unfortunately for Woolf the numbers just do not stack up – or if they do then Indulf was given a different name at birth. Indulf was baptised around the age of 10 or so.

2. At Brunanburh (in 937), Constantine's son (almost certainly Cellach) was killed and it seems not a coincidence that, as we noted above, according to the Chronicle of the Kings of Alba (dated to 906):

   > King Constantine and Bishop Cellach met at the *Hill of Belief* near the royal city of Scone and pledged themselves that the laws and disciplines of the faith,

> and the laws of churches and gospels, should be kept *pariter cum Scottis.*

So it looks as if Cellach was baptised according to Catholic rites, but by the time Indulf was born these rites had been abolished. So Constantine seized the opportunity of the gathering at Eamont Bridge, which was not Scottish soil, to have his son baptised "properly" (as he saw it) ie according to Catholic rites. So here we can see that Constantine was acutely aware of realpolitik – personally he leant towards Catholicism, but he realised that it was more than his job was worth to parade this in front of his Columban Christian people.

The earlier reference said that he retired to the "céli dé monastery of St Andrews" – this is a very lazy assumption, actually probably wrong. Given what I have suggested to be his Catholic preferences, it is more likely that Constantine joined a group of Catholic monks guarding the relics of St Andrew. These monks will not have been allowed to perform any religious ritual in public but it is likely that they were Catholic rather than Culdee – Culdees did not "do" relics. The Culdees in St Andrews had their separate church dedicated to St Mary; but we do not know exactly what the arrangements for St Andrew's relics were at this time.

As we saw in the last chapter the Scots had had to try to find ways of avoiding what was tantamount to continuous raiding by Viking pirates and even creeping settlement by them. By 810 a separate Viking state had been set up in the Hebrides and by the later 800s Caithness and Sutherland was under Viking control. On the one hand unifying Dal Raita and Pictland (and Strathclyde) would help, but also somehow a deal had to be done.

Constantine II

Note how Constantine's line included Norse names (Indulf, Olaf), while the 'other' line (from Malcolm I) did not. We know that, via a daughter, Constantine was intermarried with the dynasty of the descendants of Ragnar Lodbrok which ruled York and Dublin and which was also intermarried with the family of Guthrum, the 'other' leader of the Summer Army and later king of East Anglia. This was why Constantine helped the Vikings both at the Battle of White Hill (927) and at the Battle of Brunanburh (937). On the first occasion Athelstan was successful in wresting Northumbria from the Vikings; on the second occasion the Vikings were unsuccessful in their effort to take it back.

This much is known. But what we must now suppose is that Constantine married twice. With his first wife he had Cellach – born 900x905 (the best estimate for Constantine's birth is around 880, so the numbers fit), but then when his first wife died Constantine married into the O'Ivar dynasty – his eldest son from this marriage being Indulf.

It is normal that when a girl comes to be queen in a foreign land she brings a retinue with her including some high born close male relative to look after her interests. This is even more true when the marriage is risky – ie designed to build a peace which had been lacking hitherto. The new queen will need some land for her male relative and his retinue to give him security, a home base and a guaranteed income appropriate to her status. So my guess is that Constantine's wife's entourage was settled in North East Fife. In this case we may suppose that the 'normal' entourage was bolstered by as significant cohort of Viking troops.

Constantine was recognising the realpolitik and he was right – this move bought a good deal of peace. However it came at a cost – for the Scottish magnates did not like this excessive foreign invasion: it felt like they were being controlled by aliens. They put up with it so long as it brought them benefits they could see as 'obvious'. But the moment things go wrong the knives come out.

In this case Constantine's regalia had been on a "shoogly peg" at least ever after the debacle of Brunanburh where even his own eldest son was killed (probably aged about 32 – it appears that he died without any male heir). Constantine had committed Scottish resources to what was really a Viking adventure and they had lost disastrously. Wikipedia cites the Prophecy of Berchan saying that his resignation was not a freely taken decision. It then comes as no surprise that he would choose St Andrews for his retirement and that his son Indulf would look after his residual interests from their North Fife base.

Malcolm I (943 – 954)

The Scots took power back from the Viking hegemony and the crown went to Malcolm I. There were no personal hard feelings, but power needed to be in the right hands and the Scots needed the correct allies. Thus we find Malcolm raiding Northumberland in 952 after it had been recovered by the Vikings (under Olaf Cuaran) – he was again on the same side as Strathclyde, but this time allied to the English against the Vikings.

Quite who took against Malcolm or why is not clear – but it appears that he died battling in the North East just two years later and after just 9 years on the throne. He was succeeded by Indulf.

Indulf (954 – 962)

As we have seen it is most likely that Indulf was born towards the latter part of the period 906-916. He reigned for about 8 years and died as a result of wounds acquired battling Vikings, probably the descendants of Ragnar Lodbrok. At the time of his death (in his late 40s) his eldest son Culen was probably in his early 20s and his younger son Olaf perhaps still a teenager.

Dubh (962 – 967)

Nevertheless the Derbfine preferred not Culen but Dubh the son of Malcolm I as successor. Dub was about the same age as Indulf – so on the face of it a safe pair of hands in difficult times. However he was not up to the job and was killed just 5 years later (967) by his own people. [It has also been argued that there was some overlap between Dub and Culen – so perhaps a compromise had been sought before Dubh was dispatched.]

Culen (967 – 971)

The Duan Albanach describes Dubh as "the vehement", so he may well have been a complete pain and his courtiers decided they would prefer Indulf's son Culen. Culen himself only lasted 5 years, but this time it had nothing to do with Scottish politics or even Viking raiders. He had abducted a Strathclyde princess and vengeance was meted out, so Culen was killed in 971. This fits well with him still being quite a young man.

It should be noted that Culen had a son Constantine who went on to be King of Scotland (Constantine III), albeit even more briefly (995-7) after the death of Kenneth II (see immediately below). This Constantine must have been born around 970, so was still under 30 when he died in 997.

Dual Kingship

As we can see the Derbfine had made a series of pretty bad choices – so now we enter a very strange period when it appears that Scotland had two kings at once. On the one hand there was

Kenneth II, son of Malcolm I who became king on the death of Culen and then ruled for some 24 years, but then there was also Olaf, (brother of Culen and son of Indulf) who may have been born as late as 952 – so not 21 until 973 – who was at least a co-ruler in the period 973 – 977 when he was killed by Kenneth. Despite Olaf being 'on the throne' it was Kenneth who went to Chester in 973 to pay homage to the English king as his overlord.

By now the reader may be wondering what this has to do with the history of Fife. Well… what we have is

- Constantine II marrying a Norse princess as his second wife and needing a base for her retinue; we have his commitment to St Andrews – which given his apparent Catholic tendencies would have been a logical choice.
- And then we have his son Indulf apparently going "home" to St Andrews to die even though his body was taken on to Iona for burial.
- And then there is the matter of the significant number of Old Norse place names in Fife – which is also common in the far north – and on the Isles which were all, in effect, under Norse control, but which is not replicated elsewhere in Scotland.

My conclusion is that North Fife was their base throughout this time. It was Norse speaking courtiers who were responsible for the place name changes. While Kings Constantine II and III may have used Abernethy as their royal capital, it is likely that the headquarters of the Viking Royal Estate was at Cupar – and this is the basis for Cupar's later role as County Town. The Viking troops would have been welcomed by the Scots in general who needed the extra support and by the Mormaer of Fife in particular who had a very long coastline to defend with relatively few people.

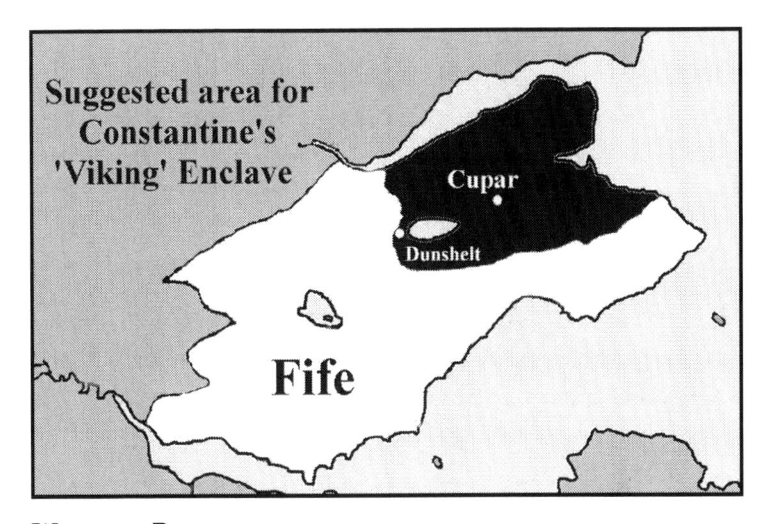

Western Border

We noted above that it is commonly claimed that Dunshelt means "Dane's Halt" because that is how far a raiding party reached. That a raiding party reached there and then turned back is possible but unlikely. Far more likely is that Dunshelt was the western limit of the Viking Royal estate as too would have been Kettle and Ormiston. The map has been drawn accordingly.

Southern Border

My initial thought was that because Fife Ness has "Ness" in its name so we should suppose that it would be included in the royal estate. However contrary to this we find that there are headlands in the Rosyth area which are now also called "ness"es: Cull Ness and Limpet Ness form a cove on the west side of the Queensferry peninsula, Rosyth Church perches on another one and others have been incorporated into the dockyard. However further upstream we find Kinniny Point and Horse Craig before we get to Culross – another "ross". My interpretation of this is that these Vikings whose first task was to support Constantine's Viking queen were later deployed by the Mormaers of Fife to provide shore patrols wherever a Viking raid may have been expected.

The 'border' could have been as far south as the Cambo Burn and Cambo Ness [Cambo: PNF 2113], but I think more likely that the border (as shown on the map) would actually have been the Kenly Burn, one of whose tributaries flows through the Lingo Den [PNF 1849].

The name Lingo

I say the name Lingo is Old Norse "Lyng" and "o" (as in Thurso) and means "the Red Whortleberry Burn" (Lingonberry Jam is a Scandinavian favourite) and as we know at that time Fife was "Fib" which means "red whortleberry".

The full argument about this is complicated so if the reader would prefer to take my word for it then feel free to pass on to the next subheading. But I know that there will be many "what about-ers" so here is my full analysis.

(a) The East Anglian Example

There is a river in East Anglia called the Ouse (a co-variant of what in Gaelic is Uisg meaning water, from which we get the word Whisky) – in other words it does not have a specific name at all. A middle section of this river was called the Grant – the gravelly river – because it runs over gravel. For this reason a town on the riverbank was called Grantchester (Grantacaster) – the fort on the river Grant – and just below it was a bridge – Grantabrygge – which was also the name of the town that grew up beside it. But the bridge was wonky and so came to be known as the Cam Brygge and so the town became known as Cambridge. Then some idiot thought "Well, if the bridge is called Cambridge it stands to reason that it must be a bridge over the River Cam!" Actually this was probably a joke in the first instance, but then repeated by people who knew nothing and cared less... with the result that then name stuck and today that stretch of the river is still called the Cam.

Now there are two tributaries of the Cam both called the Granta! Another of the tributaries is called the Rhee and it is the head of this river which is called the Source of the Cam!

In short river names can get confused; they certainly can change and it is quite normal for one water course to have different names for different stretches of the one river.

(b) The Scottish Example

There is a classic case of stupidity of this sort in Strathearn. On the south bank of the river just west of Comrie is an estate called Aberuchill (which, of course, means the mouth of the "uchil" burn (modern Welsh "uchel" means loud and this compares to many rivers called "gairnie"). Through the estate runs the so-called "Aberuchil Burn" which is a silly name because it already contains its own name – and the mouth is not the whole! But this was not enough for the self-important lairds – so they called the more substantial river to their east "the water of Ruchill". Now we should begin by noting that if it had been "Ruchil" then the estate should have been Aberruchill – with two "r"s.

Not only that, but the "Water of Ruchill" flows through Glenartney and one of the tributaries of the river is called Allt Strath a' Ghlinne. This last name means "mountain stream feeding the Strath of the river Glen (cf modern Welsh glân meaning holy/pure and glên meaning clean – there are several rivers in Scotland (especially Ayrshire) and elsewhere in Britain (eg Northumberland and Lincolnshire) with this name and meaning). [Unfortunately the Welsh have managed to confuse themselves for while "Glyn" often means Glen in the sense of Valley, the Dictionary of the Place Names of Wales (p338) is, in my view, mistaken when they try to claim that Nantglyn means "the river in the valley" when even they record the local lore that "divers Saincts were ancient Tyme buried" there.]

So what we have is a burn which in the original Pictish was called the Uchelig – the loud burn – and its mouth Aberuchelig after which the estate Aberuchill takes its name. The river now grandiosely called Water of Ruchill was originally called the Avon Glen – the pure (ie clean) river.

(c-i) And so to the Lingo

At the moment it is the Lathockar Burn which runs through the Lingo Den. The name Lathockar [PNF 1776] is not a river name and we can see that the word "burn" is Scots. So we can safely say that the name Lathokar Burn is a relatively new one and it has taken its name from the farm/estate name Lathockar.

Meanwhile there is a Ling Burn (again we can see that this is Scots and new) which runs past a farm called Lochty. The word Lochty [PNF1850] is in essence a minor variation of Pictish Lochie and means "Blackburn" – but there is no black burn in the area! Between the Ling Burn and the Lathockar Burn is a farm called Lingo. This farm has taken its name from the (original) river! But now there is no "o" in Ling Burn"!

(c-ii) So here is what happened

What is now the Ling Burn used to be called the Lochty – the Black Burn. What is now the Lathockar Burn used to be called the Lingo – which although it literally means "the Red Whortleberry Burn" actually means "the Fife Burn" – because this is where the Royal estate ended and the rest of Fife began.

Much later the Lingo was renamed the Lathockar Burn because of its importance to the Lathockar Estate.
Meanwhile another estate had been named Lingo after the Lingo – so the Lochtie was renamed to reflect the importance of the Lingo Estate.

Now as it happens the burn now called Ling Burn could have served as the boundary – but a far more "natural" boundary is likely to have been the burn through the Lingo Den.

Descendants of King Constantine III

There is another important point. Of Constantine III, Wikipedia (June 2023) says:

> Constantine is not known to have any descendants and he was the last of the line of Áed (Áed mac Cináeda) to have been king. With his death, the rivalry between descendants of Causantin and Áed gave way to a rivalry between two new royal lines, both descended from Causantin

This is trite and overly dismissive. Absence of Evidence is not Evidence of Absence – but the Wikipedia contributor (likely a well known Scottish History academic) has fallen into this trap.

Indulf is likely to have been born c916, so Constantine III, his grandson by Culen, is likely to have been born c 966, making him about 30 at the time of his short reign. It is unlikely that this Constantine III would not have had a son by this time, more likely he had more than one, but any such son would have been an infant in 996 and so in no position to be available as king until around 1010. For this reason this hypothetical son could not even have been a rival to Malcolm II being made king in 1005. But by 1030 this son of Constantine III would have been about 40 and the Derbfine might well have considered him a worthy alternative to Malcolm III's grandson Duncan – and this brings us very neatly to the next chapter!

Summary so far: The results of the Viking Settlement

North Fife was settled by Vikings, but they were not invaders and they did not fight their way in. The Vikings were the entourage of Constantine II's second wife and North Fife became the home base for Constantine's second family. Key lieutenants like Ketil and Orm were settled in the area, giving their name to some places (and now that we understand what is going on we may yet discover a few more which would fit this pattern). So too the coasts had to be guarded from different Vikings – genuine raiders. So coastal places became important strategic points to be garrisoned by these incomers – and so the headlands became known as "ness"es.

The Vikings mixed well with the community and once their original task was complete (with the death of Constantine II's queen) the Mormaer of Fife rewarded them well especially for sea defences, especially against the pirates.

In earlier chapters we saw that originally 'Fife' was really made up of North East Fife, Kirkcaldy district and Kinross; the Dunfermline area was only absorbed after 685. Now we can understand that after 100 years of broadly independent rule, North East Fife came to be a unit in its own right. The consequences of this include:

(a) the three way division of Fife we see today, albeit that this separateness was reinforced many centuries later when industrialisation overtook Kirkcaldy and Dunfermline while North East Fife retained its rural character.

(b) the establishment of Cupar as a major power centre. [Cupar was later to become the County Town of Fife which lasted until the last round of reorganisation of Local Government.]

(c) what is now Kinross-shire being out on a limb with hardly any land connection to the rest of Fife at all; this will have played a significant part in laying the foundations for the subsequent break away of Kinross as a separate shire.

(d) Abernethy too was now so isolated that it was easy for later kings to reallocate revenues from this parish (once the parish system had been established) to other religious purposes and thereafter for Abernethy to be annexed to Perthshire at a later date.

2. Exit the Vikings

It was King Malcolm II who put an end to this Viking enclave; he reigned from 1005 to 1034 – when he appears to have been murdered – at the age of 80!

Malcolm had three serious problems.

1. was the changing but continuing Viking threat.
2. was that, however naively, many of the Scottish nobles did not like the way they were being ruled more and more by Vikings.
3. was that he only had daughters and was desperate for his own genetic line to succeed to the throne;

2.1 Dealing with Jarl Sigurd and his family

At the beginning of this chapter, we saw how King Constantine II had to cosy in with the Vikings of Dublin and York who were the major players at the time. Over the course of 100 years power had shifted. The Dublin family had taken on too much and were now largely consumed by holding on to whatever they could of what they had. The new strongman threatening too much of Scotland was Jarl Sigurd the Stout of Orkney. Malcolm II had learned from his predecessor; like Constantine II he had a firm grasp of realpolitik…

Sigurd the Stout named his eldest son Hlodvir after his own father. Young Hlodvir (nicknamed Hundi – the hound) acted as Steward of the Western Isles on his father's behalf (rather like being Prince of Wales) and had at least two children: Sigurd (named after the Jarl) and Karl (presumably named after his wife's father).

In 995 Olaf Tryggvasson and his army arrived on Orkney on his way from Ireland to claim the throne of Norway from Jarl Haakon the Mighty. Olaf took Hundi and Sigurd to Norway with him – in effect as hostages — to ensure that Jarl Sigurd did what he was told. This left Hundi's younger son Karl as Steward of the Western Isles. [Olaf Tryggvasson only lasted as king for 5 years – until the year 1000.]

On Orkney and then in Norway King Olaf forced everyone to convert to Christianity – and this may have been the occasion when Hundi may have changed his name to Åsbjorn. Hundi died not long after his arrival in Norway, but not before having a daughter there (c997). He probably called her Bera.

When Hundi died, his son Sigurd became heir to his grandfather Jarl Sigurd the Stout. When Sigurd senior was killed in 1014 (at the Battle of Clontarff in Ireland), grandson Sigurd (nicknamed Digre, which also means "stout") sailed to Orkney to claim his inheritance as Jarl, but he got short shrift from his uncles (one of whom became Thorfinn The Mighty).

Lacking the forces to assert his claim Sigurd took service in England under Canute and soon (c1023) found himself installed as Earl of Northumberland (Canute had been looking to replace Eric Haakonsson) – and his name Anglicised as Siward. The Dictionary of National Biography refers to claims that he descended from a magical or fairy bear. This is probably a reference to the name Åsbjorn ("god-bear") which Hundi had adopted.

Malcolm II and Jarl Sigurd sealed their friendship in two ways:
- Sigurd's grandson Karl had married in the usual way and had had a son called Maldred, but his wife died soon thereafter. So Malcolm gave his eldest daughter, Bethoc, to the now widowed Karl. Bethoc and Karl had a son Duncan who was to become King Duncan I. King Malcolm installed Karl as Mormaer of Atholl and as Chancellor of the Exchequer by which he acquired the nickname "Crinan" (which translates into English as "moneybags" and into Romance languages as "Banquo").
- Malcolm gave another of his daughters to Jarl Sigurd as a wife. They too had a son who was to become Thorfinn the Mighty, Jarl of Orkney.

[Because Bethoc was the sister of Crinan's grandfather's wife, Crinan actually married his own great aunt!]

Summary of (2.1)

So about 1025 the situation was already looking reasonably precarious for Malcolm II. He had thrown in his lot with the Vikings:
- He was Canute's vassal
- He had given Caithness and Sutherland to his grandson Jarl Thorfinn the Mighty one of the Jarls of Orkney
- His Chancellor was Karl Hundisson, aka Crinan
- Just over the border was Crinan's brother, Siward the most powerful Earl in England.

The only "Celt" with any serious power in the land was Macbeth, Commander in Chief of the army.

No wonder the natives were restless!

2.2 Ensuring Duncan, Malcolm's Grandson, succeeded

Malcolm was desperate for his grandson Duncan to ascend to the throne after himself. He knew that the succession could only occur in one of two scenarios. Either there would need to be full scale military intervention which, while it might succeed initially would probably require excessive resources to be sustained, or the laws of the Derbhfine would obtain – and anyone descended within five generations of a previous king would be eligible, with those most closely related having the strongest claim.

So Malcolm adopted the policy of killing all those with a legitimate claim. We do not know the full list of those assassinated under this policy, but we do know from earlier in this chapter that Duncan's principal rivals were the descendants of Constantine III

We saw above that Constantine's descendants got on well with the Mormaers of Fife and from this we may suppose that there were dual alliances formed by marriage. Thus a daughter from Indulf or one of his sons will have married the son of the Mormaer and so too Indulf and/or at least one of his sons will have married a daughter of the Mormaer. The result is that any son or grandson of the Mormaer of Fife who reached adulthood during the reign of Malcolm II was a contender for the throne on Malcolm's death. So too, more obviously, any son born to Constantine III would also qualify.

Both the Mormaer of Fife and Constantine's son were not a happy men. We do not know their names, but we find this entry in the Saga of (St) Olaf Haraldsson (chapter 140):

> *Sigvat the skald was very intimate with King Canute's messengers, and asked them many questions. They answered*

> *all his inquiries about their conversation with King Olaf, and the result of their message. They said the king listened unwillingly to their proposals. "And we do not know," say they, "to what he is trusting when he refuses becoming King Canute's vassal, and going to him, which would be the best thing he could do; for King Canute is so mild that however much a chief may have done against him, he is pardoned if he only show himself obedient.* ***It is but lately that two kings came to him from the North, from Fife in Scotland, and he gave up his wrath against them, and allowed them to retain all the lands they had possessed before, and gave them besides very valuable gifts."***

The "two kings" here were Constantine III's heir and the Mormaer of Fife. Clearly the story dates to a time before Canute removed Olaf from Norway (1028). The reason they appealed to Canute can only have been that, at least by the time Siward had become Earl, King Malcolm II had in fact becoming Canute's vassal by acknowledging Canute as his overlord as part of his strategy for securing his own position. This would discourage any of Canute's pirates from raiding Scotland. But on the other hand this also means that any eg Mormaer was able 'in effect' to raise a grievance against his line manager with the real boss!

Earlier I disputed the lazy assumption that King Constantine III died without issue. Such an assumption is without merit and entirely depends on the logical falsehood 'absence of evidence is evidence of absence'. We should also bear in mind that in the Norway of that day the son of a king was accorded the title 'king'. So here we have circumstantial evidence: not only was Constantine III old enough that we should expect him to have had children, and here we have the evidence of someone living in Fife worthy of the title "king". We have also seen in Irish sources how Mormaers were also at least loosely referred to as "king" – but actually it is even stronger than that, because we have seen that intermarriages with the family of the Mormaer of Fife were actually highly likely. This means that it is plausible to suppose that under the Derbfine system both the son of Constantine III and his (notional) cousin – perhaps by now Mormaer of Fife – could have had a claim to be included in the Derbfine and as such to be a candidate to be the next king.

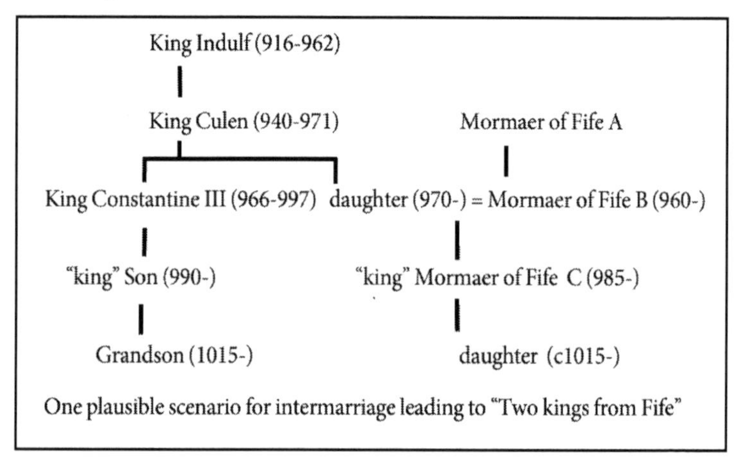

One plausible scenario for intermarriage leading to "Two kings from Fife"

The son of Constantine III was old enough to have had a son of his own – probably a teenager – so in theory it could be proposed that father and son were the "two kings" referred to in the Saga. On its own this is tenable, but then we would have to explain the 'vacancy' in Fife before 1030 (see next chapter). The simple and more elegant explanation is that the Mormaer counted as a "king" for the purposes of the saga.

So while my proposal in Chapter 12 – that the Mormaers of Fife were part of the Cenel Angus and as such not potential claimants to the throne (on which basis there was no reason for Malcolm II to kill them to secure Duncan's succession) – still stands, it is overtaken by our new understanding of the family of Constantine II. Suddenly they become prime targets – second only to the heirs of Constantine III.

The Battle of Falkland Muir

Here I suggest that the echoes of Malcolm II's killing of the two kings referred to above are still to be found in local Dunshelt legend. In previous chapters we noted the lore held by the people of Dunshelt. Their claim that Dunshelt means "Danes' Halt" is not true and I explained what it did mean. However we have seen that there was effective control by Norse people over north Fife in the second half of the 900s and into the 1000s. Here I propose, only a little tentatively, that it was the Battle of Falkland Muir which spelled the end both for the Mormaers of Fife and for the line of Constantine III – thereby "halting" the progress of the "Danes". The supreme irony of this is that this battle took place in order to ensure the succession of king Duncan I who was himself at least half Viking, probably more.

Note of caution: a previous chapter was devoted to debunking the "Battle of Raith" which did not happen. In this case legend (no more) has it that there was a Battle of Falkland Muir and I have found a space into which it slots seamlessly. However this should be understood as speculative; I may be falling into a trap similar to the way Edward Nicholson did. But at least in this case this is a "known unknown"!

Hardly anyone today has heard of "Falkland Moor", but in the Statistical Accounts for Falkland Parish, the Arraty Burn is defined as a boundary for this moor. So actually we know that Falkland Moor lay north of the Arraty Burn and south of the River Eden. In between the Eden and the Arraty lies the Ballingall Burn. I cannot say whether this or the Eden was the northern boundary of the Moor.

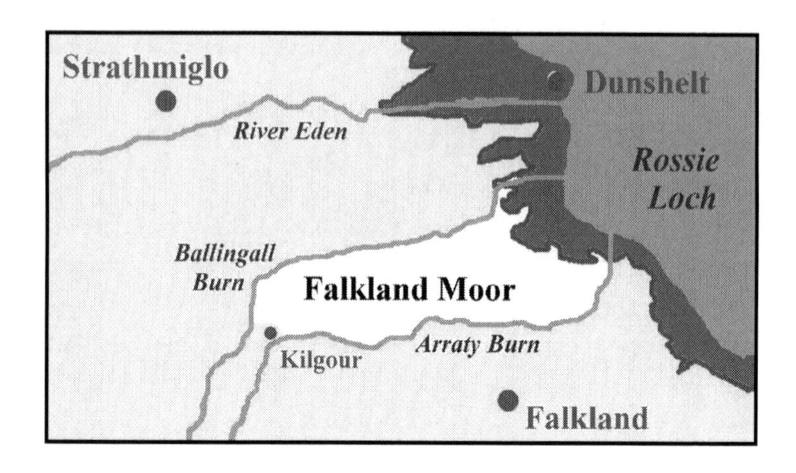

The area indicated on the map is big enough for the sort of encounter being discussed, so the Ballingall Burn probably did mark the northern boundary of the battlefield even if the moor 'officially' extended rather farther north.

SUMMARY

Participants:	King Malcolm II vs. Mormaer of Fife and descendants of Constantine III
Location:	Falkland Muir
Date:	probably between 1027 and 1030
Result:	Victory for King Malcolm II; death for his opponents (whether in battle or immediately afterwards)

AFTERMATH OF THE BATTLE OF FALKLAND MUIR

One result is that we do not any of the names of the Mormaers who ruled Fife from c850 to 1030, which is a pity because we do have at least some of the names for some of the other Mormaers. Another outcome was that Fife could be fully reunited, but there was a vacancy.

Clearly Malcolm found his subservience to Canute irksome, for, according to the Anglo-Saxon Chronicle, Canute had to get 'heavy' with him. He went to Scotland in 1031 where Malcolm II, along with Echmarcach (King of Galloway and the Isles) and Macbeth (Mormaer of Moray) became his vassals, perhaps not for the first time. Michael Swanton (Editor of the Anglo-Saxon Chronicles) prefers 1027 – but that makes no material difference to our story. Canute had been king of England from 1016 (albeit Siward was only made Earl of Northumberland around 1022/3) so there is a time window more than wide enough to accommodate this whole story.

Canute had had problems trusting his principal lieutenants and had certainly had to remove some of them summarily, so although Malcolm had ignored the guarantees Canute had given the "kings from Fife", Canute did not "owe" them anything. So given that Malcolm II reaffirmed his vassalage to Canute that would surely have been enough.

2.3 Securing his position with his vassals

With Duncan's principal competitors off the scene, becoming Canute's vassal not only went a long way to securing Duncan's succession, but also paradoxically shored up Malcolm's position within Scotland as, at least in principle, he could have called on Canute for assistance in keeping any recalcitrant Mormaer in line. Installing Crinan as Mormaer of the key central location of Atholl had been a decisive move.

Afterword

I could not resist calling this section "Exit the Vikings" but actually as will be seen in subsequent chapters people with Viking ancestry but who were not a perceived threat to the realm stayed on.

Postscript: Digression on the Arraty Burn **[PNF 1069]**
For the only occasion in this book I will quote the entire online PNF entry in order to dissect it because it betrays the danger of the Gaelo-centrism I have bemoaned throughout. T&M say:

> This name appears too late in the record for anything but a tentative etymology to be offered. It may contain G *eireachd* 'assembly, meeting' (OIr *airecht*), ending a suffix such as *–in*, 'place of' (if originally referring to a place) or 'burn of' (if to a water-course). For place-names containing this element, see Watson 1926, 439, 491 and Barrow 1981, 11–12, 21–2. However, a word related to OIr *arrachta* 'strong, vigorous, bold', should also be considered: this would aptly suit a fast-flowing burn such as the Arraty, which falls down the steep north side of the Lomonds.
>
> A comparative name is Arrat, Duns ANG, between Montrose and Brechin. There was a hospital and chapel of Mary Magdalene here, recorded as *Arrot* 1435, *Errot* 1435, *Arrot* 1456 (*Brechin Reg.* App. no. 25; and nos. 46, 87). This may be the origin of Richard *Arrath*, who held land in Balnamoon (*Balnamon*), Menmuir ANG, north-west of Brechin (c.1264 *ER* i, 26).
>
> Besides Arraty Burn OS Pathf. also shows Arraty Den and Arraty Craigs; the burn defines the southern and eastern side of the old kirkyard at Kilgour, which is situated at the confluence of the Arraty Burn and of a small burn flowing from the south-east. The Arraty Burn is also known as the *Den Burn* in 1757 (Falkland Plan/1757), at least where it ran through the small, steep-sided valley (den) between what is now Chancefield and Pillars of Hercules. The above NGR is of the point where

> the Arraty Burn meets the Maspie Burn to become the Falkland Burn. Blaeu (Pont) East Fife shows a *B<urn(e) of> Deir* which appears to correspond to the Arraty Burn, for which see FAL Introduction.

Let us dispose of the last bit first: it is perfectly normal for rivers of all sizes to have been known by different names over different stretches in historical times. It is really only with modern detailed and standardised mapmaking (based on the Ordnance Survey work of the middle 1800s) that names have been unified along their entire length.
Arraty has the form Arrat – y so our default assumption should be that the name is Pictish and that the "y" means "burn". So what of "arrat"? T&M were on the right lines when they started with "G *eireachd* 'assembly"... had they looked for a Welsh equivalent they would have found "araith" meaning "speech" or "address" and "areithio" to make a speech. We have seen several examples of the migration or evolution of meanings of words, but here we have a clear understanding that there is an assembly for the purpose of hearing a speech.

Where does this normally happen? Err... T&M seem oblivious when they note "the burn defines the southern and eastern side of the old kirkyard at Kilgour...". It is normal for an assembly to take place at any church on a regular basis to hear a speech... a congregation receives a sermon! So the name of the burn reflects the fact that it got its name and so is identified by the fact that it runs beside the old Kilgour Church.

[This also matches with the area Arrat between Brechin and Montrose identified by the then existence of the chapel dedicated to Mary Magdalene. I will not digress so far as to speculate about the date when a dedication to Mary Magdalene might have taken place, but given the bad odour in which she was held for so long by the Catholic Church we should suppose very early.]

We might consider why the church at Kilgour was so sited. If it was to cover over a druidic site it is possible that gathering for semonising took place even before Christianisation, but there is no evidence for this. As for the Arraty Den and the Arraty Craigs why T&M should regard this as problematic defeats me. In the Highlands it is normal to define and name Glens, Dens and Craigs by the associated burn – just as earlier in this chapter we deconstructed the Lingo Den.

Postscript

Mention has been made in passing of the Maspie Burn [PNF 1131]. Here I accept T&M's explanation.

14. MacBeth and the Thane of Fife

And so it is that we pick up the story of the genesis of the Kingdom of Fife about the year 1029. King Malcolm II has secured his succession by killing Duncan's Fife-based principal rivals. There is no Mormaer of Fife. And so it is that we come to one of the most famous stories in Fife's history – a story made famous by William Shakespeare in his play "Macbeth".

Here is the shocker:

- There never was a 'Thane of Fife' called "Macduff".
- No 'Thane of Fife' murdered Macbeth.

And yet, surprisingly and paradoxically, there is far more truth to Shakespeare's tale than historians will allow!

- There was a Thane of Fife
- Macbeth did kill the bulk of that thane's family
- The thane did interrogate the would-be Malcolm III to assess his potential for kingship
- It is possible that he was "untimely ripped" from his mother's womb.

The character Macduff was invented shortly before the year 1300 for very specific political purposes – but that is for another chapter, Appendix B below. In this one we will restrict ourselves to specifying what did actually happen in the relevant time period.

Much of this chapter and Appendix B is drawn from a more detailed treatment – in Book A Chapter 3 and Book C Chapter 5 in Volume II of SCLLE.

1. Background: King Duncan I's wife

Until the publication of my book SCLLE (and still for those who have not read it!) the matter of just who King Duncan I's wife was has vexed historians for a long time. Her name has been shown as "Suthen" and as "Ursula" and it seems generally accepted that she was a kinswoman of Earl Siward; she is described as Siward's sister's daughter, but the specifics of that relationship have remained controversial.

Some have alleged that she was also called Sybilla. This is no more than a misattribution – Sybilla (of Normandy, illegitimate daughter of Henry I of England) was actually the name of the wife of king Alexander I. So too we must not get too distracted by "Suthen". It was a normal Gaelic language name for the place and the time (among potential meanings are "eternal" and "gentle"). So too it was not unusual for an immigrant queen to take a new name on marriage: just two generations later, for example, we find Malcolm III's daughter Edith being renamed Matilda on her marriage to Anglo-Norman King Henry I.

First of all let us establish that she was foreign. As it is generally accepted that Malcolm III was born in 1031, Duncan I must have married in 1030 at the latest. His wife would have had to have been 15 by then and this makes her birth no later than 1015 – a time before Canute's invasion of England and long before Siward was made Earl of Northumbria. Conversely it is highly unlikely that she would be born before 1010. Hence Duncan's wife was not merely not Scottish, she was not even Northumbrian. So we may be confident that she was Norse – and we may be specific that she was Norwegian by birth. For this reason we can set the name Suthen to one side as being no more than the name she was known by in Scotland.

So now we must consider Ursula. Clearly this is Latin and hence a translation rather than her real given name. It means "she-bear". I am grateful to Dr Alex Woolf for suggesting "Bera" as the appropriate Old Norse equivalent. I shall use this henceforward.

So we have Bera, a kinswoman of Earl Siward marrying Duncan I. There were good reasons for this marriage. First as we have seen, Siward and Crinan were brothers (thus Duncan and Bera were first cousins – see pedigree chart below) so keeping the kingship firmly within the family cemented their grip on power, securing their dynasty for the future. Second there will have been great satisfaction in marginalising the new Jarls of Orkney who had deprived the brothers of their share of their inheritance. But third it was also in Canute's interest. Given the previous experience of English kings, Canute considered himself the overlord of Scotland, but Malcolm was less than ecstatic about this status. Having this extra lever on the king-to-be through his trusted lieutenant Siward was just the sort of manoeuvre Canute would have relished.

Given that Malcolm II was "all in" in his commitment to his alliance to the Jarls of Orkney this further cementing of the ties made great sense – but it also meant that he would need to be even more on his guard against the resentment of foreigners he was stoking.

The Thane of Fife identified

In the 1860s, long before he found fame and a knighthood, William Fraser began developing his trade as a family historian to the rich and genteel with a manuscript history of the Balfours (original copy still in the hands of Robert Balfour of Balbirnie).

His story starts with a "Northumbrian" called Siward who flourished "in the time of king Duncan I" and who had the lands of Balfour (just South of Milton of Balgonie and occupying the land between the rivers Leven and Ore) from which the family was later to take its surname. For a discussion of this name see below in this chapter.

When I discussed these matters with them, Major John Balfour and Dr Jean Balfour, both sadly now deceased, were amazed to hear about the legendary bear associated with Earl Siward – as this figures also in their lore (though not recorded by Fraser). Readers will readily appreciate how grateful I am to them for their giving me their time to discuss these matters and how lucky I was to be have access to such key information. Such a coincidence demands an explanation.

It is beyond peradventure that Siward Earl of Northumbria and Siward in Fife "a Northumbrian" should share such a legend and not be related. In short we may fully confident that Siward, the patriarch of the Balfour family, was the nephew of Earl Siward and the brother of King Duncan I's Queen Bera.

As we saw in the case of Constantine II's second (Viking) wife, it was normal that when a girl ventured to foreign climes to marry she would take a retinue of her own people with her. In the case of someone very important it was normal that a junior male member of the family would accompany her to ensure her interests were well safeguarded.

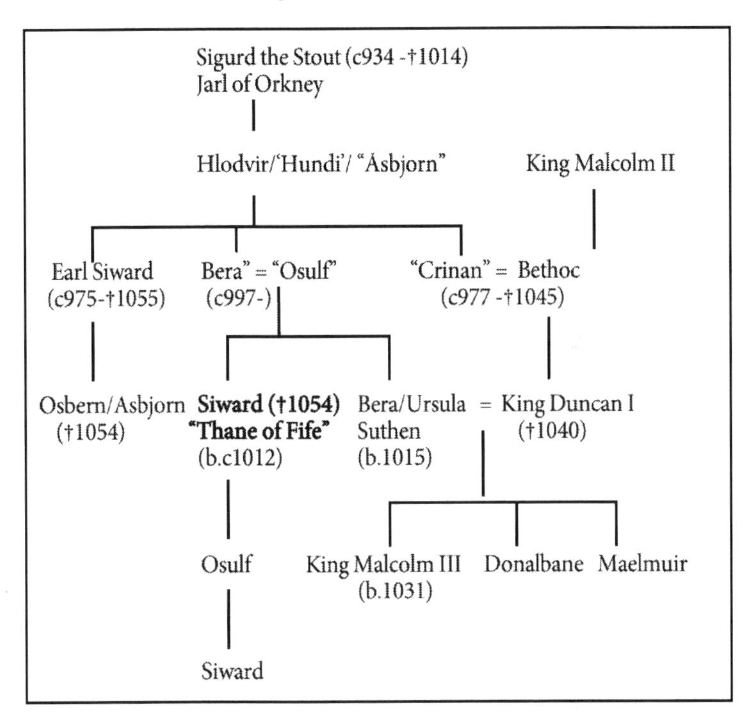

So Siward was installed as Thane of Fife. In principle this was a title which was not heritable (even though some Thanedoms were held by several generations of the same family). It was a position held directly from the crown for as long as the king thought it was a good idea. Malcolm II may have wanted to install Siward as Mormaer, but that would have been one step too far – it would have caused too much trouble with the rest of the nobility. However it is very likely indeed that Siward's wife was a very close member of the family of the old mormaers – the plan being that in due course their eldest son would be raised to the status of Mormaer.

2. The Thane of Fife and Scottish Politics

During Malcolm II's reign: So Thane Siward settled down to running Fife, first for king Malcolm II and then for king Duncan I. However Scotland was not settled. The natives were restless – and we may use that phrase because neither Crinan nor Siward nor the Queen had any Scottish blood in them at all! Malcolm's approach to realpolitik may have been sensible and practical, but it was really hard for the Scottish nobles to stomach. On the other hand Siward was a Viking and, as we saw in the last chapter, there was a substantial number of people of Viking heritage living in North Fife in particular. So having 'one of their own as it were and someone who was the brother of the future queen in charge may have gone some way to appease the resentment caused by the murder of the chiefs of both communities.

Nevertheless while all this looked good on paper, Malcolm was eventually killed at Glamis in November 1034. While the records claim that the deed was done by "bandits", we may indeed speculate as to who the so-called bandits were and what their real motivation was and who had paid them.

During Duncan I's reign: Even if he had not been murdered, Malcolm II's death at the age of 80ish was surely anticipated, so several actors will have been jostling for position. But Malcolm had been very effective in ensuring that there was no "obvious" alternative to Duncan. However the Orkneyinga Saga says that the next person who took power in Scotland was Karl Hundisson – and we know that this means Crinan – and we can see why… he was Duncan's father and he had control both of the purse strings and Atholl, the key central area of Scotland! However note the words of the saga: "took power". Crinan was never king, he merely ran affairs on behalf of his son. We know that his son from his first marriage – Maldred – played a major part and that Crinan also tried to install a relative, also, presumably, from Crinan's first wife's side of the family, in Caithness. The saga calls him "Muddan". [Wikipedia suggests that he could have been the son of a daughter from Crinan's first marriage. If so he would have been aged c30 at the time, so this is chronologically feasible.] We may be sure that our Thane Siward was also in the thick of it.

We may pause to consider this just a little further – for it is a "well known fact" that King Malcolm II had made over Caithness to Jarl Thorfinn of Orkney, his own grandson. However, as we have seen, Thorfinn was amongst the co-Jarls who had denied Siward his share of Orkney, so it would not be unreasonable for Crinan (who was, after all, Siward's brother) to have considered that all bets were off in that regard.

The death of Canute the following year left Scotland a good deal more independent – but this was bad for Duncan as the restive Scots now had more scope to flex their muscles.

Even though all this Viking stuff was too much for the Scots, they decided to give Duncan one last chance, persuading him to lead a raiding army south – but he led them to crushing defeat at Durham. So now the knives were out, but who to unite behind? In the end they settled on Macbeth. He was Mormaer of Moray, even if only by right of his wife. His claim to the throne, if any, was so flimsy that he had survived Malcolm's purges, but he was a seasoned and proven commander in the field – and he was a Scot! Crinan and Duncan saw the way the wind was blowing and intended to nip the problem in the bud, but the result of their pre-emptive strike was that Duncan was killed by Macbeth's forces at Bothnagowan near Elgin. Duncan's children were not of age, so it was easy for Macbeth to assume the crown.

During Macbeth's reign: Both Crinan and Thane Siward will have been aware that they had to tread most carefully. There was no scope for rebellion as the people of Scotland clearly backed 'one of their own' against "foreigners". Moreover Macbeth quickly did a deal with Jarl Thorfinn – effectively handing over the Western half of Scotland (the late Gunnar Henni of Edinburgh did a lot of good work trying to identify the working boundary between them, but sadly this was left unpublished). Thereby he very much strengthened his own hand in his real heartland and could call on Thorfinn for support as and when needed.

Crinan was too big a fish to be left alone, but Thane Siward had no claim on the throne so he was in a position to keep his head down for a few years longer.

Wikipedia (accessed 19 Nov. 2022) says:

> *In 1045, Crínán of Dunkeld rose in rebellion against Macbeth in support of his 14-year-old grandson, Malcolm III's claim to the throne. However, Crínán, by then an elderly man, was killed in a battle at Dunkeld, as was his son Maldred of Allerdale.*

What nonsense. Malcolm was indeed no more than 14 years old. Only an idiot would stage such a stunt at such a time. Not only that but the three boys were not around. The eldest, Malcolm, may well have gone to the court of King Edward the Confessor as soon as Edward had taken the English throne (1042) – it is not impossible that he might even have been in the court of Edward's predecessor Hardecanute. This would have been a normal arrangement to make. Tradition says that Donalbane, perhaps Maelmuir also, were sent to the Western Isles (perhaps with their mother), presumably for their own safety immediately after Duncan's death.

Crinan and Maldred were ambushed and killed in 1045. The idea that they were on their way to a feast at Macbeth's invitation may be Shakespeare's invention, but the murders were indeed at MacBeth's instigation. Doubtless Thane Siward was on the hit list also, but as it happens he was not there – so then he needed to be hunted down.

The Thane of Fife escapes from MacBeth

In Shakespeare's MacBeth we are told about the escape of "MacDuff" and the murder of his wife and children by MacBeth. The story told follows Holinshed and others who relate that "MacDuff" fled for his life; when MacBeth's men reached his castle, his wife delayed them until she could see he had put to sea safely, soon after which she and her children were butchered. Let us consider the feasibility of this story. Proponents of what has come to be the "accepted" version of the legend suggest that "MacDuff" fled from Rires castle via Earlsferry.

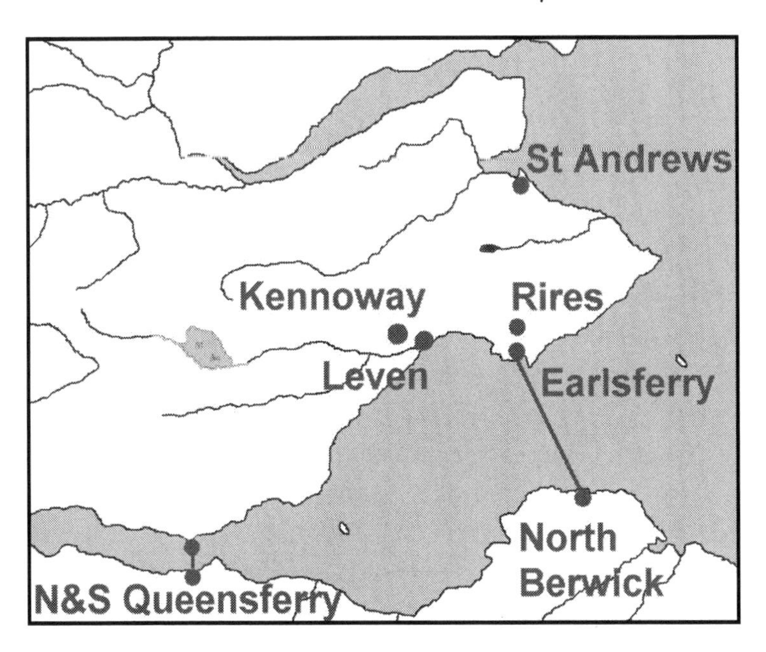

There are several problems with this. By its name, Earlsferry was founded by an Earl – but there were no earls in Scotland at this time. They were not introduced until after the death of Malcolm III in 1093. Indeed we know that Earlsferry was set up to echo Queensferry in assisting pilgrims travelling to St Andrews – so nothing to do with any escape. When I went to visit the site, a local worthy advised me that the MacDuff legend was associated not with Earlsferry itself, but with nearby MacDuff's cove. However the view from the site of Rires Castle is such that a craft would need to be many miles out to sea before there was a line of sight – too far, frankly, to be visible. [Telescopes had yet to be invented.]

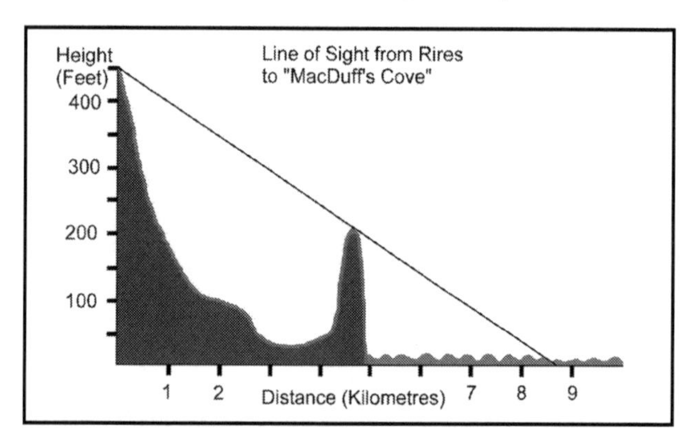

An excellent page on the John Gray Centre website informs us that the Earlsferry crossing was actually set up in 1150 by Earl Duncan I who also owned the land at North Berwick. This could be seen as a pious deed, but given that at one point some 10,000 pilgrims were using the facility each year this should be seen as a major money maker – in essence it was a hard-nosed tourist business. The page claims that at 10 miles, this was the "shortest" crossing of the Firth of Forth. Strictly this is not true – the Queensferry crossing is just over one mile – but pilgrims coming up the east coast would save themselves what would otherwise be a detour of about 60 miles – several days' journey on foot, so we can see the attractiveness of the offering.

To this we may add that there was no need for Earlsferry before 1150. As we saw in chapter 11 there is good reason to suppose that there was a well worn 'tourist' route taking pilgrims from North Berwick to Anstruther whereafter there was a very straight road just 8 miles in length to take them to St Andrews. It was only the upscaling of this trade which meant that more capacity was required – so the original "HS2" was created even if it was a little less convenient for the pilgrim: it enhanced the income of the earls and it freed up the existing harbours to get on with the day job rather than being clogged up with tourists.

However...

Both Fordun and Boece, however, tell us that "MacDuff" escaped from Kennoway. Professor Richard Oram of Stirling University has argued that the motte at Kennoway was probably built post 1067 by Maerleswein, the refugee former Sheriff of Lincoln, as two generations later it was in the hands of another Maerleswein, presumably his grandson. I find this argument attractive and it fits well with the idea of Thane Siward's hall having been destroyed by Macbeth's men any time after 1045. Very near the motte there is a trig point on a bluff with good natural defences on two sides and good views all round. This is site of the old Dunipace Hill fort we have discussed before and I propose that this was the site of Thane Siward's hall.

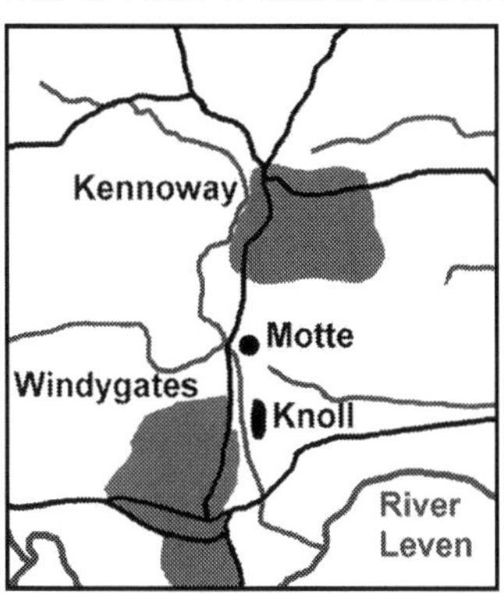

The view from the Kennoway trig point to Leven harbour is short and straightforward. A hoisted sail could be seen immediately. Moreover Rires is not a convenient place from which to govern Fife, while Kennoway is about as central as it is possible to be – the Motte reinforcing the point.

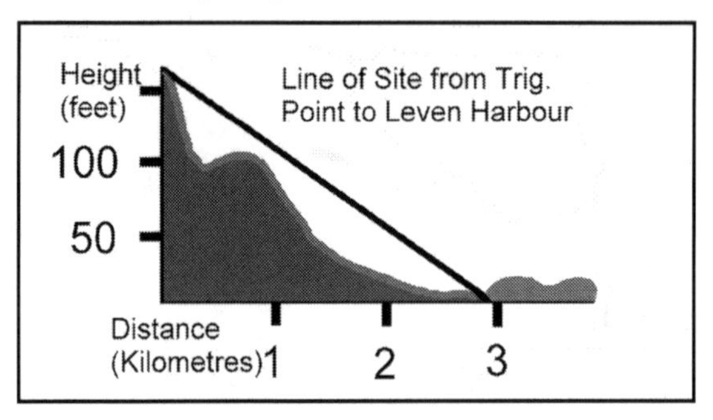

And so it was that Thane Siward DID manage to escape and naturally he sailed straight to his uncle Earl Siward in the first instance. The Balfour genealogy says he was survived by his son Osulf so this suggests that Osulf escaped with him. Assuming that Thane Siward's firstborn was a son c1032x1036+, even by 1045 that son would have been more than old enough to have accompanied his father when Siward fled for his life from Kennoway. Nevertheless there is no reason to disbelieve Shakespeare's claim that Siward also had several young children 'available' with their mother, as it were, for Macbeth's henchmen's murderous depredations.

[Because we don't know any better we may easily assume that Osulf was the name of Thane Siward's father. However Osulf is also the name of the Lord of Bamburgh who died in 1067. So Siward and Lord Osulf would probably be fairly close contemporaries. Earlier I suggested that most likely Siward's wife was a girl from the family of the Mormaers, and given that he moved to Scotland aged just 15 or 16 that remains the best bet. But Lord Osulf is likely to have had a grandfather by the same name who may have been very important in Thane Siward's early life in Northumbria. So Osulf the son of Siward may have been named not after his grandfather, but after a godfather type figure.]

What then was Thane Siward to do? He had no good reason to return to Scotland. He was about 35 years old. Doubtless he could have lived out the rest of his life in relative anonymity somewhere in England. The only "job" to be done would be to help his nephew gain the throne – but would the effort be worth it? So Shakespeare's scene of "MacDuff" and Malcolm testing each other, probably represents a process that really did occur.

The later-to-be King Malcolm III came of age in 1052. Thane Siward was full of renewed vigour to make good his life's work by seeing his nephew take the throne of Scotland. With Edward the Confessor's blessing, Earl Siward organised an invasion in 1054. The Chronicle of Worcester tells us that amongst the fallen (at Dunsinane) were Earl Siward's son Osbern and "Siward, Earl Siward's sister's son" – at which point Shakespeare takes full advantage of his poetic licence.

Although Thane Siward was killed in 1054, his son Osulf regained at least a foothold in part of his father's lands – at Balfour. He continued to play a major part in the administration of the territory, his descendants becoming hereditary Sheriffs of the Kingdom (of Fife) – just about the closest thing to 'Thane' by any other name.

While Bera was born c1015, it is possible that Siward was a year or two older. However if he was "untimely ripped" from his mother's womb then the clear implication is that he and

Bera were twins. It is not feasible for Thane Siward to have been younger than Bera – aged 12 would not be old enough to come to Scotland to look after your 15 year old sister's interests.

From c1030 Siward was the Thane of Fife – the King's representative. It is a remarkable measure of stability, as we approach 2030, that Robert W Balfour – Siward's direct line descendant – is the Lord Lieutenant of Fife, the king's representative!

POSTSCRIPT ON THE BALFOURS

The Balfour legacy was further secured by Osulf's son Siward when (c1098), at King Edgar's behest, he captured and executed "Ottar the Dane", otherwise Olaf Hemingsson, progenitor of the Siol Alpin clans and a principal lieutenant for Kings Edmund and Donalbane. Siward's reward was a vast estate based at Balfour (immediately across the river Leven from Milton of Balgonie) from which the family took its surname, their coat of arms reflecting this (see colour plates). [Blazon: Argent, on a chevron sable an otter's head erased of the field.] See also SCLLE vol. I especially chapter B3.

[**Notes on the name Balfour**: The name Balfour is a typical Gaelic/Pictish hybrid of the sort discussed in previous chapters – "Bal-" is Gaelic essentially meaning "farmstead" while "-four" comes from "pour" (the "p" softening to "f" in the Gaelic genitive, so "phuir") meaning "pastureland" – contrary to the assertions of many "historians" it has nothing at all to do with the River Ore.

Of the River Ore, T&M [PNF11] say:

> *Given that monosyllabic river-names are amongst the oldest names in the landscape, it is possible that this*

*derives from a Pictish, or even Pritenic (i.e. very early or proto- Pictish) *or...*

In the Neo-Celtic languages (Irish, Gaelic, Welsh) or developed the meaning 'border, limit, edge'. ......We cannot now know whether the earlier or later meaning was uppermost in the minds of those who named the Ore, but from the earliest historical period there is no indication that the Ore was ever a boundary.

I accept all this, but as we may see from previous maps, the Ore is in fact the one river which crossed the traditional boundary between the Caledonians and the Maeatae – quite an unusual thing for rivers to do and remarkable enough to be identified as "special". So T&M are right to say that there is no evidence that it was a boundary and hence the etymology offered is probably not correct in this case.]

Contrary to T&M [PNF1460], while the "Bal-" is Gaelic, the "-four" is NOT Gaelic, but from Pictish "pur" (cf modern Welsh "pawr" = pasture, "pori" = to graze and "porio" = to pasture). Compare this to Purin Hill, Purin Farm and the Purin Den on the east side of East Lomond which, again contrary to T&M [PNF1145], were the Common Grazings for the feuars of Freuchie and which are wholly unsuitable for arable purposes. See also Pitfour in Aberdeenshire.]

Away with the nonsense!

The story of a MacDuff, descendant of king Dubh, as peddled by the likes of Bannerman and, more lately, Alison Chapman is, frankly, patently absurd – for if there had been such a person, King Malcolm II would have had him killed, and ironically thereby creating a vacancy *inter alia* for the governance of... Fife!

It is well known – and undisputed – that it was Malcolm III himself who was responsible for the killing both of Macbeth and of Lulach.

Concluding Summary

1. There was a Thane of Fife
2. His name was Siward
3. He was Earl Siward's sister's son and the brother of Bera, Duncan I's queen.
4. He was Crinan's nephew and so Duncan I's first cousin.
5. He was king Malcolm III's uncle
6. He was the progenitor of the Clan Balfour.
7. His bases included Balfour and Kennoway.
8. Macbeth did hunt him down, but he escaped. Macbeth did not spare his wife and children.
9. Thane Siward died on Dunsinane Hill in battle against Macbeth's forces in 1054, aged c39.
10. It was Malcolm III himself who killed Macbeth.
11. Malcolm II did indeed kill or arrange for the killing of both the Mormaer of Fife and any sons and any sons of king Constantine III and the sons in subsequent generations. In short Fife was actually Malcolm's main killing field – the basis of the legend that emerged.

15. Fife Becomes a "Kingdom"

1 The reign of Malcolm III

King Malcolm III had a major task on his hands sorting out the mess he was confronting – and we may be confident that it was only possible due to the major logistical support he was receiving from Edward the Confessor. It took three years to catch and kill Macbeth and another year to kill Lulach, MacBeth's successor and choice of the Scots as the non-Viking option. Moray was inherited by Maelsnectan as Mormaer, but he was ousted in 1078 (see below).

Fortunately for Malcolm there were "vacancies": Atholl had been given to Crinan and so had been, in effect, vacant since his murder. Malcolm divided this between his brothers: Gowrie for Donalbane and Atholl 'proper' for Maelmuire; Fife had been vacant as discussed in the last chapter. Siward had been the Thane until Macbeth had forced his exile. It has been covered on a locum basis by The Mormaer of Angus as the titular boss and Osulf as the man in day to day charge. In Strathearn the original mormaers stayed put, doubtless swearing undying fealty to Macolm – as did Mar and Buchan.

Another slice of luck for Malcolm III was that Jarl Thorfinn died the next year (1055 – the Orkneyinga Saga, composed so many years later, greatly exaggerated Thorfinn's life) meaning that Orkney would not pose an immediate threat of any serious nature. But to make sure, Malcolm married Ingebjorg, Thorfinn's widow, and very quickly they had three boys – Duncan, Malcolm and Donald.

Ingibjorg died just at the time when a rebellion against William the Conqueror, by Anglo-Saxons supported by the Norse had flared briefly and then failed. A number of VIP refugees fled to Scotland.

One of the refugees was a man called Maerleswein, who had been Sheriff of Lincoln before briefly finding exile in Northumberland. He settled in Fife and it was he who built the motte at Kennoway right next to the site of the hall where Macbeth's men had killed Siward's family.

Malcolm took a great fancy to Margaret Atheling – another of the refugees. They were soon married (1071 at the latest) and many children resulted. We should note carefully the male members of her family: Her father was Edward Atheling, her uncle Edmund. Her grandfather was King Edmund Ironside and her great-grandfather King Aethelred II ('The Unready'). She also had a brother Edgar – who had actually been elected as King of England, but had been unable to take it up due to the Norman conquest.

Malcolm and Margaret's sons, in birth order, were: Edward, Edmund, Aethelred, Edgar, Alexander and David. [The reader will find many 'authorities' who will dispute this order, but they have their own agenda. The real story is out there – merely discounted. Some of these will be examined in this chapter.]

The Treaty of Abernethy

From William the Conqueror's point of view it was bad enough having these rebels living next door. Now that Margaret was married to Malcolm surely only more trouble was to be expected. So in 1072 William arrived in force in Fife, requiring Malcolm to sign the Treaty of Abernethy (still an integral part of Fife at that time). As part of this, King Malcolm became King William's vassal – ie feudal inferior. To try to make sure that Malcolm stuck to his word, his eldest son, Duncan, just into his teens, was taken to the English court as a hostage.

Appanages

Today in this country it is normal for the eldest son of the monarch to be appointed Duke of Cornwall more or less at birth. Of course a young child is not capable of administering a Dukedom, but with good advisors it is an excellent preparation for the subsequent job of king – and it can provide a generous income.

So too it was like this over 1,000 years ago: Duncan I had been appointed King of Strathclyde (by then a client kingdom) at the age of 5 (which is why Symeon of Durham calls him "the King of the Cumbrians").

Malcolm III followed the same practice. Duncan, his eldest son, was invested in Strathclyde. Similarly Malcolm was given all Lorne/Argyll. [Wikipedia (19/11/22) calls Malcolm an "apocryphal" character and claims that he died in 1085. This is nonsense. He was alive and well enough in 1096 to sign the Coldingham Charter and in 1103 to negotiate with Norwegian king Magnus Barelegs.] I do not know about his third son, Donald, but the pattern implies that he would have had Kintyre.

When Duncan became a hostage in England a 'vacancy' arose – presumably filled by Edward. I do not understand exactly how this worked, because, as we shall see, these sons were moved around quite a bit – so I cannot account for Edmund (perhaps he had Cumberland?). But clearly Malcolm wanted to put his own family in wherever he could (ie without upsetting the locals to the point of rebellion). Lothian was an easy one. It was newly acquired and was not part of the "system" – a space which Edgar was able to fill. So too Alexander seems to have had charge of the bulk of the old Manau (today's Falkirk Clackmannan, and Stirling).

Fife was being run effectively by Osulf as Thane and, after 1070, with Maerleswain as an experienced side-kick. It was Aethelred who was initially pencilled in for Fife, but this was not to last long as a bigger opportunity arose.

At the very top of Malcolm's to-do list was Moray. Before he was king, Macbeth had been Mormaer of Moray by right of his wife. Lulach had presumably been at least acting Mormaer of Moray (by right of his father) for some time while his stepfather was king. Lulach is normally counted as a "king of Scots" even though there is no evidence of any acclamation by the nobles and no coronation at Scone, so I would count his inclusion in the list as "unofficial". When Lulach too was killed, his son Maelsnectan was at least Mormaer of Moray.

Malcolm had, in effect, invaded Moray to attack Macbeth and then Lulach (in 1057 and 1058). His writ did not actually run there. On the other hand Maelsnectan had not been approved by any Debhfine as "king of Scots". We can see from this mess how Irish annalists were correct in calling him "king" of Moray. Malcolm even arranged for a chain of beacons starting at

Craigelachie (by Aviemore) so that the rest of Scotland could be warned quickly if any armed force were to come up the Spey intending trouble (see SCLLE Volume I). Maelsnectan was in practice answerable to no-one – so he was indeed a king of sorts.

It was not until 1078 that Malcolm was sure enough of his ground to stage a proper annexation of Moray. Maelsnectan was forced to resign (though he did not die until 1085 so at least a potential threat remained).

It looks as if Moray remained under direct rule until Maelsnectan had died, but immediately afterwards Aethelred was posted there and was married to Lulach's daughter (Maelsnectan's sister), Gruoch. Aethelred was very young, but the numbers do stack up! In Moray he shortened his name to Aedh – a good Gaelic name – and the Moraymen quickly rallied around him. Their eldest son was Angus. All was set for a nice life and the start of a new dynasty of Mormaers. As a result there was a 'vacancy' in Fife.

HERALDRY

There are five coats of arms which will help our understanding – for which see the colour plates:

The Lion Rampant Undifferenced (Fife, now Wemyss)
The Lion Rampant debruised with a Ribbon Sable (Abernethy)
The Lion Rampant surrounded by a Double Tressure (the Royal coat of arms)
Gules two Chrevrons Or (Earls of Strathearn)
Gules three Ancient Crowns Or (Chiefs of Grant)

Vassalage is shown by the reversal of the colours

Edward the Confessor was the first person in England to adopt a coat of arms. He did so because when he came of age he was an exile in the French court where coats of arms were already normal. Malcolm III was the first Scot to adopt a coat of arms: A red lion rampant on a gold ground. He did so because when he came of age he was an exile in Edward the Confessor's court.

The arms he chose are the arms of the Counts of Flanders in the colours of the Counts of Boulogne (the reasons need not concern us here, but for the detail see SCLLE Vol. II).

Aethelred chose a variation on his father's arms: a red wildcat rampant on a gold ground (and Maelmuir chose a red wolf rampant on a gold ground).

Other very early adopters included the Earl of Stathearn and Olaf Hemingsson (the progenitor of the Grants and other clans). Because they were vassals and not members of the royal family their arms had their colours reversed (ie the background was red and the image(s) were gold).

2. 1093 – DISASTER AT ALNWICK AND ITS AFTERMATH

In 1093 Malcolm III and his son Edward, his choice as successor, were killed while taking part in a siege of Alnwick. They had no business being there in the first place, of course, but the story is that they were killed treacherously under a flag of truce.

Who should be king? Malcolm had clearly favoured his sons by Margaret, but Duncan was his eldest son and so naturally claimed to be "the" heir. The Scots wanted a champion of their independence; in England, King William II 'Rufus' wanted someone compliant – who would behave like the vassal Malcolm III was supposed to have been. Duncan was well schooled in and had adopted Norman ways – he had even been knighted.

The leaders of Scotland wanted someone who understood them and their ways, choosing Malcolm's brother Donalbane – as they had every right to do. But William had other ideas and sent up an army under the command of Edgar Atheling to install Duncan. What were the Scots to do?

One of Malcolm's chief assistants had been Olaf Hemingsson, nicknamed Grento. In Duncan's entourage was Heming, previously an assistant to Edward the Confessor and now the sub-prior of Worcester. He was Olaf's father. Between them they brokered a deal. The Scots would accept Duncan, but on the basis that he sent home all his Norman retainers.

Six months later it was clear that Duncan was not sticking to his side of the bargain. So the writing was on the wall for Olaf: "You got us into this mess, so you'll need to get us out of it!" And so it was that Olaf's son Maelpedair, now Mormaer of the Mearns (he had married the Mormaer of Angus' daughter and the Mormaerdom had been divided) killed Duncan II at Mondynes (in his own patch 7 miles down the A90 from Stonehaven).

The Scots were once again able to choose their own king – and they chose two! Donalbane was re-enthroned along with Malcolm's next-in-line son Edmund. Broadly they split the country between them, Donalbane taking charge of the north, Edmund the south. The Scots were delighted, but Edmund's younger brothers Edgar, Alexander and David were far from happy. They left for England – and to plot a coup.

3. 1097 – Serious business

King William Rufus was not a happy man, and this time it would be hardball. He equipped another army, again under Edgar Atheling but this time to install Edgar as king. Edgar was happy to be as compliant and as good a vassal as William could ask for.

The invasion was effective… up to a point. To reinforce control Alexander was installed as Regulus of the South. Donalbane was blinded, emasculated and imprisoned at Rescobie where he died soon afterwards. Edmund was spared death on the basis of becoming a monk in Somerset. Olaf Hemingsson was hunted down and executed.

When I said "up to a point" above, the "point" was Moray. Edgar's usurpation of the throne was utterly illegitimate whichever way you looked at it. First of all Edmund and Donalbane were appointed kings in the proper Scottish way, so Edgar had no right to interfere. Second, if we were to set aside the Scottish way and adopt Norman male-line primogeniture then apart from Malcolm, still vey much alive and well in Argyll, Aethelred certainly had a superior claim the throne compared to Edgar's. Maelpeder fled Edgar's realm to seek Aethelred's protection.

Backed by a very large proportion of the Scots people, Aethelred and his son Angus decided to press their claim – and this military adventure came to be known as the Moray Risings. Edgar and his younger brothers were only able to hold on by importing more and more Anglo-Saxons and Normans and Flemish from the realms of the Norman kings of England.

During their reigns, Edgar, Alexander and David also introduced feudalism. What this meant was that parcels of land could be made smaller and smaller – an earl need not control a whole province – so he was able to reward more and more lackeys, even foreign ones; and it gave the king more and more control, for feudal lands were held directly from the king and during the king's pleasure even if they could be passed on to future generations provided that the earls behaved well. So land was feudalised at any opportunity (for example whenever there was no heir) and many Mormaerdoms vanished in a short period of time. I urge the reader not to believe those who would tell you that there is no difference between an earl and a mormaer.

4. 1130 – Exhaustion

The Moraymen were on a hiding to nothing. Every time they got beaten they lost men, but King David (for by now it was he) who was also Earl of Huntingdon essentially had limitless support from England and, via England, from the continent. It all came to a head in 1130 at Stracathro, two miles south of Edzell where the Moraymen were beaten soundly in a battle in which Mormaer Angus himself was killed (we do not know when his father died). Angus' heir was his nephew Duncan who was still a minor, so it was his uncle Gillemichael, another of Angus' brothers who took charge of negotiating a peace with King David. Here are the terms agreed:

- The rightful Mormaer of Moray would become the Earl of Fife, but he would hold his land "by the Grace of God"
- The Earls of Fife would have the right to crown the kings of Scotland.
- The Earl of Fife would have the right to bear King Malcolm III's arms undifferenced.
- The Earl of Fife would have the right to lead the right wing in the Scots army
- The Earl would operate the Sanctuary at MacDuff's cross, Abernethy (see below)
- In exchange for this the Earl gave up any claim to the throne for himself or his descendants.

It is worth pausing here to consider the implications of some of these items of agreement

By the Grace of God

Who is authorised to validate the rule of a monarch? In Old Norse society it was often done by acclaim; in the modern day UK that right has been usurped by the church, supposedly acting on behalf of God. The time we are discussing was a transition time in Scotland. It had been the Derbhfine – the group of people who could claim to be within five generations of a former king who would, in effect elect the next king from within their own number. It was at least echoing this practice that had been the basis upon which Donalbane and indeed Edmund had become kings. On the other hand, particularly from Malcolm II the kings themselves were looking to male line primogeniture (and, in due course, willing to look to the (Catholic) church to support this).

Here we can see that the king was acknowledging that it was God who had installed the Earls of Fife in place – and so woe betide any mortal (including any king) who should challenge their position. At least in theory the Earl was not a vassal of the king.

Crowning the King

Many readers will be familiar with the Ceremony of the Keys in Edinburgh. When the King arrives in Edinburgh the Lord Provost will present "his" keys to the City of Edinburgh to him. He then has a think about it and decides that the Lord Provost is the person best placed to look after them for him and so (re-) consigns them to his keeping.

So too with the coronation. The right to crown the king is saying "I am really the king, but I am authorising you to carry out my functions on my behalf". So this is a reinforcement of the superiority of the Earl over the King.

The Earls' Coat of Arms

1. By accepting that the Earls of Fife had the right to bear Malcolm III's arms undifferenced (ie in their pure and simple form) the King was recognising that the Earl represented the 'senior' line.
   [The Lion Rampant undifferenced are now the arms of Michael Wemyss of Wemyss Castle who descends from Michael, more likely Gillemichael (born c1140), the second son of Earl Duncan I. So (barring any "extramarital event" along the way) he should, therefore, be able to trace his YDNA back to Eystein Glumra, King of Trondheim in Norway in the 800s.]

2. As Mormaers of Moray Aethelred and Angus had borne "or a catamountain rampant gules" (this is my conjecture – but for the rationale see immediately below) a red rampant wildcat on a gold ground. But now they could upgrade as they were entitled to "or a lion rampant gules" in its pure and original form.

3. The wildcat did not disappear – it was 'relegated' to the crest and eventually all the clans in the "Clan Chattan" federation used a wildcat in one pose or another as their crest. [Shaw, 'the mac an Toiseach' and progenitor of the Mackintoshes was a junior son of the Earl Duncan II of Fife. The Mackintoshes also still have the undifferenced Lion Rampant in the pronomial quarter of their arms.]

4. Their plant badge was the Red Whortleberry – which in Gaelic is "fib" the proper Gaelic name for Fife which does appear in charters witnessed by the early earls.

It should be remembered that the original line of the Earls of Fife died out in 1346. Thus the right to bear the undifferenced "Or a Lion Rampant Gules" went sideways via junior lines and now resides with the head of the family of Wemyss. Many other coats of arms have evolved over the years due for example to reflect intermarriage via quartering. Crests often varied to reflect eg an allegiance to a new feudal superior.

[As the reader will know, the Royal coat of Arms is the Lion Rampant surrounded by a "double tressure". This was introduced when Alexander II married Marie de Coucy (as his second wife) in 1239 (the double tressure featured in the de Coucy arms). This made the coat of arms sufficiently different from that of the Earls of Fife that it no longer needed to be "differenced" with a mark of cadency.]

Sanctuary

The concept of Sanctuary is badly misunderstood, because the way it worked evolved so much over a relatively short period of time. I mention this because, for example, the MacDuff entry in the Scottish Clan and Family Encyclopaedia claims that in addition to the privileges agreed above was

> *"the right of sanctuary for all his kinsmen, even for the crime of murder, if they reached the cross near Abernethy, after which a small fine would be levied instead of more severe penalties."*

As it stands this is nonsense.

First we need to recognise that sanctuary was already a tradition of long standing which existed all over Scotland, certainly going back to Pictish – and almost certainly to Druidic, ie pre-Christian – times.

As he toured his domains, part of a king's job was dispensing justice. 'Normal' justice was a rough and ready affair (a good comparison might be with the "wild west" as portrayed in countless films). Local bosses could do more or less whatever they wanted and there was no comeback. 'Due process' was a rarity – all too often what served as convictions were determined on the basis of lies and personal spite; the punishments arbitrary and often grotesquely excessive. Long running feuds resulted in the spilling of copious amounts of blood. Even the Mormaers did not necessarily have the day to day control needed to sort this out.

So the best that could be done was to set up local sanctuaries. If someone could reach such a place they were immune to local law enforcement; they could get a fair hearing in front of the king when he next came to the area, particularly for that purpose. He would hold as fair a trial as was possible and then decide on the punishment; the local population was required to accept the king's decision as final.

So initially the purpose of sanctuary was solely an attempt to ensure a fair trial and a reasonable punishment in the case of conviction. The idea that King David thought it would be OK for a kinsman of an Earl of Fife to get away with murder is nonsensical and the opposite of the purpose of sanctuary.

The point of this right was that the Earls of Fife had the 'royal' right to dispense justice within their 'kingdom' – in other words people living in Fife could not appeal to the king for justice, they had to accept that the Earl had sufficient – and absolute – authority.

Next we should recognise that even in our own times our tabloid newspapers are full of the grieving relatives of murder victims claiming that the sentence of the court was unreasonably lenient. This is the context in which we should see the phrase "small fine". In fact the court-sanctioned payment of "blood money" was a common practice in eg Old Norse society and indeed remains in place in, for example, some Muslim countries to this day. If it is the case that in practice the Earls were especially lenient to close relatives, this too should not really surprise us.

Third we should notice that the text on the cross (to which we no longer have access) was garbled – so much so that it has been translated in several different ways. Chapman says that the text seems to be a mixture of Latin and 'Saxon' – which suggests that it dates to the period after 640, but long before 850. While one translation she cites mentions the name MacDuff, the fact is that that word is not to be found – and, of course, particularly given the date, we should not be surprised. Clearly we should assume that the sanctuary area was fairly large and dates from a time when Abernethy served as the 'capital' of Fife.

[King David I was keen on sanctuaries and spread them widely, especially in the newly acquired parts of Scotland (eg Lothian). He was also very amenable to the increasing powers of the Catholic Church. So all too soon more and more church grounds became sanctuaries – gathering large crowds of miscreants. But the justice system was not up to the task *(plus ça change!)* and the church was not authorised to dispense "justice" in non-ecclesiastical cases, so sanctuaries became chaotic masses of people living there for far too long. The system was not fit for purpose.]

Fife had acquired an ambiguous status. The Earl of Fife held his lands "by the Grace of God", so his lands were a kingdom – and yet he was an Earl and his lands were an integral part of Scotland.

Footnote on Freuchie

In Chapter 12 I noted that Freuchie was most likely a transferred name. The proto-Grants were evicted from what is now Glen Quaich for supporting Edmund and Donalbane against the English-backed king Edgar and his younger brothers. Malpedair (eldest son of the executed Olaf Hemingsson) in particular sought refuge with Aethelred and Angus, the Mormaers of Moray, he and his descendants becoming significant supporters/lieutenants. When Duncan I became Earl of Fife, uncle Gillemichael was settled at Abernethy. Freuchie became the main base for the proto-Grants for some 20 years or so until, with the help and sponsorship of the Earl, they were able to acquire their own estate on the shores of Loch Ness (see SCLLE). [The name Freuchie was later also transferred to both to Stratherrick and then to Strathspey.]

Postscript: The true ancestry of the 'Celtic' Earls of Fife

Aethelred (3rd son of King Malcolm III with his wife St Margaret Atheling) became Mormaer of Moray and had four sons:

Angus	b. c1087	no heirs
Duncan	b. c1090	his son, also Duncan who became 1st Earl of Fife was born 1115

Gillemichael	b. c1093	son Aeth: progenitors of the Abernethy family
Malcolm	b. c1096	successors became Earls of Ross and led MacHeth rebels

Angus: was killed at the Battle of Stracathro (1130) where the Moray Risings ended.

Duncan: too was dead by this time, whether killed in the same battle or earlier. Duncan had had a son, also called Duncan, who was born in 1115. We know Duncan's position in the family because he was described as "the second of that name" (by Lachlan Macintosh reporting to Nisbet for his "System of Heraldry") . Otherwise the assumption would have been that he was Angus' son.

Gillemichael: After the death of Angus and Duncan, Gillemichael was the functioning head of the family until young Duncan came of age. So it was Gillemichael who was responsible for negotiating the agreement with King David I to end the Moray risings. [By this time young Duncan the heir was a teenager, so there would have been plenty of discussion between uncle and nephew.] Gillemichael's status and his commitment is demonstrated by his (post 1130) coat of arms: the same Lion Rampant, but "differenced" by a black ribbon – a mark of 'cadency' to show his junior status.

Gillemichael named his son Aedh – essentially after and in honour of his father (which was the normal thing to do) and the family became the Abernethys. [Lazy writers dismiss Aedh as "Hugh". While it is true that people called Hugh were often referred to as Aedh in the Gàidhealtachd (Gaelic speaking areas) there is no connection between the names.

- Aedh is a bona fide Gaelic name (a variation of Aodh meaning "fire" – Aedan is a diminutive) – albeit in this particular case it was a Gaelicisation of Aethelred.
- Aethelred (Æðelrǽd) is Anglo-Saxon combining the elements éðel meaning 'homeland' and rǽd meaning 'advice'/'wisdom'.
- Hugh derives from the Anglo-Saxon 'hyġe' (and ON 'hugr') meaning "mood, mind, spirit" (compare this with the word 'hug' and modern Danish 'hygge'/'hugge')

This resolves Bannerman's confusion (represented by one set of question marks) on his family tree (p33 chapter "MacDuff of Fife" in Grant and Stringer's 1993 "Mediaeval Scotland: Crown, Lordship and Community").

Malcolm and The Mac(H)Eth rebellions

This leaves Malcolm, who bridled at the agreement. King David tried to assuage him. On the one hand he wanted him out of the way, but on the other hand he did not want to humiliate his nephew. So he made Malcolm Earl of Ross. Unfortunately Malcolm (mac Aedh) was not satisfied; if Gillemichael had abdicated Duncan's and his own rights to the throne this left him, Malcolm, as the claimant (as he saw it) and so thereafter followed the so-called "mac Heth" rebellions. [Malcolm's heirs ended up as the Clan Mackay even farther away from the 'action' in Strathnaver.]

Note: None of these people was "MacDuff" – whether by name or by patrimony! We will come to the family tree from Duncan the 1st Earl later.

Establishment of the "kingdom"

Gillemichael, son of Aethelred, looked after all young Duncan's affairs until he came of age in 1136 – and this included 'running'

Fife once the agreement ending the Moray Risings had been reached in 1130.

Before 1130 there had been Mormaers and Thanes of Fife and locums taking charge, many of whom may have been rendered "Comes" in Latin. But, despite it being a "kingdom", Duncan was the first "Earl" of Fife.

And so it was that Fife became a Kingdom.

Appendix A: Dunfermline Abbey

There are two readily accessible major sources of information here:

- "The Annals of Dunfermline" by Ebernezer Henderson (1879) and
- "Registrum de Dunfermelyn" by Cosmo Innes for the Bannatyne Club (1842)

Fortunately both are online at archive.org.

Controversy has surrounded the foundation of Dunfermline Abbey for many hundreds of years. This is because of its foundation charter, reproduced in the "Annals" (p. 16)

> *"In name of the Holy Trinity, I Malcolm, by the Grace of God, King of Scots, of my Royal authority and power, with the confirmation and testimony of Queen Margaret, my wife, and of the Bishops, Earls, and Barons of my kingdom, the clergy also and the people acquiescing: Let all know, present and future, that I have founded an Abbey on the hill of the Infirm, in honour of God Almighty, and of the Holy and undivided Trinity, for the safety of my own soul and the souls of all my ancestors, and for the safety of the soul of Queen Margaret, my wife, and of all my successors; for I have granted, and by this my Charter confirmed, to the foresaid Abbey, all the lands and town of Pardusin, Pitnaurcha, Pittecorthin, Petbachichin, Laur, Bolgin, and the shire of Kirkaladunt, and Inneresc the Lesser, with the whole of Forthriff and Muselburge, and all*

their pertinents; as well in Chapels, in Tithes, and other oblations; as in all other things justly belonging to these lands, towns, and shires, as freely as any King ever granted or conveyed any gift from the beginning of the world until this day.—Witnesses, Ivo, Abbot of the Culdees; Macduff, Earl; Duncan, Earl; Araldo, Earl; Neis, son of William; Marleswain.

This charter has been widely dismissed as a fake – so much so that on his "Annals of Dunfermline A.D. 1069 – 1878", (John Tweed, Glasgow 1879) Ebenezer Henderson, LL.D sought to address the objections (Annals p709-12). It is hard to say whether Henderson represented the objectors' cases fairly, but his dismissal is supercilious. And one major problem left unaddressed was whether the copy to hand was supposed to be "the" original, or a faithful copy.

There are two unassailable proofs that the charter is a fake.

1. **"Abbey":** Malcolm III is quoted as saying "I have founded an Abbey". Yet in subsequent charters it continued to be referred to as the "Church" of the Holy Trinity. The Annals Appendix J (p723) shows the roll of Abbots – and the first entry dates to 1124. This is a crass mistake on the part of the forger. It was King David I who raised the church to Abbey status.

2. **Witness List:** The problem above is exacerbated by a detailed examination of the witness list:

Ivo, Abbot of the Culdees

I have no information about Ivo. "Ivo" is a Norman form of name rather than a Gaelic (or Brythonic) one. There was a handful of Norman knights in Scotland from 1052 (when they were expelled from Edward the Confessor's court), but there was no reason for any of them to espouse Culdee ways and certainly no time for any of their number to have risen to the rank of Abbot less than a generation later.

However the Worcester Chronicle under the year 600 says: "Ivo the apostolic doctor and truly an ambassador from heaven and a renowned prelate, died; born like the Star from the East, in Persia, he was destined by God for the Western limits of Britain" Clearly this Ivo was a Catholic and very much not a Culdee.

The problem is that I do not think that the forgers would have simply plucked the name out of thin air. So we may suppose that at some time there probably was someone called Ivo who was the Abbot, but we do not know when. As the Culdees were more and more oppressed and contained by the Catholic church, it could easily be that an Abbot Ivo was imposed upon them – but clearly not in 1075 or any time soon thereafter.

Earl MacDuff

- Malcolm III came to a Scotland which did not recognise the title "Earl". The only real title below King was Mormaer and there was the salaried title Thane (which was normally not hereditary). Malcolm was careful not to appoint foreigners to too high a rank – he appointed his brothers and some of his sons as Mormaers; the one notable half-exception to this was Maelpeder mac Olaf/ Aulay who was made Mormaer of the Mearns (as noted in a previous chapter) but his entrée was via marriage to the daughter of the Mormaer of Angus. Earldoms were introduced to replace mormaerdoms as part of the process

of feudalisation which actually started under Edgar (so post 1095), gathering pace under David I.
- As we have seen in a previous chapter there was no MacDuff as Thane of Fife, never mind his being an Earl (but for earls called MacDuff see next chapter).
- The ancestor of the Earls of Fife who slew Macbeth was Malcolm III himself.

Earl Duncan

In the case of Fife, the first Earl was indeed called Duncan, but his appointment dates to 1130 – the end of the Moray Risings (see previous chapter), and he was a minor at the time – only coming of age in 1136. So if he were a proper signatory to this charter it would need to be after that date. This Duncan (I) Earl of Fife died in 1154 – so again it is likely that the 'charter' dates to a time when details about him were already long forgotten – ie at least well into the 1200s (his son, also Duncan, did not die until 1203).

And then, of course, there is the problem that there seem to be two people simultaneously being Earl of Fife!

Earl Harald

The only potential candidate is Harald Maddadarson, Earl of Orkney and Mormaer of Atholl. His dates are c1134-1206 (so not an adult until 1155). His father was Maddad (variously Matad), Earl of Atholl. There is good reason to suppose that it is this Harald who is intended – the reason being that Maddad himself ("Madeth Comes") is a signatory to the first of the accepted charters in the Dunfermline Register.

Neis son of William

There was no-one in Scotland called William before the Norman conquest of England; the first Scot of that name was

William the Noble, who was born in the period 1090-1094 and who was later to become Earl of Moray. His father was King Duncan II. Given his birth epoch his (illegitimate) son Neis (who was made Lord of Leuchars) could not have been born before 1105 – more likely some time after 1110 – and was not an adult until after 1126 (likely 1135). So the 'charter' could not have been written until Ness had been dead so long that the forgers had forgotten his dates – this suggests a time substantially after 1200.

Merleswein

This is a potentially credible witness. We noted in the last chapter a Merleswein who had been Sheriff of Lincoln – a major noble in England – before 1066; he came to Scotland 1068 with the other refugee nobles who had rebelled against William the Conqueror. There were other later Merlesweins – presumably descended from him including a son of Colban who was infeft with Ardross, Fife in 1173; in the 1170s he gave the church in Kennoway to St Andrews; he had a son also called Merleswein.

Conclusions

(i) We may assert categorically that the Charter is indeed a forgery

(ii) The discussion of the errors points to a date no earlier than 1200, with the strong likelihood for it to be much later.

(iii) At the time of the forgery the name MacDuff was already in circulation.

(iv) We cannot rely on the spelling of Kirkcaldy here as reliably "original".

Why the forgery?

In the earliest 'reliable' charter in the Dunfermline Register, dating to around 1130, King David confirms gifts made by his parents

(King Malcolm III and Queen Margaret who both died in 1093) and by his brother Duncan (who died in 1094) and other brothers – but they were to a church, not an abbey. These gifts would have been made using charters to these effects. So if this is the case, why would the monks want to lie to add less than another maximum 20 years to their existence? It makes no good sense.

Fortunately, the Annals of Dunfermline come to our rescue, for under the years 1303 and 1304 is recorded:

> *1303 EDWARD I., KING OF ENGLAND, with his Court, arrive in Dunfermline.—There is a discrepancy in the accounts of some early historians regarding the month and day of Edward's arrival in Dunfermline on the "expedition of his." Langtoft's Chronicle, p. 332, and Tytler's History of Scotland, vol. i. p. 201, give 6th November, 1303, as the day and month of his arrival, while Hailes, in his Annals of Scotland, vol. i. p. 275, quoting from Prynne and Rymer, &c., gives 11th December, 1303. We think the first the correct date, because it will be seen by next entry that Edward, on 5th December (six days before the 11th), gave a donation to the Boy-Bishop enactment. So far as we have been able to ascertain, this visit is the fourth one of Edward to Dunfermline: the first, in 1291, the second and third, in 1296; and the fourth, in 1303.*
>
> *1304.—DUNFERMLINE MONASTERY BURNED!—King Edward I. of England, after a sojourn of ninety-seven days in the Monastery of Dunfermline, with his retinue of courtiers, took his departure, early on the morning of February 10th, for Cambuskenneth, when he gave orders to destroy the Monastery by fire. This barbarous order was obeyed, and*

in a few hours the magnificent Monastery, and adjacent buildings on the east, were a heap of smoking ruins.

1306.—CHARTULARY, or Register of the Abbey, which appears to have been much neglected for a long series of years, begins this year to have more frequent entries, probably on account of the coronation of King Robert the Bruce, and an anticipated settled state of public affairs. It appears singular how this MS. Register was prevented from falling into Edward's hands.

Conclusion

We should suppose that the fake founding Charter was written in 1305 or 6 and that this was done to recreate/replace the original which had been stolen or burned in the course of King Edward's depredations. Even the senior monks in place at the time had little idea of who would have witnessed the original, so they plucked names out of the air that seemed reasonable.

In short it was a forgery, but in so far as this is possible it was an 'honest' forgery. Those who fabricated it had no intention to deceive. All they were seeking to do was to try to ensure the enforcement of their historical rights in the new political environment following the chaos of the last several years and the senseless destruction at King Edward's instructions.

Postscript

1. The Kirkcaldy Seal

Dunfermline Abbey has been remodelled extensively over the years. However the "Shire" of Kirkcaldy was a part of the estates which supported it. The town seal was designed to represent the abbey.

2. Fothriff

The first thing to say is that there is a very important error in the translation – an error caused by lack of attention to detail on the part of Cosmo Innes.

Henderson says "…the whole of Forthriff…"
while the Latin text (Annals p 15) says "tota schira de fothriff".

This is very important: Fothriff is called a "shire" (to be compared with eg Kirkcaldy and, perhaps bizarrely Goatmilk, now part of Glenrothes). [This is to be contrasted with a "burgo" such as Dunfermline or St Andrews.]

Here are the subsequent references in the charters:

Charter #	Registrum page	Entry extract
27	15	Cain from "fif & fothrif & de Clacmanan"
28	16	"fif & de fothrif"
35	20	"fif & de fothrif"
50	29	"fif & de fothrif"
74	41	"de fif & de fotha"
81	47	"fyf & de fotheryf" "pochiam tota fotheref"
237	152	"fif & de fothif" "Totam pochiam de fothif"
274	175	"fif & fothif"
376	259	"de ffyf & de ffothryf"

From these entries we may note that:

- Fothriff is described as a "parish" (p'ochiam = parochiam). [Parishes did not exist under the Columban system so only began to be introduced certainly after 1055, in earnest really only after 1070, and taking some time to roll out.]
- Fothriff is mentioned in connection with Fife and with Clackmannan.

I hope that the reader will see that this is fully consistent with the proposition I offered in the chapter about the Romanisation of the early 700s..

Nevertheless Henderson (Annals p 2,3) says:

> *There still remains a name of doubtful origin, viz., "Fothriff," sometimes spelt "Fothric," "Fothrick," "Patrick," &c. This name covered a very large extent of country, stretching from the mouth of the Leven to some miles above Alloa in length, and from the Forth to the base of the Ochils in breadth, thus comprehending within its area the greater part of the counties of Kinross and Clackmannan, and the whole of what is now known as the "Western District of Fife." (For etymology, &c., see local histories of Dunfermline and of Fife; also Appendix to "Annals of Dunfermline" This territory, or a certain division of it, was bestowed on the Church of the Holy Trinity (the Abbey), at the time of its erection {circa, 1070-1080). In some old [p3] works, Dunfermline Abbey is represented as standing in Patrick Muir.*
>
> *In conclusion, the Forth, about the beginning of the Christian era, and for a great length of time afterwards, appears to have been known as the "Sea of Bodotria" which name was succeeded by that of 'Scotwater," and afterwards by "Phorth," "Firth of Forth," &c., which last*

appellation it has retained for at least these 900 years past.

I hope the reader will see how crass this analysis is.

The Firth of Forth

Before getting into the substance let us deal with his last paragraph which is largely irrelevant nonsense.

"Sea of Bodotria" is from Ptolemy and is a scribal error for "Sea of Godotria" – ie the Gododdin/Godoðin/Votadini's sea – which would be a natural name to give it. Cramond was established as a base by Agricola because it was already in friendly – ie Gododdin – territory. The fact that the Romans gave it this name tells us nothing about what the Maeatae may have called it (just as the name "English Channel" tells us nothing about why the French call it "La Manche").

We know that in the 600s it was known to the Angles (as recorded by Bede and others) as "Sea of Iudeu" or "Sea of Giudi". It had this name because of the strategic importance of Blackness. This variation in spelling tells us that this was not an Anglic invention, but rather the name being used by the Gododdin at the time the Angles overwhelmed them (638). While this also makes clear that this was a Pictish language name, it does not tell us what the Picts themselves called the Firth.

The name "Scotwater" is an English language name, hence applied by the Angles, and could only become relevant once the Scots had a presence on the north shore – ie after 850. However It would be useless as a term after the Battle of Carham (1018) because as a result of that battle that time Scots controlled both shores as well as so many other firths, so this would not be a helpful name.

The River Forth

We must start by noting the general case that many rivers have – or have had – different names for different stretches of their length (as discussed in different contexts in previous chapters). In different cases these names can 'migrate' in different ways until in recent times, particularly with the development of accurate mapping, map makers have chosen which name to apply to the whole course.

In the case of the Firth of Forth we need to understand why the River Forth should have taken precedence over other rivers draining into it – eg the River Teith and even the Allan Water. The whole of the Forth/Teith valley was a giant bog with very few routes through it. One famous route centres on the Fords of Frew (near Kippen). The word "ford" comes from the Welsh "ffyrdd" (say 'forth') meaning 'road' or 'route', so I suspect that the river took its name from this crossing point.

On the other hand Wikipedia tells us that the River Forth takes its name from Proto-Celtic (ie Pictish or even earlier!) **Vo-rit-ia* (slow running), which Gaels may have rendered as *Foirthe.* However when the Scots came along they called at least one stretch Abhain Dhu – the Black River.

Whatever the etymology, the clear implication is that the Firth was already recognised as the estuary of this river before the Scots took over – ie before 850, making a nonsense of the reference to 'Scotwater' as "the" name to anyone but Angles.

So why was 'Forth' preferred over "Teith" or, indeed "Alan" for the firth? The answer is probably simple: the establishment of the Lennox in 498 left the Britons of Strathclyde in command of the bulk of the Campsie and Kilsyth Hills. For nearly another 200 years places like Myot Hill were in Maeatae territory rather than Pictish territory as such. Because of the lie of the land, the River Forth therefore acted as the de facto southern boundary of Pictland even if at least in theory the foothills at Gargunnock and Kippen were in their territory. So there is a logic in continuing that name into the Firth.

I think that the purpose of Henderson's paragraph was examine a possible link between the name Fothriff and the name of the River Forth – indeed on occasion Fothriff was written as 'Forthriff' etc.

Back to Fothriff

First of all he proposes that Fothriff is no mere "parish", but covers more than half the county of Fife! So we may dismiss this out of hand. It is ridiculous to suppose a single parish of this size. So too with "Schyres" of this date – indeed the Shyres of Kirkcaldy and Goatmilk seem to lie within it!

The cause of the misunderstanding is easy to discern: with the development of abbeys and cathedrals all over Scotland, funds were needed to support them. All too soon, but not before a Catholic Church structure had been established, much of the lands of Fothriff were alienated to support this building project elsewhere – which is why Culross and Tulliallan parishes were actually exclaves of Perthshire until local government reorganisation in 1891.

The problem was that the church in Fife was already organised with Fothriff as one important income stream – a Deanery. So small parcels of land all over the county became a virtual church "schyre" in the sense that the funds from these places were funnelled into the stream which Fothriff had provided previously. What Henderson and indeed others to this day have done is to see these small scattered parcels of land and assumed that they must all have been geographically contiguous - and because they are clearly not, that all the intervening land must also have been part of Fothriff. But this is not the case.

There is an exact parallel with the way a computer stores memory. As amendments and additions take place over time, a large file cannot be stored in one unit - so what appears to the user as one file is in fact stored all over the place in small packets - which is why 'defragmentation' and compacting of such files is a good thing to do from time to time.

More than 30 years ago the idea that Fothriff was, frankly, more than half of Fife had already been shown to be even more risible by Ian B Cowan, who died in 1990 ("The Medieval Church in Scotland" (Ed: James Kirk) 1995 p152) who says, regarding a reorganisation of deaneries, that

> "These deaneries... were known as Atholl and Drumalban, Angus and Fife, Fothriff and Strathearn, and their first deans were apparently appointed on 22nd April 1505."

Conclusions

1. The name Fothriff has the etymology I have proposed
2. The original Fothriff was one contiguous piece of land as I proposed.
3. The church in Fife found it convenient to maintain its existing financial structure after Fothriff had been Balkanised and much of the funds it was generating re-allocated (eg to Dunblane).
4. What more modern scholars have been wrestling with is the virtual structure rather than the real one. This has nothing directly to do with the Fothriff referred to in the charters we have been examining.

3. PATRICK MUIR

Henderson says (above):

> *In some old works, Dunfermline Abbey is represented as standing in Patrick Muir.*

[NB This has nothing to do with Pattiesmuir, shown on old maps as Pettymuir.]

Here Henderson seems to be trying to see whether the name Fothriff may be a corruption of "Patrick Muir". No... Precisely the same argument applies to Patrick Muir as applied in the case of Kirkcaldy Old Kirk, dedicated to St Patrick probably soon after 850 which then had St Bryce superimposed when it was fully incorporated into the Catholic structure in 1244. The name Patrick Muir suggests that there was a church here, established some time after 850 – it may well have been the church in which Malcolm III and Margaret were married. It would be unsurprising, given that it was Margaret who drove the building of the new church, then, that no trace of the old building would be left. Indeed we may even speculate more about the difference. Into the 1500s many churches were still wooden structures. If St Patrick's Church, Dunfermline were built in this manner, of course it would be taken down to make way for a stone built structure. Conversely if the original Old Kirk in Kirkcaldy had been built of stone reused from the Caer y Caledy, then rededication rather than demolition would be the logical and economical thing to do.

4. THE CULDEES

Margaret and subsequent kings wanted to suppress the Culdees as a separate and potentially hostile faction (necessary if Catholicism were to become "the" faith), but they did not want to be seen to attack them for fear of fomenting unrest.

So on the contrary the early charters specify that the gifts made must not impinge on the existing rights of any Culdee establishment(s).

Considerably later than the raising of the church at Dunfermline to Abbey status, the Culdees at Abernethy were corralled and neutralised, becoming a chapter of canons in St Andrews cathedral; much of the revenue from the lands they had held was diverted to support the building of Arbroath Abbey. So we may take the inclusion of the witness "Ivo, Abbot of the Culdees" as implying that there had been Culdees in the areas from which Dunfermline Abbey drew its revenue – and this is probably Culross. Conversely given that we understand "Patrick Muir" correctly then we may be confident that the Culdees were in Culross and not in Dunfermline until the Abbey was established.

There is no reason for any Culdee to have been involved in the foundation of the church of the Holy Trinity, but by 1306 there was very good reason for the Culdees to be seen to have been on board with the foundation of the Abbey, especially if they had been or still were – now an integral part of it.

The foundation charter was fabricated well after the Abernethy Culdees had been absorbed by St Andrews and we may imagine that the Culdees at Culross had by this time been absorbed similarly. We noted above the problem with the name "Ivo" which is clearly of Norman rather than Gaelic or Pictish origin. It may be that the name of the Abbot who had been imposed upon these Culdees to manage them into subjugation was called Ivo but that he belongs to a period some generations after the foundation.

Appendix B: Confecting the Macduff myth

1. Foreword

In Chapter 14 the true story about the Thane of Fife was set out, thereby refuting the story of "Macduff" so now we know the real person around whom who the tale was built. In this appendix I explain how why and when the myth was confected.

2. Why we are still talking about it

It was the late John Bannerman of Edinburgh University who breathed new life into the lies about "Macduff" in his chapter "MacDuff of Fife" in Grant and Stringer's 1993 "Mediaeval Scotland: Crown, Lordship and Community". Bannerman's proposition was heavily acknowledged and learnt upon by Alison Chapman in a booklet "MacDuff, Thane of Fife: History and Legend" published by Fife Council in 1997. The result is that the internet is awash with pages mindlessly rehearsing the nonsense.

Even by the turn of the new millenium, Dr Michael Brown, then of St Andrews University, knew that it was all wrong. But seeking perfection did not publish on the matter before I came to my own general conclusions in SCLLE. He did publish in 2011 (see quotation below). However in this chapter I have extended the study much more deeply.

3. Recapitulation

In earlier chapters we have seen that:

1. King Kenneth mac Alpin placed both Fife and Angus in the responsibility of the Cenel Angus when he replaced the local kings after he had murdered them (c850).
2. The Mormaer of Fife sought the protection of Canute because he feared King Malcolm II. Unfortunately for him this was ineffective and by c1030 there was a "vacancy".
3. There was a Thane of Fife in Macbeth's time – he was King Duncan I's brother-in-law (so he was King Malcolm III's uncle) and his name was Siward. He was killed in battle in 1054.
4. It was King Malcolm III who actually killed Macbeth and indeed Lulach (in 1057 and 1058).
5. The Heraldry by itself is enough to prove that the Earls of Fife descended from Aethelred, the third of King Malcolm III's children with Margaret Atheling. With the death of his elder brother Edward and the abdication of his other elder brother Edmund, neither of whom had children, Aethelred's line was the senior one if the matter is to be judged by male line primogeniture and if Malcolm's sons with Ingibjorg were to be discounted. However the claim to the throne which this position in the pedigree supported was renounced in 1130.
6. King Malcolm II had ensured the succession of his grandson King Duncan I by murdering anyone with a viable claim. Had there been anyone if the sort of lineage claimed by believers in the "MacDuff" legend that person would have been murdered before 1034.
7. A new vacancy arose in Fife when Aethelred was posted to Moray. This was probably when Maelsnectan died – in 1085 – when Aethelred would have been about 15. The fact that his wife was twice his age was neither here nor there – a 15 year age gap is not very remarkable even today and she was still very fertile. And in any case this was a dynastic matter.

3.1 Examining the "Evidence" for the fake legend

When all the romanticised wittering about "knidreds" is set to one side, Alison Chapman cites just three items of evidence. She says:

- Dufagan, supposed to be the Earl of Fife signed the Charter of Scone Priory in 1114
- Constantine, son of Dufagan died in 1129
- Gillemichael MacDuff witnessed the foundation Charter of Holyrood Abbey in 1128. He died in 1139
- A grandson of King Dubh is labelled "Mac Duff" when really he was "mac Kenneth (III)".

To this we may add from Bannerman:

- Constantine Earl of Fife, Chief Justice of Scotland arbitrated a case in 1128.

And now to the facts (See "Early Scottish Charters" by Sir Archibald Lawrie (1905)):

- In the Charter dating to 1114x20 Dufagan is described as "Earl". There is no reference to Fife.
- Gillemichael is described as "Earl" in the 1128 Charter. There is no mention of Fife or of MacDuff.
- Even if we accept that Constantine was the son of Dufagan the only "evidence" that he died is that a Gillemichael was in charge of affairs in Fife from 1130.
- Bannerman's reference is accurate.

The term "Earl" is problematic here. It is really a translation of the Latin 'comes' which could mean Mormaer.

What Bannerman (and so Chapman) did was to take a handful of facts and force them into a pre-conceived scenario that they wanted to be true. In order to do this they ignored the heraldry and scattered the name "MacDuff" about on no basis at all.

3.2 True Ancestry of Duncan the 1st Earl of Fife

This has been set out in detail in the postscript to chapter 13.

3.3 Mormaers of Angus

Because Angus and Fife were both part of the Cenel Angus, they were expected to help each other out in the case of any trouble – or gap in the leadership. In broad terms the kings of Scots would have expected this. And we have noted that Malcolm II did not attempt to make Siward a "Mormaer" – he remained a Thane only. Thus if the problem was in Fife then it would be to Angus that the king would turn for a 'locum'.

[The one previous exception had been when Malcolm II made Crinan Mormaer of Atholl – but even then Atholl was in the "Royal" Cenel Ghabrain, so it could be argued that he was not out of line even here.]

Unfortunately the line of the Mormaers of Angus is patchy. At the very least we know of one who escaped the attention of the author of the relevant Wikipedia page (November 2022). He was called Sinill (variously Sinhil) and his daughter, Finngualla, married King Lulach. The Chronicle of the Kings of Alba notes the death of Dubucan mac Indechtraig in 937.

In attempting to reconstruct the early line of the Mormaers I have followed the normal "average" 25 year inter-generational gap which works as a general guide. In the case of Indechtraig I suppose that Dubucan will have delayed marriage, taking (she will have had no choice in the matter) a daughter of the previous Pictish incumbent to bind in the subsequent line. So too there is no reason to suppose that Finnguala was the eldest of Sinhill's children. From such sources as we have we may reconstruct the early generations. The bold entries are those attested one way or another elsewhere. I have interpolated the others.

Name	Birth Era	Death Era
Dubucan I	820	890
Indechtraig	850	915
Dubucan II	875	**937**
	900	
Dubucan III	925	
Conchar	950	**995**
Dubucan III	975	
Sinhill	1000	1050
Finnguala	**1030**	

"Conchar" (variously Conchúr) is a variant of "Conchob(h)ar" – a normal Gaelic name including that of several kings.

Sinhill looks like a representation of the Cinhill we find at the start of the pedigree of the Strathclyde kings which is a rendition of the Roman name Quintilian.

What is proposed here is that Dubucan I was the senior representative of the Cenel Angus who, at the peak of his young adult powers, was (perhaps with his father) one of Kenneth mac Alpine's lieutenants in the conquest of Pictland. His reward was Angus (which at that time included the Mearns). As he was the progenitor it is unsurprising that we should find his name or variations (eg Duff and Dufagan) of it repeating down the generations. Dubucan/Dufagan is a diminutive/pet form of Dubh/Duff.

Subsequent generations: Mystery surrounds the death of Sinhill, so my working hypothesis is that he was amongst the casualties at Dunsinane Hill in 1054.

Gen	Name	Birth Era	Fife Locum	Angus Mormaer from	Death Era
0	Sinill	1000			1054?
1	"Duff" Finghuala	1025 1030	 (m. Lulach)		c1095
2	Dufagan Geirmunda	1050 c1065	1085-<1095 (m. Malpeadar)		<1120
3	Gillemichael Constantine	1075 1078	1095-<1120 c1120-1130	<1120	1139
4	"Dufagan" Ete	1100 1098	 (m. Gartnait)	1139	?1148
5	Gillebrigte	1125		?1148	1187
6	Adam Gillechrist	c1150 c1155		1187 1189	1189 <1206

[By the time of the end of this table we are well beyond our timeframe for the genesis of Fife as a Kingdom and we are in any case entering the era in which the regular records can take over.]

1. "Duff": born c 1025 Sinhill's son (we do not know his name, hence the quotes).
    - He becomes Mormaer of Angus on the death of his father c1054
    - He continues in post until he dies about 1095
    - [His daughter Geirmunda (b. c1065) married Malpeadar mac Aulay.]

2. Dufagan: born c 1050 Sinhill's grandson.
   - In 1085 (aged 35) he is called as locum 'Earl of Fife' when Aethelred moves to Moray
   - In 1095 (aged 45) he relinquishes Fife to take over from his father as Mormaer of Angus
   - In 1114 (aged 64) as Mormaer of Angus he witnesses the foundation of Scone Priory.
   - He has died by 1120 (when he would have been 70)

3. Dufagan had two sons:

3(a) Gillemichael mac Duf(agan) born c1074

- In 1095 (aged 21) he takes over from his father as locum 'Earl of Fife'
- In 1120 (aged 46) he succeeds his father as Mormaer of Angus
- In 1128 (aged 54) as Mormaer he witnesses the foundation of Holyrood Abbey
- He dies in 1139 aged 65

3(b) Constantine mac Duf(agan) born c 1078

- In 1120 (aged 42) he takes over from his brother as locum "Earl" of Fife
- (1128/9?) Defends Kirkcaldy by force from Dunfermline Abbey
- 1128 (aged 50) he is also Chief Justice of Scotland
- In 1130 (aged 52) he relinquishes Fife in favour of Duncan.
- There is no reason to suppose an early death for him.

4. Two problems resolved

4.1 Three contemporary Gillemichaels

We can see that one basis for confusion is the existence of three broadly contemporary Gillemichaels.

- One was the son of Aethelred Mormaer of Moray – patriarch of the Abernethy family (his son was "Aedh" variously "Hugh").
- A second was the second son of Dufagan, Mormaer of Angus;
- The third was the second son of Earl Duncan I, patriach of the Wemyss family (his sons were "Big John" of Methil and Duncan)

So it would be all too easy for someone who had not looked at the matter carefully to assume that any two of these were one and the same person. But this was not the case. Thus the (Angus line locum) Gillemichael who witnesses Holyrood in 1128 is not the same as the (Moray line guardian) Gillemichael 'comite de Fif' who witnesses a Dunfermline Charter c1133 who was standing in for his nephew Duncan.

4.2 Rogue Charter

There is one outstanding problem: There is a charter purporting to date from 1095 (#15 ESC p12) in which "king" Edgar gives his "mansio" of Berwick (ie including several surrounding villages) to the monks of Durham. This is the charter in which Constantine is called son of "Magdufe". However Lawrie calls the Charter "spurious". It is bizarre that Edgar is already claiming to be King of Scots. Given that at this time his older brother Edmund was a king, Edgar had no claim whatsoever – so it is very hard to see any basis for him even to make such a claim.

There is another bit of a giveaway with this charter. The substance of the text starts "Ego, Edgarus…" in other words "I, Edgar…" throughout the charter there are references to "my…" relatives etc. However when it comes to the signatures, the text reads "Signum Edgari Regis, Signum Alexandri fratris ejus" – "HIS" brother!! Given the "Ego" really it should have been "fratris mei".

Despite this problem there is, as we have seen, a potential way in which Constantine could have been "mac mhic Duibh" – so this need not concern us and certainly does not interrupt the flow of the narrative.In short we may accept the general view that this charter is spurious and suppose the fabrication to date to a time when the Macduff myth had already gained currency.

Summary

This extended treatment is designed to show that the alternative scenario I propose here is entirely consistent with all the facts such as we know them and is a far more elegant explanation than that proposed by Bannerman and Chapman.

5. Line of the Earls of Fife

So now I hope that the confusion about the ancestry of the Earls of Fife has been made clear, we can consider the family tree of the Earls themselves – and it has been quite a complex matter to sort out! The reader is warned that the Wikipedia pages (accessed November 2022) about these people are mostly a disaster, but unfortunately the contributors mostly have nonsense to draw on.

Here is my revised pedigree of the Earls with their birth and death dates:

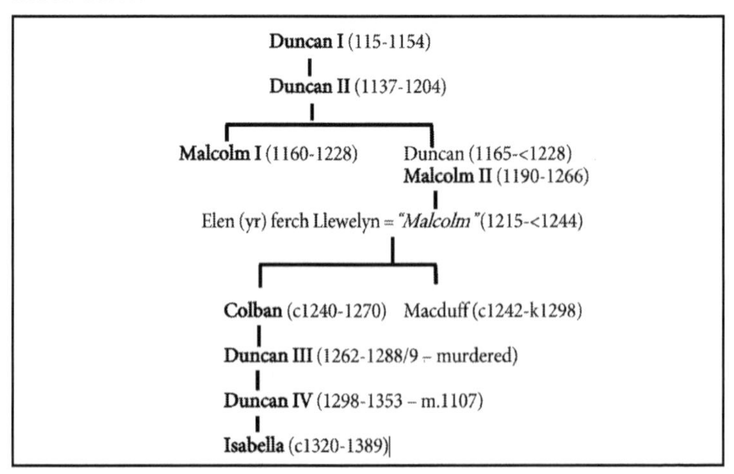

Notes

Earl Duncan IV: was born posthumously to his father in 1289 and married in 1307 when still a minor. His wife was Mary de Monthermer (b 1297), a granddaughter of king Edward I through his daughter Joan of Acre (who was Gilbert de Clare's 2nd wife). They were not to have a child until 1320.

Earl Duncan III succeeded when only 8 years old – making his birth epoch 1262. He will be discussed below. He married Joan (1264 – 1302<) daughter of Gilbert de Clare 7th Earl of Gloucester (from his 1st marriage) making him King Edward I's step grandson.

Errr… so Earl Duncan IV was his father's step-brother-in-law as well as being his son!

Earl Colban: Ludicrous claims have been made that Colban was only born in 1247x53, making him potentially just 9 years old when he fathered his son Duncan III and 11 when he was knighted (by Alexander III in 1264)! Clearly Colban must have been born before 1241, but given the family tradition almost certainly not long before. We shall rely on Matthew Hammond for telling us that his wife was Anna a daughter of Alan Durward,

Isabella (not shown in the table above) wife of John Comyn, 3rd Earl of Buchan (c1260-1308). The Wikipedia page tells us that she was the daughter of Duncan IV. Had this been true her dates would have been born c1285, married c1300. But this is ridiculous. Clearly Isabella was the daughter of Colban – so born c1265, married c1280 – and a sister of Duncan III. This then makes more sense of her arriving a day too late to crown Robert Bruce in 1306 (the ceremony was repeated). Her nephew, Earl Duncan IV would have been only 17 at the time.

Earl Malcolm II must have been old enough to succeed his uncle, so born before 1207, with the 1190 date above being far more likely.

Elen and her husband: Elen was the daughter of Llywellyn the Great ap Iorwerth (1173-1240). There is some doubt as to whether or not her mother was his wife Joan (an illegitimate daughter of King John of England). If so she had an older full sister of the same name and a full sister in Gwladus Ddu. Gladys Ddu means "Black Gladys" so we can see that dark colouring was in the family. This is why her children were called Colban ("black leg") and Macduff ("son of the black one").

It is reported that after the death of Earl Malcolm II, Elen married Donald I Earl of Mar. Something does not add up. She had 5 children with Donald. Their eldest, Gartnait, had a daughter Margaret b 1270, so Gartnait must have been born before 1249, probably born c1245. This means that Elen could not have been married to Earl Malcolm II because he did not die until 1266! Not only that, but she must have had her two Fife sons before 1243 and her husband must have died by 1244.

Correction: *"Malcolm"*: To solve the problems above I have interpolated an extra "*Malcolm*". Given the lack of records it is easy for anyone to conflate two successive Malcolms. Not only that but Elen must have married the younger *"Malcolm"*, making her birth date likely 1225 (and this agrees with the Welsh family tree).

MacDuff, brother of Colban

I doubt that the name Colban actually meant that the earl had a black leg – rather the name would have been given both because of its appropriateness due to his complexion and because it was already a name in circulation amongst the aristocracy (there had been, for example, a Colban Earl of Buchan). Macduff was given his name because he was the son of a very dark woman.

This then supports the claim of Dr Michael Brown of St Andrews University (in "Aristocratic Politics and the Crisis of Scottish Kingship, 1286–96" in *The Scottish Historical Review*, Volume XC, 1: No. 229: April 2011, p18n) who says:

> There remains a debate around the name of Macduff. Bannerman argues that it was a title denoting headship of the kindred of the earls of Fife, referred to in the fourteenth century as *Clenmcduffe*. This role may have entitled the holder to legal and military authority over the kindred. In the absence of an adult earl, Macduff may have held this role. Rather than a name, he was '*MacDuib* of Fife'. However, the absence of any name for him except Macduff, and the uniform references to him by this term in narratives and official records, both Scottish and English, makes it less likely that it was not a personal name
> (Bannerman, 'Macduff of Fife', in Grant and Stringer (eds), *Medieval Scotland*, 20–38).

The minute anyone does the sums, one realises just how stupid too many of the assertions made about the Earls and their families have been. We don't know about the wives of Duncan and his son Earl Malcolm II because when they married no-one had any idea how important they would become and so the facts were not recorded. Probably their wives were not from very important families.

6. Why and how the 'MacDuffs' faked their history

So now we have a clear understanding of the family of the Earls, we can go on to consider why they faked their history and "whodunit?". At what point would the Earls of Fife want to retain the claim that it was their ancestor who killed Macbeth, but to deny that that ancestor was King Malcolm III? Had there been hard evidence there would not have been all the speculation and rival propositions. So we have no option but to resort to hopefully informed speculation.

6.1 Narrowing the window

Let us try a bit of triangulation.

(a) After 1266

Surely we must be confident that Earl Malcolm I, grandson of the first earl would not have entertained any nonsense of this sort, so we can impose another date – 1228. So too not only is there no reason for Earl Malcolm II to make anything up. On the contrary, given the way he was able to arrange such a powerful marriage for his son *"Malcolm"*, he would be emphasising his royal connections.

(b) Before 1298

The first mention of MacDuff in history is that recorded by John of Fordun writing around 1380. Had John been aware of any fakery, surely he would not have recorded it as true, so the story must have predated him. Earl Duncan IV had only died 25 years earlier and his daughter Isabella, born c1320, was still alive. There was no good reason for Isabella to perpetuate a lie that she was aware of and given that she was 30 years old when her father died surely she would have been privy to any family secret that he might have known. So our first conclusion must surely be that the fakery pre-dated 1298 (the death of Macduff) .

(c) Before 1289

We have seen that the "Foundation Charter" for Dunfermline Abbey was faked around 1306. So where did the monks get the idea to include "MacDuff" from? It can only have come from Duncan IV or a representative – and this then closes the window by another ten years because by this time Earl Duncan IV was not old enough to have made it up himself. So the fabrication must pre-date him.

Thus we can pin the fakery on Earl Duncan III.

6.2 The Earl and Tides in Scottish Politics

Selected Contemporary Scottish Annals

We now need to understand what was going on in Scottish politics during the key period.

1241: Birth of the future King Alexander III (KAIII)
1249: KAIII (age 7) becomes king on the death of his father
1251: KAIII (age 10) marries Margaret, daughter of King Henry III of England
1261: 1st child (Margaret) born to KAIII
1262: KAIII comes of age.
1263: (Oct) Battle of Largs
1264: (Jan) 2nd child (Alexander) born to KAIII
1266: Treaty of Perth – peace between Scotland and Norway following Battle of Largs.
1270: Prince Alexander made Earl of Fife (age 6)
1273: 3rd child (David) born to KAIII
1275: Death of KAIII's Queen Margaret
1281: Death (age 11) of David son of KAIII
1281: (Aug) Margaret (age 20) marries King Eric II (age 14) of Norway. Margaret and any children specified as heirs presumptive to Scottish throne.

1282: (Nov) Prince Alexander (age 16) marries Margaret of Flanders

1283: (April) birth of Margaret Maid of Norway to Margaret Queen of Norway

1283: Earl Duncan III comes of age.

1283: Death (age 22) of Margaret daughter of KAIII now Queen of Norway, shortly after childbirth

1284: (Jan) Death (aged 20) of Prince Alexander (his marriage childless)

1284: (Feb) KAIII convenes the magnates, requiring them to recognise the Maid as heir presumptive

1285: (Oct) KAIII marries Yolanda de Dreux

1286: (March) KAIII killed by falling off his horse at Pettycur, Kinghorn [A monument on the A921 road marks the place where he fell down the cliff.]

1286: (March) Parliament at Scone appoints Guardians of Scotland. The two Earls elected are Duncan III and his brother-in-law Alexander Comyn of Buchan. One of the two Barons is Alexander's cousin, John Comyn of Badenoch.

1286: (Nov) Queen Yolanda suffers a still birth.

1286: (Nov) Margaret Maid of Norway (age 3) becomes Queen of Scotland

1288: Earl Duncan III murdered

1287-90: Marriage negotiated between Maid of Norway and Edward son of King Edward I of England.

1290: Death of the Maid of Orkney

1292: Guardians of Scotland demitted office when John Balliol became king.

Earl Duncan III (1262-1288) was only eight when he inherited the title. His uncle, MacDuff, acted as his tutor. But on the death of Colban (1270) the title Earl of Fife was vested temporarily in King Alexander's son Alexander (b. 1264); enough of the management of Fife was devolved onto William Wishart, Bishop of St Andrews to allow him to take advantage of the situation and to confiscate some of the Earl's lands. This would prove to be a nagging unresolved issue essentially for the rest of his life. [Wishart demitted office in 1279, but the Church kept hold of the land.]

Duncan III came of age in 1283 and was murdered just 5 years later. He was described in the Lanercost Chronicle as "cruel and greedy beyond the average" but even from the few lines about him above we can see only too easily how these character traits would have developed. He was murdered – assassinated – "by his own people" at Pitillock in 1288 or 1289. One of those principally implicated was his kinsman Sir William de Abernethy.

The family troubles we have noted were badly compounded by the state of Scotland. Full marks must be given to Alexander III for doing his best with regard to succession planning. When his son David died he ensured that written into Margaret's marriage contract was that she and her children would retain their claim to the Scottish throne. As soon as Prince Alexander died he wasted no time in making all the magnates in Scotland swear to accept Margaret and any children she might have as their Queen if his male line failed (Prince Alexander's wife was pregnant and, as it turned out, their child was still born) – what foresight (or presentiment).

When the worst case scenario did indeed come to be in 1286, and a parliament was convened it is very clear that the "people's choice" would have been Earl Duncan III. He was the premier earl; his line had been passed over once already. No wonder he became a Guardian despite his youth and inexperience. But he had sworn to support the claim of the Maid of Norway and immediately it was clear that he would not be able to resist the marriage already brewing between her and the son of King Edward I. Unfortunately he was the wrong generation to stake a claim of his own and in any case his own family had close connections to the English crown:

Summing up Duncan III's experience

1. He had been treated with disdain by the Crown who gave away HIS land and HIS position – even if only temporarily – to Prince Alexander even though Fife was held "by the Grace of God", so really King Alexander was exceeding his authority.
2. He had been treated with disdain by the Church which had stolen some of his land
3. Foreigners (like the Bruces, Comyns and Stewarts) were limbering up to battle it out for Scotland. Earl Duncan might have had the support of the people, but he did not have the wealth or the strength of numbers to compete.
4. He did have split loyalties – on the one hand he was the last bastion of the old Scottish ways and so was supported by the 'ordinary people' and even the last of the Celtic magnates, but on the other hand he did not want to pick a fight with the English because of his very close family connections.
5. Despite all of the above he had given his solemn word to support the Maid of Norway.

In short he was very disappointed that he was not able to fulfil the role he thought he should. He was embittered. So no wonder he would 'kick the dog' – ie take out his frustration on those unable to fight back. [Note to reader: please don't copy this!] No wonder he would decide that all that was left to him was to look after himself. No wonder, then, that people would see him as cruel and greedy.

Under these circumstances trying to maintain the family's proud heritage was even more pointless than it had been during the Moray risings. So how best to get out of this? The answer was to abandon the project as a fool's errand. Why carry the burden of your heritage when there is no advantage to anyone?

The rot set in as early as 1270 when Prince Alexander was put in over his head. 140 years after the agreement which ended the Moray Risings, it was clear that Alexander III did not respect the Earls of Fife. To make things worse Duncan was two years older than Alexander!

The seed was probably sown in 1281 with King Alexander's presentiments about the future. He then had plenty of time to talk things over with his uncle Macduff. They noticed the coincidence of "mag Duffe" etc. in the old charters and his uncle's name. Matilda, the last of the line of the Angus Mormaers, had died in 1247 so there was not going to be any dissent from that quarter.

The decision was probably taken in 1284 when he "read the room" when Alexander called the magnates together to make them swear their allegiance to The Maid.

The new story was probably promulgated from the first meeting of the Guardians in 1286.

We noted above Duncan III's selfishness and the reasons for this. Owing to this he discussed the whole thing only with his uncle and his wife. but his selfishness meant that he failed to consider the implications of his lie for his kinsmen. In due course the Mackintoshes would reinvent their own story, pretending that their "Clan Chattan" nickname derived from Gillechattan Mor – a descendant of Somerled.

But remember the MacHeths! When Gillemichael negotiated away the Morays' claim to the throne on behalf of Duncan I, the junior line did not accept it. Gillemichael might rescind the claim on his and Duncan's behalf, but it was not up to him to do so on behalf of those who became the MacHeths and after them the MacWilliams.

So it was again this time. Earl Duncan III might deny his heritage on behalf of himself and his own, but for others that really only meant that the baton should pass to someone qualified and willing to take it up – in this case the Abernethys. So outraged was William de Abernethy that his heritage should be swept away from under his feet that there was only one thing for it: Duncan III would have to go. He was able to secure support from others locally who had suffered from Duncan's petty nastiness to them and Duncan was murdered. Ironically it may be because of the sanctuary privilege that he got away with his life, merely spending the rest of it in prison.

PS: In the Family of Strathbogie, descended from a younger son of Earl Duncan I and from whom stem the Duffs of Braco (later Earl and Duke of Fife), the first individual to adopt the surname Duff (NB not MacDuff) was John, probably born c 1335 – so coming of age c1350.

So I propose that the fiction was conceived and gestated through the early 1280s and was born in late 1286.

Appendix C: The End of the Kingdom

Macduff was able to promote the new story up to his death in 1298, by which time Duncan IV had been imbued with it. Whether or not he believed this – and surely he must have been told that it was not true – is not important. He could see that it was to his advantage to maintain it. There was no reason not to. The "Special Position" had already been trodden on all over from 1270. And it was about to get worse.

Notwithstanding the close family connections, in 1292 King Edward I was utterly disdainful of the prestigious position of the Earls of Fife. When John Balliol was to be crowned no effort was made to find at least a representative of the infant Duncan IV to perform the coronation as was the post-1130 tradition. He could have summoned Macduff; he could have summoned Duncan III's widow; he could even have asked William of Abernethy to stand in… the list goes on. But no… instead the job was handed to John St John the father of the first Baron St John of Basing who really had no connection to Scotland – even if he was later to have an important part to play for Edward on the England/Scotland border. Perhaps John Balliol would have fared better had he been crowned "properly"!

So disdainful was the later panel of Guardians that King Edward I needed to order them return to the confiscated lands.

In 1315 Robert Bruce found a pretext to require Duncan IV to resign the earldom to him for a regrant. The last vestige of the pretence about Fife being "a kingdom" was over. Wikipedia cites Boardman *The Early Stewart Kings*, p13, quoting English chronicler Sir Thomas Gray who claimed that Duncan "had forfeited the earldom to the crown during the reign of Robert I for the murder of an esquire named Michael Beaton and had received it back as a male entail which had reverted to the crown on Duncan's death". As we shall see, that was not quite true…

Earl Duncan IV had no options here. Bruce was ruthless about taking lands away from nobles whose loyalty was in doubt; the earls' connection to the English crown was enough for a "shoogly peg" scenario – and indeed their Strathbogie cousins had their lands forfeited.

This dubiety may have held on both sides, for after King Robert Bruce's death Edward Balliol with English backing landed at Burntisland (then known as Wester Kinghorn) on 6th August 1332. Balliol was hoping for defections, especially from the Earl of Mar; the support of Earl Duncan IV might also have been hoped for. In the event Earl Duncan fought against Balliol and lost despite having a considerably greater number of men (probably c1500 men for Balliol, more than 4000 for Earl Duncan). [The English-backed army then plundered Dunfermline before marching north to Dunning and Forteviot then crossing the Earn where they were met on Dupplin Moor (11th August). Again the Scots had the overwhelming superiority of numbers, but again they were soundly beaten with thousands of Scots killed. Fortunes then swung back and forth until Balliol finally left for exile in England in 1336.]

When Earl Duncan IV died in 1353 he left no male heir. His daughter Isabel became Countess of Fife in her own right. She married four times and each of her husbands became Earl of Fife "de iure uxoris". In 1371 Isabella resigned the Earldom of Fife to Robert Stewart, 1st Duke of Albany, the third son of King Robert II and the younger brother of King James I.

Robert Stewart held the earldom until his death in 1420, when it was inherited by his son Murdoch. However his estates were forfeit on his execution for treason at the behest of King James I in 1425 at which time the earldom became extinct and reverted to the crown.

Birth of Kinross as a separate shire

According to Robert Sibbald

> "The country called the Shire of Kinross was made a distinct shire from Fife about the year 1426..."

At the start it comprised only the parishes of Kinross, Orwell and Poprtmoak and was not enlarged until 1685. The juxtaposition of this and the end of the Earldom cannot be coincidental (see https://archive.org/details/historyancientmo00sibbiala/page/270/mode/2up).

Afterword

The title "Earl of Fife" was not to be revived until 1759 by which time it was irrelevant to Fife, not least because it was in the Peerage of Ireland! It was claimed by a descendant of the Strathbogie family descended from a junior son (probably called David) of Earl Duncan I. This title too has since become extinct.

Appendix D: Another Name Change for Fife

Recap

We do not know what name Fife or any part of it had before 200BCE

We do know that around 200BCE the part of Fife and Kinross north of Kirkcaldy was occupied by the Falcon tribe whose name in Pictish was Uip/Vep etc. so the 'name' for Fife was probably "Uipu"

We do know that around 850 Uip was taken over by Kenneth MacAlpine's henchmen who did not know or care to find out what "Uip" meant. So far as they were concerned it sounded like "Fib" – meaning "red whortleberry" / "lingonberry" and that is how it stayed until into the 1200s where it appears in this form in charters.

The reader is encouraged not to listen to so-called experts who will try to tell you that "fib" is the genitive of something else. This is nonsense and, as we have seen, we know this because the Earls of Fife used the red whortleberry as their plant badge (which was the way their soldiers recognised each other) and this remains the plant badge of Mackintoshes, collateral descendants from Earl Duncan I.

However...

The way we pronounce words changes over time. When I came to Fife I got to know people who pronounced "daughter" as "dochter" and weight as "wecht". Years ago this was normal, but now, mainly due to television and partly due to schools, such people are certainly even thinner on the ground than they were those decades ago. But we should note the overlap between the two pronunciations.

Neil Macgregor gave me an excellent parallel example from the past in Gaelic. South of Crossford is the farm Pitliver [PNF 520]. The "Liver" comes from the Gaelic Lebor meaning book – but often you will find the word for book spelled "leabhor" where the hard "b" has softened to "v". [The suggested implication of this name is that the income from this estate which went to Dunfermline Abbey was to be used in a way directly connected to the writing and copying books.]

In all these cases the pronunciation changed – and in the days before spelling was standardised in Scotland people tended to write down what they heard, and even more so when they were writing in a language they did not necessarily understand.

These changes represent a change in pronunciation parallel to the dauter/dochter shift we noted above. In the case of Pitliver the charters show that this process of changing pronunciation was already under way by 1124.

Many people will know that two separate words are in use for one plant: bramble and blackberry. Some people recognise these as the same thing, but others will be aware of one and not the other. The same applies to Fib, for Dwelly cites Cameron's Gaelic Names of Plants (1909) as his source – and in his dictionary against "Fib" he says "see Lus-nam-braoileag". In other words Dwelly regarded "fib" as less well known. For all we know there may have been very few people living in Fife even in 1100 who actually knew what "fib" actually meant. So when the new way of speaking came along "Fib" came to be pronounced "Fiobh" and even "Fiobha" people started writing what they heard. Meantime incomers were also writing "Fyf" and "Fyffe" and several other variations.

When "Lebor" became "Leabhar" everyone still knew what they meant, so the meaning "book" remained attached to the new spelling. But in the case of Fib the people who started saying "Fiobh" and "Fiobha" had no clue what the word actually meant – so now you will not find it in a dictionary except as the Gaelic way of spelling Fife.

I have rather laboured this explanation because there is a danger that the reader may have come across a so-called historian who wrote:

> "In the course of the ninth century, Pictish Fib became Gaelic Fiobh. And since bh in Gaelic is sounded like an f Fife began to sound more like itself."

Oh dear… Fife only became Fib in the 9th century; Fib was always Gaelic and not Pictish. The same author claims that "Fib" is a personal name because the legend of Cruithne and his seven sons mention "him". The problems include (i) that there never was anyone called Cruithne; (ii) the legend was concocted some time after 900 CE as a deliberate attempt to weld Pict and Scot together in one nation (see my paper on the legend for a detailed examination) and (iii) Fib was as non-existent as Cruithne.

We know that "Fib" was still in use (eg in charters) in the 1200s, so it is likely to have continued in use as long as the Earls were in place – after which Gaelic was already in decline as Scots came to the fore.

[The word "fife" does have a meaning in English, of course – it is a wind instrument, "a small shrill flute". So too a "fifer" is someone who plays a fife. But this is wholly coincidental – this word derives from the Germanic "pfeife".]

So eventually amongst Anglophones the name standardised as "Fife" while in the Gàidhealtachd "Fiobh(a)" became the norm.

Appendix E: Pedigree of the Earls of Fife &c.

In Appendix B I set out the line of the Earls. Here I consider the family rather more widely. This is the result of serendipitous research done at different times into other people. My confidence is greatly increased not least because it all slots together so well when brought together in this context.

There are many omissions and errors in what is presented on the internet and even in books. Often those responsible have a story they want to tell and are impervious to advice – or the facts! Some websites will only accept correction from authorities they would recognise – I understand that they cannot make emendations on the basis of an (often wild) allegation made to them. So we end up in zugswang (as chess players would call it). Of course the original Earls of Fife bear a good deal of responsibility for the chaos because it is they who made up a story, putting pressure on others to corrupt their own narratives to fit.

Ancestry of the Earls of Fife Part 1 –
Ancestry of King Duncan I and his Queen Bera

Generations				c. birth	Name	Title/Comment
1				770	Ivar	Of the Uplands
2				792	Eystein	King of Trondelag aka 'Glumra',
3				820	Ragnald	Jarl of the Uplands ('bloodeagled' 861/2)
4				848	Ivar	
5				868	Einar	Jarl of Orkney aka 'Turf'
6				890	Thorfinn	Jarl of Orkney aka 'Skullsplitter'
7				912	Hlodvir	Jarl of Orkney
8				944	Sigurd	Jarl of Orkney aka 'The Stout',
9				954	Hlodvir	'Hundi'
	10			975	Sigurd	Siward Earl of Northumbria
	10			977	Karl	'Hundisson', 'Crinan', Mormaer of Atholl
		11		1006	Maldred	(from m1)
			12		Gospatric	Earl of Northumberland => Earls of Dunbar
		11		**1009**	**Duncan I**	(from m2, Bethoc) King of Scotland
	10			997	Bera	
		11		1012?	Siward?	Thane of Fife => Balfours
		11		1015	**Bera**	Queen of Duncan I: aka Ursula & Suthen
9				955x90	Sumarlidi Brusi Einar	Co-Jarls with Thorfinn in the early days
9				99	Thorfinn	Jarl of Orkney aka 'The Mighty'

King Duncan I and his queen Bera were first cousins.

Ancestry of the Earls of Fife Part 2 –
Ancestry of Earl Duncan I of Fife

Generations				c. birth	Name	Title/Comment
11	King Duncan I and Queen Bera					
12				1031	Malcolm III	
	13			1055 to 1068	Duncan II Malcolm Donald	King Mormaer of Argyll (sons of 1st wife Ingebjorg)
	13			1068 to 1071	Edward Edmund	Eldest with Margaret Atheling
	13			1072	Athelred	Mormaer of Moray aka Aedh
		14		1093	Angus	Mormaer of Moray k.1130
		14		1095	Duncan	d. <1130
			15	**1115**	**Duncan**	**Ist Earl of Fife**
			15	1120	?daughter?	m. Gilla Brigte co-Lord of Galloway
		14		1097	Gillemichael	Lord of Abernethy
			15	1118	Aedh/ "Hugh"	Lord of Abernethy => Clan Abernethy
		14		1100	Gruaidh	m. William the Noble son of Duncan II
			15		Donald	=> MacWilliam rebels
		14		1099	Malcolm	Earl of Ross
			15	1120	Aedh	=> Mac(H)eth Rebels
	13			1073 to 1085	Edgar Alexander I Edith David I Mary	King King m. King Henry I of England King m. Count Eustace of Boulogne
12				1033	Donalbane	King & Mormaer of Gowrie m. Hextilda
	13			1075	Bethoc	=> Comyns (via Tynedale)
12				1036	Maelmuir	Mormaer of Atholl => Clan Donnachie

For the full justification of all this see my SCLLE in which, however, there are two mistakes: I had not appreciated that (i) there were three Gillemichaels and so had presumed the Wemyss family descended from Abernethy (ii) Earl Duncan I must have been the son of Duncan rather than Angus.

Ancestry of the Earls of Fife Part 3 – Descendants of Earl Duncan I of Fife

Generations						c. birth	Name	Title/Comment
15	Duncan I Earl of Fife (1115-1154)§							
16						1137	Duncan II	2nd Earl of Fife
	17					1160	Malcolm I	3rd Earl of Fife
	17					1162	Duncan	
		18				1190	Malcolm II	4th Earl of Fife
			19			1215	“Malcolm”	died before father: m. Elen
				20		1240	Colban	5th Earl of Fife (son of “Malcolm”)
					21	1262	Duncan III	6th Earl of Fife
					22	1289	Duncan IV	7th Earl of Fife
					23	1320	Isabella	(8th) Countess of Fife d 1389 (m.x4)
				20		1242	Macduff	Twice tutor; killed in battle 1298
16						1139	Gillemichael	aka Michael => Wemyss‡ family
	17					1164	John	“Big John” of Methil & Wemyss
16						1141	Shaw§	“Mac an Toiseach” => Mackintoshes
16						1143	“John§”	=> family of Strathbogie
16						1145	Adam	m. Orabilis nic/‘fitz’ Neis
16						1135x45	Aufreka§	m. Harald Maddadarsson (Atholl)
16 or 17						1150x60	Dervorguilla§	m. Aulay Grant => Grants

Notes

** David de Strathbogie was born c1240. His father was John about whom little is known – but logically it is likely he was born c1215. The story of this branch of the family can be found online and it was from this line that the Duffs of Braco take their descent. Quite where this family breaks off from the main line is not clear.

Given David born in 1240, it is likely that his ancestry includes earlier Davids born in, say, 1190 and 1140. The earlier date is more likely because it was probably given in honour of King David I. What we know is that because of the Arms, the progenitor of this line must be "junior" to the Wemyss family. A birthdate around 1190 would not be possible because then "David" would be senior to the Wemyss family. So there are really only two possible scenarios: this "David" could have been

(i) a younger son of Earl David I (so a younger brother both of Earl Duncan II and of Gillemichael of the Wemyss family) – but there are already 6 children in generation 16; putting "David" into Strathbogie would match sending Shaw to Inverness. Putting both these men into Moray would help to calm things down in the context of the MacHeth rebellions and the imposition of foreign Earls.
(ii) a younger son of Earl Duncan II, but in that case he would need to have been younger than both Malcolm I and Duncan and so not born until about 1165 which makes the idea not impossible but less likely to have had an inheriting grandson also called David in 1240. Not only that but with David long dead the relevance of the name was much diminished.

This is the reasoning for the position I have placed him in the table – but it is tentative.

‡Thus the head of the Wemyss family fell heir to the Lion Rampant undifferenced arguably in 1353 on the death of Earl Duncan IV or at the very latest in 1389 on the death of

the Countess Isabella. For later generations of the Wemyss family see: https://archive.org/details/memorialsoffamil01fras/page/814/mode/2up

§ We are not told the name of the wife of Earl Duncan I, but we can probably work it out. The Wikipedia page (March 2023) on Fergus, Lord of Galloway (he was born c1090 and died in 1161), says that Fergus' son "Gilla Brigte may have been wed to a daughter or sister of Donnchad II, Earl of Fife…". This is unrealistic because Earl Duncan II would not have had marriageable children before 1160, while Gilla Brigte was born around 1120.

No… Gilla Brigte could only have been married to a sister of Duncan I (her father would still have been called Duncan). However we can see that the marriage must have taken place well after the end of the Moray Risings when Duncan I was indeed Earl of Fife.

If we now look at the other names with a § we find:

(i) **Aufreka** – which is in essence the same as Affraic, the name of a daughter or Fergus of Galloway (she married Olaf Guthrothsson, King of Man and the Isles). This is a 'normal' Irish name (also the name of two Abbesses of Kildare). It means "pleasant".

(ii) **Dervorguilla** – which is another Irish name which means "daughter of Forgall" (who was a semi-mythic Irish hero – he features in the "Tochmarc Emire"). There was a Dervorguilla of Galloway, a great granddaughter of Fergus, who became King John Balliol's queen. It is theoretically possible that "our" Dervorguilla was daughter of Duncan II because she was not married until 1174, so could have been born c1159x60. Either way from this we may reasonably suppose that Earl Duncan I married a daughter of Fergus of Galloway and there is a very fair chance that her name was Dervorgilla.

We can go on from there to consider

(iii) **Shaw.** At face value this is a silly name. But we should bear in mind that Affraic was rendered as Aufreka, so we can be a little creative. The only word in Scottish Gaelic which comes really close is "Seaghag" (say Shaw-uc) meaning Peregrine Falcon; while for reasons now obvious to the reader it would be wonderful if this were the explanation and while the "-ag" is a diminutive so we should expect a root word "Seabh" meaning something similar, it is not to be found. The word is there, but it is a verb meaning "to stray" (which fits with the "Peregrine") – so not a name for a son. [Some websites try to offer "hawk" or "hawklike" for Shea/O'Shea, but the relevant Irish words are sebac and seboc (meaning hawk/sparrowhawk) – and, as with the Scottish Gaelic, it is not easy to lose the "-c". "Shea" in the Irish surname O'Shea" is held to mean "fortunate".]

However now that we know that Irish Gaelic is available to us and that a desirable description is acceptable (Affraic meaning pleasant), in eDil we find "ségda" meaning "happy/lucky" etc. and "seaghdha" meaning "learned". Wikipedia goes on to say that the name originates in the Corcu Duibne of County Kerry – who are Cruithin and, as we know, the Novantes of Galloway were Cruithin. So it may be that the name was endemic in Galloway for 1 000 years before it reached Fife. I think the more likely meaning of "our" Shaw is "learned" – which would be a good aspiration for a man to have for his son.
[Gaelic is a language very rich in allusion. I suspect that the root of this word (from Dwelly) is "seagad" meaning 60. From

this comes "sean" meaning "old/ancient" (I suggest originally literally over 60 years old). In those days the old were respected and the general understanding was that wisdom came with age – so Dwelly has "seagh" meaning "esteem/value/respect" which originally came from having reached the age of 60 and "seagach" means weighty or prudent – the sort of qualities one might expect to come with age and experience. The Irish "seaghdha" too is not a stretch at all, never mind a long one. One small extra extension and we come to "seannachaidh" who was the keeper of knowledge, especially about family histories etc. and who would recite these at gatherings.]

So to sum up

What we see is a double marriage, with Duncan marrying Fergus' daughter and Gilla Brigte marrying Duncan's sister, perhaps in a dual ceremony in 1136 (perhaps contracted even earlier). This is likely to have been arranged by King David I because, at this time, Galloway was still independent of Scotland and was being pulled in three directions simultaneously – by the kings of England (Fergus' wife was Elizabeth, an illegitimate daughter of Henry I), and Man and the Isles (see Affraic above) as well as Scotland. David I would have hoped that these liaisons would tip the balance in Scotland's favour. [Scotland had the inherent geographical advantage here because of the long common and ill-defined border.]

Epilogue

We know nothing of our Stone Age ancestors. All we have of them are such of the marks they made on the landscape which have survived. So too all we know of our Beaker People ancestors is a little archaeology. Of the Caledonians we know far too little and such as we do know is largely that which was recorded by foreigners. Perhaps forging a connection with the Calata of Transylvania might help – but only a little. It has taken this book to identify our Falcon ancestors; perhaps we may hope that forging a connection with the Valais canton in Switzerland or the Lens area in Belgium give us some insight – but by its nature it will be peripheral.

The Romans', the Angles' and King Arthur's impacts were shallow and transient, but Christianity wiped out all understanding of what had gone before in our religious life – and only with this book's highlighting Medocus may we perhaps begin to identify at least one strand of this aspect of our past.

The Scots not only destroyed our Pictish culture – albeit itself less than truly authentic – they also misrepresented themselves leaving us with very little; largely hiding their dependence on Irish mercenaries, they minimised our understanding of their impact which was so culturally devastating.

The Vikings left far more of a mark on and in Fife than Scots in particular have been happy to acknowledge and we are the poorer for our failure to embrace this. Then feudalisation under Norman-influenced and Norman-intermarried mac Malcolm kings added yet another destruction layer before, belatedly, we enter the realm of recorded history – and even here we see obfuscation and denial as too many of today's historians seek to label as untrue too many of the few records which have come down to us as they try to construct their tartan-and-shortbread Panglossian fantasy history.

We are the products of past generations. The more we understand them the better we will know ourselves – and knowledge brings power.

In this book I have been able to do no more than scratch the surface of Fife's origins, of the many influences and the many cover ups. But hopefully at least we now have a rather better grasp of what we know we do not know!

Acknowledgements

I am grateful to the many people who have assisted me on my journey to the writing of this book.

The list below is not exhaustive because it does not include those who contributed to the background papers I had to write – my thanks to them is recorded on the various papers (see Bibliography).

While it is invidious to be selective from this list I really must pick out for special mention three people who have particularly indulged me with enormous quantities of their time:

Dr Alex Woolf of St Andrews University has been very generous with his time over many years. His prodigious memory is a wonder to behold. Many of the insights I have been able to bring to the reader stem from steers he has given me.

Neil Macgregor is one of the foremost scholars of Gaelic of our times who has kept – or put – me right on many occasions and has been indulgent in allowing me to test out many of my potentially more outlandish ideas.

Ron Greer has brought to me his expertise both as an ecologist with a deep understanding of Scotland's environment going back to the ice age and, though his membership of the Antonine Guard Roman Re-enactors, a knowledge and personal experience of the Romans and their ways and hence of military matters more generally pertinent throughout the period discussed in this book.

But this is not to diminish the value each of those mentioned below have contributed to the richness of the narrative and detail I have been able to place before the reader in these pages. I am very grateful to them all.

William Adkins
Willie Anderson
Dr Jean Balfour
Robert W Balfour
Rev. Canon Liz Baker
The Barr family
Donal Bateson
John & Nan @ Betty Nicols
Eva Bennett
Paul Bennett
Linda Bissett
Clare Houseman du Boulay
Prof Ian Bradley
Andrew Breeze
Philip Brooks
Dr Jasper de Bruin
David Bruton
Andrew Calder
Ailsa Campbell
Donald Campbell
Prof Thomas Clancy
William Clark
Tim Clarkson
Ewen Crawford
Dr Martin Counihan
Charlotte Dales
Hugh Dales
Linda Docherty
Cara Donald
Ken Donnelly
Andrew Dowsey
Michael Duncan
Roxanne @ Elite Falconry
WJ Ferguson
David Forbes
Gillian Forbes
David Ford
Helen Fox
George Geddes
Michael Given
Lavinia Gordon
Sandra Gordon
Cllr Jimmy Gray
Ron Greer
Marco Grilli
Joe & Jenny Harper
Andrew Hawke
Lynsey Haworth
Alan Hay
Dr Bridget Heal
David Henry
Kristina Herz
WG Hepburn jr
John Harrison
Clare Hopkins
Prof. Carole Hough

Oliver House
Christopher Hughes
Dr Fraser Hunter
Florence Hutchison
Harold Ingram
Neil Kennedy
Jake King
Ken Lang
Nigel Lindsay
Peter Littwin
Mindy Lynch
Neil Macgregor
Elma Macintyre
Diane MacKenzie
Duncan MacKenzie
Alan MacNiven
Libby MacRae
Donna Maguire
Gilbert Markús
Colin Mayall
Dr Bruce McAndrew
Sharon McColl
John & Pam McDairmid
Heather McHaffie
Steve McHardy
Alastair McIntyre
Peter McNaughton
Dr Dic Mortimer
Dr Anne Mouron
John Murray
Beth Newman
Sophie Nicol
Elisabeth Novitski
Peter Peacock
Sheila Pitcairn
Alan Pollock
Anne Porteous
David Potter
Rosemary Potter
Tommy Pringle
George Proudfoot
Kelly Rae
Dr John Raven
Guto Rhys
Ginny Reid
Rev. Mary Ann Rennie
Elizabeth Rhodes
Simon Rodway
Mike @ RomanBritain
Eilidh Scammell
Kevin Scott
Alan Sinclair
Samantha Smart
Ainslie Smith
Allan Stephen
Alan Stephens
Alan Stewart
Douglas Speirs
Helen Spencer
Ninian Stuart
Dr Simon Taylor
Bill Thayer
Dr Tom Turpie
George Way of Plean
Patrick & Louise Wedderburn
Michael Wemyss

Margaret West
Nicholas Williamson
Prof David Willis
Maggie Wilson
Nicola Wilson
Stan Wolfson
Dr Alex Woolf
Andrew Wooton
Kat Wright

Bibliography

This will not be a 'normal' bibliography. Very often bibliographies can be measured by 'weight' and are designed to show off rather than to inform. Not only that, but in this case I was faced with a serious problem: in order to write this book I had to overturn a lot of "well known facts" about Scottish History. Not only would this have doubled the size of the book, it would not be directly relevant to a large proportion of readers. These papers are accessible online at

https://independent.academia.edu/AdrianGrant1

and are referred to in the text. The individual papers are heavily referenced, especially via embedded hyperlinks.

Reference is also made to two of my previous books, synopses for which can also be found with my papers. Some readers will still be disappointed, but that is because so much of this work is entirely original: there simply are no sources to refer to.

Omitted from this list also are those references detailed where they occur in the text.

My Books

SCLLE: Scottish Clans: Legend, Logic & Evidence (Fastprint 2012)
ALLE: Arthur: Legend, Logic & Evidence (Fastprint 2017)

Those of my papers which provide relevant background for this book

OPS: *The Origins of The Picts and The Scots: A Comprehensive Outline Narrative*
PS1: *Who were the Picts? Who were the Scots? v1 -Time to cut the Gordian Knot*
PS2: *Who were the Picts? Who were the Scots? Part 2 – A Dissection of the Mythology*
Cruith: *The Legend of Cruithne and his Seven Sons*
LKP: *The Legendary Kings of the Picts – a Reconsideration*
Brochs: *The Smertae and the need for the Brochs of Scotland*

Schiehallion: *Schiehallion -NOT a "fairy hill" at all*
NES: *The Political Geography of North East Scotland in Roman Times v3*
Fortriu: *Why Fortriu Was Misplaced By Historians Of Old v2*
Bones: *The Culdees, the Bones of St Andrew and the Council of Nicea*
Atholl: *Towards an Understanding of the Place Name 'Atholl'*
Atholl+: *Atholl Addendum*
Argyll: *Argyll -What's in a name*

Siege: *Dating the Siege of Lindisfarne v3*
Urbs Iudeu: *Locating Urbs Iudeu / Giudi and Winwaedfeld Disposing of false conflation and false dichotomy*
Penda: *Encomium_Pendae_Regis_Penda_of_Mercia_Not_All_Angles_Were_The_Same*
Caer Greu: *Caer_Greu_and_the_loss_of_the_kingdom_of_Ebrauc_York*
Daegsastane: *In_search_of_the_battlefield_of_Degsastan_603_AD_*

Camp1: *Whence Came the Campbells*
Camp2: *Clan Campbell -Addendum*

https://www.nhm.ac.uk/discover/news/2018/february/the-beaker-people-a-new-population-for-ancient-britain.html
http://www.britishmuseum.org/research/collection_online/collection_object_details.aspx?objectId=1363164&partId=1
https://www.theoi.com/Phylos/Hyperborea.html
http://www.old-north.co.uk/Holding/celt_personalnames.html
https://penelope.uchicago.edu/Thayer/E/Roman/Texts/Cassius_Dio/77*.html
https://hillforts.arch.ox.ac.uk/
https://www.royal.uk/alexander-iii-r-1249-1286
http://history-books.weebly.com/uploads/6/9/9/0/6990231/new_information_on_wallace_and_the_guardians___the_breaking_of_britain.pdf

"The Chronicle of the Picts and Scots" (ed. WF Skene 1867)
"Roman Camps in Scotland" Rebecca H Jones (Soc. of Antiquaries of Scotland 2013)
"Copper Parchment and Stone" https://eprints.gla.ac.uk/128834/14/128834.pdf
"The History, Ancient and Modern of the Sheriffdoms of Fife and Kinross" Sir Robert Sibbald London 1803

Index of Place Names

There are some out-and-out reference books whose indexes make up a very substantial proportion of the whole book - almost a case of the tail wagging the dog. When I did my initial trawl to create the index, the list ran to about 440 places. Many of these are not directly relevant to the narrative and are mentioned for the sake of background or comparison. For this reason I have decided to exclude them from this index in the hope that the result will be a lot less unwieldy. Thus only a few names outside Fife and Kinross are retained.

Index of Personal Names

In this work, too many people share just a few names. I regret that to avoid rewriting the book in this index, compromise has been necessary. Thus (i) tribal names, their mythical progenitors and pagan gods are not included; (ii) this index does not discriminate between different people with the same name – thus it is largely an index of personal names rather than of people as such. I hope it will nevertheless prove to be of some use. It should also be noted that the great majority of the historical people referred to are mentioned only in the chapter(s) pertaining to the times they lived in.

This book is printed on paper from sustainable sources managed under the Forest Stewardship Council (FSC) scheme.

It has been printed in the UK to reduce transportation miles and their impact upon the environment.

For every new title that Troubador publishes, we plant a tree to offset CO_2, partnering with the More Trees scheme.

For more about how Troubador offsets its environmental impact, see www.troubador.co.uk/sustainability-and-community